A
Semantic
Web
Primer

Cooperative Information Systems
Michael P. Papazoglou, Joachim W. Schmidt, and John Mylopoulos, editors

Advances in Object-Oriented Data Modeling
Michael P. Papazoglou, Stefano Spaccapietra, and Zahir Tari, editors, 2000

Workflow Management: Models, Methods, and Systems
Wil van der Aalst and Kees Max van Hee, 2002

A Semantic Web Primer
Grigoris Antoniou and Frank van Harmelen, 2004

Aligning Modern Business Processes and Legacy Systems
Willem-Jan van den Heuvel, 2006

A Semantic Web Primer, second edition
Grigoris Antoniou and Frank van Harmelen, 2008

A
Semantic
Web
Primer

second edition

Grigoris Antoniou

and

Frank van Harmelen

The MIT Press
Cambridge, Massachusetts
London, England

This book was set in 10/13 Palatino by the authors using LATEX 2$_\varepsilon$.
Printed and bound in the United States of America.

Library of Congress Cataloging-in-Publication Data

Antoniou, G. (Grigoris)
A semantic Web primer / Grigoris Antoniou and Frank van Harmelen. – 2nd ed.
    p. cm. – (Cooperative information systems)
Includes bibliographical references and index.
ISBN 978-0-262-01242-3 (hardcover : alk. paper)
1. Semantic Web. I. Van Harmelen, Frank. II. Title.
TK5105.88815. A58   2008
025.04–dc22

                                             2007020429

10 9 8 7 6 5 4 3 2 1

Dedicated to Konstantina

G.A.

Brief Contents

Contents

List of Figures

Series Foreword

The traditional view of information systems as tailor-made, cost-intensive database applications is changing rapidly. The change is fueled partly by a maturing software industry, which is making greater use of off-the-shelf generic components and standard software solutions, and partly by the onslaught of the information revolution. In turn, this change has resulted in a new set of demands for information services that are homogeneous in their presentation and interaction patterns, open in their software architecture, and global in their scope. The demands have come mostly from application domains such as e-commerce and banking, manufacturing (including the software industry itself), training, education, and environmental management, to mention just a few.

Future information systems will have to support smooth interaction with a large variety of independent multivendor data sources and legacy applications, running on heterogeneous platforms and distributed information networks. Metadata will play a crucial role in describing the contents of such data sources and in facilitating their integration.

As well, a greater variety of community-oriented interaction patterns will have to be supported by next-generation information systems. Such interactions may involve navigation, querying and retrieval, and will have to be combined with personalized notification, annotation, and profiling mechanisms. Such interactions will also have to be intelligently interfaced with application software, and will need to be dynamically integrated into customized and highly connected cooperative environments. Moreover, the massive investments in information resources, by governments and businesses alike, call for specific measures that ensure security, privacy, and accuracy of their contents.

All these are challenges for the next generation of information systems. We call such systems *cooperative information systems*, and they are the focus of this series.

In lay terms, cooperative information systems are serving a diverse mix of demands characterized by *content—community—commerce*. These demands are originating in current trends for off-the-shelf software solutions, such as enterprise resource planning and e-commerce systems.

A major challenge in building cooperative information systems is to develop technologies that permit continuous enhancement and evolution of current massive investments in information resources and systems. Such technologies must offer an appropriate infrastructure that supports not only development but also evolution of software.

Early research results on cooperative information systems are becoming the core technology for community-oriented information portals or gateways. An information gateway provides a "one-stop-shopping" place for a wide range of information resources and services, thereby creating a loyal user community.

The research advances that will lead to cooperative information systems will not come from any single research area within the field of information technology. Database and knowledge-based systems, distributed systems, groupware, and graphical user interfaces have all matured as technologies. While further enhancements for individual technologies are desirable, the greatest leverage for technological advancement is expected to come from their evolution into a seamless technology for building and managing cooperative information systems.

The MIT Press Cooperative Information Systems series will cover this area through textbooks, and research editions intended for the researcher and the professional who wishes to remain up-to-date on current developments and future trends.

The series will include three types of books:

- Textbooks or resource books intended for upper-level undergraduate or graduate level courses

- Research monographs, which collect and summarize research results and development experiences over a number of years

- Edited volumes, including collections of papers on a particular topic

Data in a data source are useful because they model some part of the real world, its subject matter (or *application*, or *domain of discourse*). The problem of *data semantics* is establishing and maintaining the correspondence between a data source, hereafter a *model*, and its intended subject matter. The model may be a database storing data about employees in a company, a database schema describing parts, projects, and suppliers, a Web site presenting information about a university, or a plain text file describing the battle of Waterloo. The problem has been with us since the development of the first databases. However, the problem remained under control as long as the operational environment of a database remained closed and relatively stable. In such a setting, the meaning of the data was factored out from the database proper and entrusted to the small group of regular users and application programs.

The advent of the Web has changed all that. Databases today are made available, in some form, on the Web where users, application programs, and uses are open-ended and ever changing. In such a setting, the semantics of the data has to be made available along with the data. For human users, this is done through an appropriate choice of presentation format. For application programs, however, this semantics has to be provided in a formal and machine-processable form. Hence the call for the Semantic Web.[1]

Not surprisingly, this call by Tim Berners-Lee has received tremendous attention by researchers and practitioners alike. There is now an International Semantic Web Conference series,[2] a Semantic Web Journal published by Elsevier,[3] as well as industrial committees that are looking at the first generation of standards for the Semantic Web.

The current book constitutes a timely publication, given the fast-moving nature of Semantic Web concepts, technologies, and standards. The book offers a gentle introduction to Semantic Web concepts, including XML, DTDs, and XML schemas, RDF and RDFS, OWL, logic, and inference. Throughout, the book includes examples and applications to illustrate the use of concepts.

We are pleased to include this book on the Semantic Web in the series on Cooperative Information Systems. We hope that readers will find it interesting, insightful, and useful.

John Mylopoulos
jm@cs.toronto.edu
Dept. of Computer Science
University of Toronto
Toronto, Ontario
Canada

Michael Papazoglou
M.P.Papazoglou@kub.nl
INFOLAB
P.O. Box 90153
LE Tilburg
The Netherlands

1. Tim Berners-Lee and Mark Fischetti, *Weaving the Web: The Original Design and Ultimate Destiny of the World Wide Web by Its Inventor.* San Francisco: HarperCollins, 1999.
2. <http://iswc.semanticweb.org>.
3. <http://www.semanticwebjournal.org>.

Preface

The World Wide Web (WWW) has changed the way people communicate with each other, how information is disseminated and retrieved, and how business is conducted. The term *Semantic Web* comprises techniques that promise to dramatically improve the current WWW and its use. This book is about this emerging technology.

The success of each book should be judged against the authors' aims. This is an introductory textbook about the Semantic Web. Its main use will be to serve as the basis for university courses about the Semantic Web. It can also be used for self-study by anyone who wishes to learn about Semantic Web technologies.

The question arises whether there is a need for a textbook, given that all information is available online. We think there is a need because on the Web there are too many sources of varying quality and too much information. Some information is valid, some outdated, some wrong, and most sources talk about obscure details. Anyone who is a newcomer and wishes to learn something about the Semantic Web, or who wishes to set up a course on the Semantic Web, is faced with these problems. This book is meant to help out.

A textbook must be selective in the topics it covers. Particularly in a field as fast developing as this, a textbook should concentrate on fundamental aspects that can reasonably be expected to remain relevant some time into the future. But, of course, authors always have their personal bias.

Even for the topics covered, this book is not meant to be a reference work that describes every small detail. Long books have already been written on certain topics, such as XML. And there is no need for a reference work in the Semantic Web area because all definitions and manuals are available online. Instead, we concentrate on the main ideas and techniques and provide enough detail to enable readers to engage with the material constructively and to build applications of their own.

That way readers will be equipped with sufficient knowledge to easily get the remaining details from other sources. In fact, an annotated list of references is found at the end of each chapter.

Preface to the Second Edition

The reception of the first edition of this book showed that there was a real need for a book with this profile. The book is in use in dozens of courses worldwide and has been translated into Japanese, Spanish, Chinese and Korean.

The Semantic Web area has seen rapid development since the first publication of our book. New elements have appeared in the Semantic Web language stack, new application areas have emerged, and new tools are being produced. This has prompted us to produce a second edition with a substantial number of updates and changes. In brief, this second edition has the following new elements:

- All known bugs and errata have been fixed (notably the RDF chapter (chapter 3) contained some embarrassing errors).

- The RDF chapter now discusses SPARQL as the RDF query language (with SPARQL going for W3C recommendation in the near future, and already receiving widespread implementation support).

- The OWL chapter (chapter 4) now discusses OWL DLP, a newly identified fragment of the language with a number of interesting practical and theoretical properties.

- In the light of rapid developments in this area, the chapter on rules (chapter 5) has been revised and discusses the SWRL language as well as OWL DLP.

- New example applications have been added to chapter 6.

- The discussion of web services in chapter 6 has been revised and is now based on OWL-S.

- The final outlook chapter (chapter 8) has been entirely rewritten to reflect the advancements in the state of the art, to capture a number of currently ongoing discussions, and to list the most challenging issues facing the Semantic Web.

We have also started to maintain a Web site with material to support the use of this book: <http://www.semanticwebprimer.org>. The Web site contains slides for each chapter, to be used for teaching, online versions of code fragments in the book, and links to material for further reading.

Acknowledgments

We thank Jeen Broekstra, Michel Klein, and Marta Sabou for pioneering much of this material in our course on Web-based knowledge representation at the Free University in Amsterdam; Annette ten Teije, Zharko Aleksovski and Wouter Jansweijer for critically reading early versions of the manuscript; and Lynda Hardman and Jacco van Ossenbruggen for spotting errors in the RDF chapter.

We thank Christoph Grimmer and Peter Koenig for proofreading parts of the book and assisting with the creation of the figures and with LaTeX processing.

For the second edition of this book, the following people generously contributed material: Jeen Broekstra wrote section 3.9 on SPARQL; Peter Mika and Michel Klein wrote section 6.3 on their openacademia system; some of the text on the Bibster system in section 6.4 was donated by Peter Haase from his Ph.D. thesis; and some of the text on OWL-S was donated by Marta Sabou from her Ph.D. thesis.

Also, we wish to thank the MIT Press people for their assistance with the final preparation of the manuscript, and Christopher Manning for his LaTeX 2_ε macros.

1 *The Semantic Web Vision*

1.1 Today's Web

The World Wide Web has changed the way people communicate with each other and the way business is conducted. It lies at the heart of a revolution that is currently transforming the developed world toward a knowledge economy and, more broadly speaking, to a knowledge society.

This development has also changed the way we think of computers. Originally they were used for computing numerical calculations. Currently their predominant use is for information processing, typical applications being database systems, text processing, and games. At present there is a transition of focus toward the view of computers as entry points to the information highways.

Most of today's Web content is suitable for human consumption. Even Web content that is generated automatically from databases is usually presented without the original structural information found in databases. Typical uses of the Web today involve people's seeking and making use of information, searching for and getting in touch with other people, reviewing catalogs of online stores and ordering products by filling out forms, and viewing adult material.

These activities are not particularly well supported by software tools. Apart from the existence of links that establish connections between documents, the main valuable, indeed indispensable, tools are search engines.

Keyword-based search engines such as Yahoo and Google are the main tools for using today's Web. It is clear that the Web would not have become the huge success it is, were it not for search engines. However, there are serious problems associated with their use:

- High recall, low precision. Even if the main relevant pages are retrieved, they are of little use if another 28,758 mildly relevant or irrelevant documents are also retrieved. Too much can easily become as bad as too little.

- Low or no recall. Often it happens that we don't get any relevant answer for our request, or that important and relevant pages are not retrieved. Although low recall is a less frequent problem with current search engines, it does occur.

- Results are highly sensitive to vocabulary. Often our initial keywords do not get the results we want; in these cases the relevant documents use different terminology from the original query. This is unsatisfactory because semantically similar queries should return similar results.

- Results are single Web pages. If we need information that is spread over various documents, we must initiate several queries to collect the relevant documents, and then we must manually extract the partial information and put it together.

Interestingly, despite improvements in search engine technology, the difficulties remain essentially the same. It seems that the amount of Web content outpaces technological progress.

But even if a search is successful, it is the person who must browse selected documents to extract the information he is looking for. That is, there is not much support for retrieving the information, a very time-consuming activity. Therefore, the term *information retrieval*, used in association with search engines, is somewhat misleading; *location finder* might be a more appropriate term. Also, results of Web searches are not readily accessible by other software tools; search engines are often isolated applications.

The main obstacle to providing better support to Web users is that, at present, the meaning of Web content is not *machine-accessible*. Of course, there are tools that can retrieve texts, split them into parts, check the spelling, count their words. But when it comes to *interpreting* sentences and extracting useful information for users, the capabilities of current software are still very limited. It is simply difficult to distinguish the meaning of

I am a professor of computer science.

from

I am a professor of computer science, you may think. Well, . . .

Using text processing, how can the current situation be improved? One solution is to use the content as it is represented today and to develop increasingly sophisticated techniques based on artificial intelligence and computational linguistics. This approach has been followed for some time now, but despite some advances the task still appears too ambitious.

An alternative approach is to represent Web content in a form that is more easily machine-processable[1] and to use intelligent techniques to take advantage of these representations. We refer to this plan of revolutionizing the Web as the *Semantic Web* initiative. It is important to understand that the Semantic Web will not be a new global information highway parallel to the existing World Wide Web; instead it will gradually evolve out of the existing Web.

The Semantic Web is propagated by the World Wide Web Consortium (W3C), an international standardization body for the Web. The driving force of the Semantic Web initiative is Tim Berners-Lee, the very person who invented the WWW in the late 1980s. He expects from this initiative the realization of his original vision of the Web, a vision where the meaning of information played a far more important role than it does in today's Web.

The development of the Semantic Web has a lot of industry momentum, and governments are investing heavily. The U.S. government has established the DARPA Agent Markup Language (DAML) Project, and the Semantic Web is among the key action lines of the European Union's Sixth Framework Programme.

1.2 From Today's Web to the Semantic Web: Examples

1.2.1 Knowledge Management

Knowledge management concerns itself with acquiring, accessing, and maintaining knowledge within an organization. It has emerged as a key activity of large businesses because they view internal knowledge as an intellectual asset from which they can draw greater productivity, create new value, and increase their competitiveness. Knowledge management is particularly important for international organizations with geographically dispersed departments.

---

1. In the literature the term *machine-understandable* is used quite often. We believe it is the wrong word because it gives the wrong impression. It is not necessary for intelligent agents to *understand* information; it is sufficient for them to process information effectively, which sometimes causes people to think the machine really understands.

Most information is currently available in a weakly structured form, for example, text, audio, and video. From the knowledge management perspective, the current technology suffers from limitations in the following areas:

- Searching information. Companies usually depend on keyword-based search engines, the limitations of which we have outlined.

- Extracting information. Human time and effort are required to browse the retrieved documents for relevant information. Current intelligent agents are unable to carry out this task in a satisfactory fashion.

- Maintaining information. Currently there are problems, such as inconsistencies in terminology and failure to remove outdated information.

- Uncovering information. New knowledge implicitly existing in corporate databases is extracted using data mining. However, this task is still difficult for distributed, weakly structured collections of documents.

- Viewing information. Often it is desirable to restrict access to certain information to certain groups of employees. "Views," which hide certain information, are known from the area of databases but are hard to realize over an intranet (or the Web).

The aim of the Semantic Web is to allow much more advanced knowledge management systems:

- Knowledge will be organized in conceptual spaces according to its meaning.

- Automated tools will support maintenance by checking for inconsistencies and extracting new knowledge.

- Keyword-based search will be replaced by query answering: requested knowledge will be retrieved, extracted, and presented in a human-friendly way.

- Query answering over several documents will be supported.

- Defining who may view certain parts of information (even parts of documents) will be possible.

1.2.2   Business-to-Consumer Electronic Commerce

Business-to-consumer (B2C) electronic commerce is the predominant commercial experience of Web users. A typical scenario involves a user's visiting one or several online shops, browsing their offers, selecting and ordering products.

Ideally, a user would collect information about prices, terms, and conditions (such as availability) of all, or at least all major, online shops and then proceed to select the best offer. But manual browsing is too time-consuming to be conducted on this scale. Typically a user will visit one or a very few online stores before making a decision.

To alleviate this situation, tools for shopping around on the Web are available in the form of shopbots, software agents that visit several shops, extract product and price information, and compile a market overview. Their functionality is provided by wrappers, programs that extract information from an online store. One wrapper per store must be developed. This approach suffers from several drawbacks.

The information is extracted from the online store site through keyword search and other means of textual analysis. This process makes use of assumptions about the proximity of certain pieces of information (for example, the price is indicated by the word *price* followed by the symbol $ followed by a positive number). This heuristic approach is error-prone; it is not always guaranteed to work. Because of these difficulties only limited information is extracted. For example, shipping expenses, delivery times, restrictions on the destination country, level of security, and privacy policies are typically not extracted. But all these factors may be significant for the user's decision making. In addition, programming wrappers is time-consuming, and changes in the online store outfit require costly reprogramming.

The Semantic Web will allow the development of software agents that can *interpret* the product information and the terms of service:

- Pricing and product information will be extracted correctly, and delivery and privacy policies will be interpreted and compared to the user requirements.

- Additional information about the reputation of online shops will be retrieved from other sources, for example, independent rating agencies or consumer bodies.

- The low-level programming of wrappers will become obsolete.

- More sophisticated shopping agents will be able to conduct automated negotiations, on the buyer's behalf, with shop agents.

1.2.3   Business-to-Business Electronic Commerce

Most users associate the commercial part of the Web with B2C e-commerce, but the greatest economic promise of all online technologies lies in the area of business-to-business (B2B) e-commerce.

Traditionally businesses have exchanged their data using the Electronic Data Interchange (EDI) approach. However this technology is complicated and understood only by experts. It is difficult to program and maintain, and it is error-prone. Each B2B communication requires separate programming, so such communications are costly. Finally, EDI is an isolated technology. The interchanged data cannot be easily integrated with other business applications.

The Internet appears to be an ideal infrastructure for business-to-business communication. Businesses have increasingly been looking at Internet-based solutions, and new business models such as *B2B portals* have emerged. Still, B2B e-commerce is hampered by the lack of standards. HTML (hypertext markup language) is too weak to support the outlined activities effectively: it provides neither the structure nor the semantics of information. The new standard of XML is a big improvement but can still support communications only in cases where there is a priori agreement on the vocabulary to be used and on its meaning.

The realization of the Semantic Web will allow businesses to enter partnerships without much overhead. Differences in terminology will be resolved using standard *abstract domain models*, and data will be interchanged using translation services. Auctioning, negotiations, and drafting contracts will be carried out automatically (or semiautomatically) by software agents.

1.2.4   Wikis

Currently, the use of the WWW is expanded by tools that enable the active participation of Web users. Some consider this development revolutionary and have given it a name: Web 2.0.

Part of this direction involves *wikis*, collections of Web pages that allow users to add content (usually structured text and hypertext links) via a browser interface. Wiki systems allow for collaborative knowledge creation because they give users almost complete freedom to add and change information without ownership of content, access restrictions, or rigid workflows. Wiki systems are used for a variety of purposes, including the following:

- Development of bodies of knowledge in a community effort, with contributions from a wide range of users. The best-known result is the general-purpose Wikipedia.

- Knowledge management of an activity or a project. Examples are brainstorming and exchanging ideas, coordinating activities, and exchanging records of meetings.

While it is still early to talk about drawbacks and limitations of this technology, wiki systems can definitely benefit from the use of semantic technologies. The main idea is to make the inherent structure of a wiki, given by the linking between pages, accessible to machines beyond mere navigation. This can be done by enriching structured text and untyped hyperlinks with semantic annotations referring to an underlying model of the knowledge captured by the wiki. For example, a hyperlink from *Knossos* to *Heraklion* could be annotated with information *is located in*. This information could then be used for context-specific presentation of pages, advanced querying, and consistency verification.

1.2.5   Personal Agents: A Future Scenario

The following scenario illustrates functionalities that can be implemented based on Semantic Web technologies.

Michael had just had a minor car accident and was feeling some neck pain. His primary care physician suggested a series of physical therapy sessions. Michael asked his Semantic Web agent to work out some possibilities.

The agent retrieved details of the recommended therapy from the doctor's agent and looked up the list of therapists maintained by Michael's health insurance company. The agent checked for those located within a radius of 10 km from Michael's office or home, and looked up their reputation according to trusted rating services. Then it tried to match available appointment times with Michael's calendar. In a few minutes the agent returned two proposals. Unfortunately, Michael was not happy with either of them. One therapist had offered appointments in two weeks' time; for the other Michael would have to drive during rush hour. Therefore, Michael decided to set stricter time constraints and asked the agent to try again.

A few minutes later the agent came back with an alternative: a therapist with a good reputation who had available appointments starting in two days. However, there were a few minor problems. Some of Michael's less important work appointments would have to be rescheduled. The agent offered to make arrangements if this solution were adopted. Also, the therapist was not listed on the insurer's site because he charged more than the insurer's maximum coverage. The agent had found his name from an independent list of therapists and had already checked that Michael was entitled to the insurer's maximum coverage, according to the insurer's policy. It had also negotiated with the therapist's agent a special discount. The therapist had only recently decided to charge more than average and was keen to find new patients.

Michael was happy with the recommendation because he would have to pay only a few dollars extra. However, because he had installed the Semantic Web agent a few days ago, he asked it for explanations of some of its assertions: how was the therapist's reputation established, why was it necessary for Michael to reschedule some of his work appointments, how was the price negotiation conducted? The agent provided appropriate information.

Michael was satisfied. His new Semantic Web agent was going to make his busy life easier. He asked the agent to take all necessary steps to finalize the task.

1.3   Semantic Web Technologies

The scenarios outlined in section 1.2 are not science fiction; they do not require revolutionary scientific progress to be achieved. We can reasonably claim that the challenge is an engineering and technology adoption rather than a scientific one: partial solutions to all important parts of the problem exist. At present, the greatest needs are in the areas of integration, standardization, development of tools, and adoption by users. But, of course, further technological progress will lead to a more advanced Semantic Web than can, in principle, be achieved today.

In the following sections we outline a few technologies that are necessary for achieving the functionalities previously outlined.

1.3.1   Explicit Metadata

Currently, Web content is formatted for human readers rather than programs. HTML is the predominant language in which Web pages are written (directly or using tools). A portion of a typical Web page of a physical therapist might look like this:

```
<h1>Agilitas Physiotherapy Centre</h1>
Welcome to the Agilitas Physiotherapy Centre home page.
Do you feel pain? Have you had an injury? Let our staff
Lisa Davenport, Kelly Townsend (our lovely secretary)
and Steve Matthews take care of your body and soul.

<h2>Consultation hours</h2>
Mon 11am - 7pm<br>
Tue 11am - 7pm<br>
Wed 3pm - 7pm<br>
Thu 11am - 7pm<br>
Fri 11am - 3pm<p>
But note that we do not offer consultation
during the weeks of the
<a href=". . .">State Of Origin</a> games.
```

For people the information is presented in a satisfactory way, but machines will have their problems. Keyword-based searches will identify the words *physiotherapy* and *consultation hours*. And an intelligent agent might even be able to identify the personnel of the center. But it will have trouble distinguishing the therapists from the secretary, and even more trouble finding the exact consultation hours (for which it would have to follow the link to the State Of Origin games to find when they take place).

The Semantic Web approach to solving these problems is not the development of superintelligent agents. Instead it proposes to attack the problem from the Web page side. If HTML is replaced by more appropriate languages, then the Web pages could carry their content on their sleeve. In addition to containing formatting information aimed at producing a document for human readers, they could contain information about their content. In our example, there might be information such as

```
<company>
  <treatmentOffered>Physiotherapy</treatmentOffered>
  <companyName>Agilitas Physiotherapy Centre</companyName>
  <staff>
    <therapist>Lisa Davenport</therapist>
    <therapist>Steve Matthews</therapist>
    <secretary>Kelly Townsend</secretary>
```

```
    </staff>
  </company>
```

This representation is far more easily processable by machines. The term *metadata* refers to such information: data about data. Metadata capture part of the *meaning* of data, thus the term *semantic* in Semantic Web.

In our example scenarios in section 1.2 there seemed to be no barriers in the access to information in Web pages: therapy details, calendars and appointments, prices and product descriptions, it seemed like all this information could be directly retrieved from existing Web content. But, as we explained, this will not happen using text-based manipulation of information but rather by taking advantage of machine-processable metadata.

As with the current development of Web pages, users will not have to be computer science experts to develop Web pages; they will be able to use tools for this purpose. Still, the question remains why users should care, why they should abandon HTML for Semantic Web languages. Perhaps we can give an optimistic answer if we compare the situation today to the beginnings of the Web. The first users decided to adopt HTML because it had been adopted as a standard and they were expecting benefits from being early adopters. Others followed when more and better Web tools became available. And soon HTML was a universally accepted standard.

Similarly, we are currently observing the early adoption of XML. While not sufficient in itself for the realization of the Semantic Web vision, XML is an important first step. Early users, perhaps some large organizations interested in knowledge management and B2B e-commerce, will adopt XML and RDF, the current Semantic Web-related W3C standards. And the momentum will lead to more and more tool vendors' and end users' adopting the technology.

This will be a decisive step in the Semantic Web venture, but it is also a challenge. As we mentioned, the greatest current challenge is not scientific but rather one of technology adoption.

1.3.2   Ontologies

The term *ontology* originates from philosophy. In that context, it is used as the name of a subfield of philosophy, namely, the study of the nature of existence (the literal translation of the Greek word $Ov\tau o\lambda o\gamma i\alpha$), the branch of metaphysics concerned with identifying, in the most general terms, the kinds of things that actually exist, and how to describe them. For example, the observation that the world is made up of specific objects that can be grouped

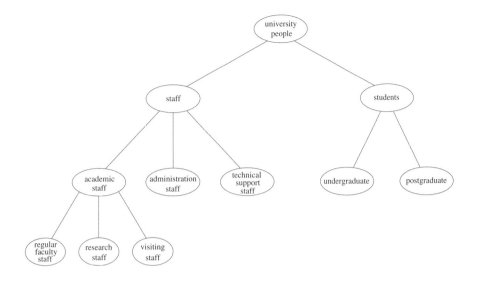

Figure 1.1   A hierarchy

into abstract classes based on shared properties is a typical ontological commitment.

However, in more recent years, *ontology* has become one of the many words hijacked by computer science and given a specific technical meaning that is rather different from the original one. Instead of "ontology" we now speak of "*an* ontology." For our purposes, we will use T. R. Gruber's definition, later refined by R. Studer: *An ontology is an explicit and formal specification of a conceptualization.*

In general, an ontology describes formally a domain of discourse. Typically, an ontology consists of a finite list of terms and the relationships between these terms. The *terms* denote important *concepts* (*classes* of objects) of the domain. For example, in a university setting, staff members, students, courses, lecture theaters, and disciplines are some important concepts.

The *relationships* typically include hierarchies of classes. A hierarchy specifies a class C to be a subclass of another class C' if every object in C is also included in C'. For example, all faculty are staff members. Figure 1.1 shows a hierarchy for the university domain.

Apart from subclass relationships, ontologies may include information such as

- properties (X teaches Y),

- value restrictions (only faculty members may teach courses),

- disjointness statements (faculty and general staff are disjoint),

- specifications of logical relationships between objects (every department must include at least ten faculty members).

In the context of the Web, ontologies provide *a shared understanding of a domain*. Such a shared understanding is necessary to overcome differences in terminology. One application's zip code may be the same as another application's area code. Another problem is that two applications may use the same term with different meanings. In university A, a course may refer to a degree (like computer science), while in university B it may mean a single subject (CS 101). Such differences can be overcome by mapping the particular terminology to a shared ontology or by defining direct mappings between the ontologies. In either case, it is easy to see that ontologies support semantic interoperability .

Ontologies are useful for the organization and navigation of Web sites. Many Web sites today expose on the left-hand side of the page the top levels of a concept hierarchy of terms. The user may click on one of them to expand the subcategories.

Also, ontologies are useful for improving the accuracy of Web searches. The search engines can look for pages that refer to a precise *concept* in an ontology instead of collecting all pages in which certain, generally ambiguous, keywords occur. In this way, differences in terminology between Web pages and the queries can be overcome.

In addition, Web searches can exploit generalization/specialization information. If a query fails to find any relevant documents, the search engine may suggest to the user a more general query. It is even conceivable for the engine to run such queries proactively to reduce the reaction time in case the user adopts a suggestion. Or if too many answers are retrieved, the search engine may suggest to the user some specializations.

In Artificial Intelligence (AI) there is a long tradition of developing and using ontology languages. It is a foundation Semantic Web research can build upon. At present, the most important ontology languages for the Web are the following:

- RDF is a data model for objects ("resources") and relations between them;

it provides a simple semantics for this data model; and these data models can be represented in an XML syntax.

- RDF Schema is a vocabulary description language for describing properties and classes of RDF resources, with a semantics for generalization hierarchies of such properties and classes.

- OWL is a richer vocabulary description language for describing properties and classes, such as relations between classes (e.g., disjointness), cardinality (e.g., "exactly one"), equality, richer typing of properties, characteristics of properties (e.g., symmetry), and enumerated classes.

1.3.3 Logic

Logic is the discipline that studies the principles of reasoning; it goes back to Aristotle. In general, logic offers, first, *formal languages* for expressing knowledge. Second, logic provides us with *well-understood formal semantics*: in most logics, the meaning of sentences is defined without the need to operationalize the knowledge. Often we speak of declarative knowledge: we describe *what* holds without caring about *how* it can be deduced.

And third, automated reasoners can deduce (infer) conclusions from the given knowledge, thus making implicit knowledge explicit. Such reasoners have been studied extensively in AI. Here is an example of an inference. Suppose we know that all professors are faculty members, that all faculty members are staff members, and that Michael is a professor. In predicate logic the information is expressed as follows:

$$prof(X) \rightarrow faculty(X)$$
$$faculty(X) \rightarrow staff(X)$$
$$prof(michael)$$

Then we can deduce the following:

$$faculty(michael)$$
$$staff(michael)$$
$$prof(X) \rightarrow staff(X)$$

Note that this example involves knowledge typically found in ontologies. Thus logic can be used to uncover ontological knowledge that is implicitly given. By doing so, it can also help uncover unexpected relationships and inconsistencies.

But logic is more general than ontologies. It can also be used by intelligent agents for making decisions and selecting courses of action. For example, a shop agent may decide to grant a discount to a customer based on the rule

$$loyalCustomer(X) \rightarrow discount(X, 5\%)$$

where the loyalty of customers is determined from data stored in the corporate database. Generally there is a trade-off between expressive power and computational efficiency. The more expressive a logic is, the more computationally expensive it becomes to draw conclusions. And drawing certain conclusions may become impossible if noncomputability barriers are encountered. Luckily, most knowledge relevant to the Semantic Web seems to be of a relatively restricted form. For example, our previous examples involved *rules* of the form, "If conditions, then conclusion," where conditions and conclusion are simple statements, and only finitely many objects needed to be considered. This subset of logic, called Horn logic, is tractable and supported by efficient reasoning tools.

An important advantage of logic is that it can provide *explanations* for conclusions: the series of inference steps can be retraced. Moreover AI researchers have developed ways of presenting an explanation in a human-friendly way, by organizing a proof as a natural deduction and by grouping a number of low-level inference steps into metasteps that a person will typically consider a single proof step. Ultimately an explanation will trace an answer back to a given set of facts and the inference rules used.

Explanations are important for the Semantic Web because they increase users' confidence in Semantic Web agents (see the physiotherapy example in section 1.2.5). Tim Berners-Lee speaks of an "Oh yeah?" button that would ask for an explanation.

Explanations will also be necessary for activities between agents. While some agents will be able to draw logical conclusions, others will only have the capability to *validate proofs*, that is, to check whether a claim made by another agent is substantiated. Here is a simple example. Suppose agent 1, representing an online shop, sends a message "You owe me $80" (not in natural language, of course, but in a formal, machine-processable language) to agent 2, representing a person. Then agent 2 might ask for an explanation, and agent 1 might respond with a sequence of the form

   Web log of a purchase over $80

Proof of delivery (for example, tracking number of UPS)

Rule from the shop's terms and conditions:

$$purchase(X, Item) \land price(Item, Price) \land delivered(Item, X)$$
$$\rightarrow owes(X, Price)$$

Thus facts will typically be traced to some Web addresses (the trust of which will be verifiable by agents), and the rules may be a part of a shared commerce ontology or the policy of the online shop.

For logic to be useful on the Web it must be usable in conjunction with other data, and it must be machine-processable as well. Therefore, there is ongoing work on representing logical knowledge and proofs in Web languages. Initial approaches work at the level of XML, but in the future rules and proofs will need to be represented at the level of RDF and ontology languages, such as DAML+OIL and OWL.

1.3.4   Agents

Agents are pieces of software that work autonomously and proactively. Conceptually they evolved out of the concepts of object-oriented programming and component-based software development.

A personal agent on the Semantic Web (figure 1.2) will receive some tasks and preferences from the person, seek information from Web sources, communicate with other agents, compare information about user requirements and preferences, select certain choices, and give answers to the user. An example of such an agent is Michael's private agent in the physiotherapy example of section 1.2.5.

It should be noted that agents will not replace human users on the Semantic Web, nor will they necessarily make decisions. In many, if not most, cases their role will be to collect and organize information, and present choices for the users to select from, as Michael's personal agent did in offering a selection between the two best solutions it could find, or as a travel agent does that looks for travel offers to fit a person's given preferences.

Semantic Web agents will make use of all the technologies we have outlined:

- Metadata will be used to identify and extract information from Web sources.

- Ontologies will be used to assist in Web searches, to interpret retrieved information, and to communicate with other agents.

Today   **In the future**

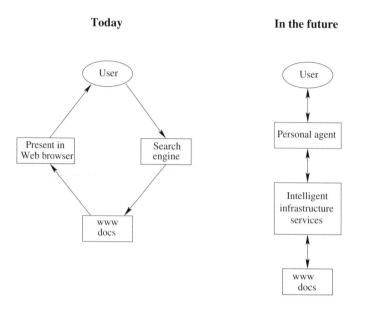

Figure 1.2   Intelligent personal agents

- Logic will be used for processing retrieved information and for drawing conclusions.

Further technologies will also be needed, such as agent communication languages. Also, for advanced applications it will be useful to represent formally the beliefs, desires, and intentions of agents, and to create and maintain user models. However, these points are somewhat orthogonal to the Semantic Web technologies. Therefore they are not discussed further in this book.

1.3.5   The Semantic Web versus Artificial Intelligence

As we have said, most of the technologies needed for the realization of the Semantic Web build upon work in the area of artificial intelligence. Given that AI has a long history, not always commercially successful, one might worry that, in the worst case, the Semantic Web will repeat AI's errors: big promises that raise too high expectations, which turn out not to be fulfilled (at least not in the promised time frame).

This worry is unjustified. The realization of the Semantic Web vision does not rely on human-level intelligence; in fact, as we have tried to explain, the challenges are approached in a different way. The full problem of AI is a deep scientific one, perhaps comparable to the central problems of physics (explain the physical world) or biology (explain the living world). So seen, the difficulties in achieving human-level Artificial Intelligence within ten or twenty years, as promised at some points in the past, should not have come as a surprise.

But on the Semantic Web partial solutions will work. Even if an intelligent agent is not able to come to all conclusions that a human user might draw, the agent will still contribute to a Web much superior to the current Web. This brings us to another difference. If the ultimate goal of AI is to build an intelligent agent exhibiting human-level intelligence (and higher), the goal of the Semantic Web is to assist human users in their day-to-day online activities.

It is clear that the Semantic Web will make extensive use of current AI technology and that advances in that technology will lead to a better Semantic Web. But there is no need to wait until AI reaches a higher level of achievement; current AI technology is already sufficient to go a long way toward realizing the Semantic Web vision.

1.4   A Layered Approach

The development of the Semantic Web proceeds in steps, each step building a *layer* on top of another. The pragmatic justification for this approach is that it is easier to achieve consensus on small steps, whereas it is much harder to get everyone on board if too much is attempted. Usually there are several research groups moving in different directions; this competition of ideas is a major driving force for scientific progress. However, from an engineering perspective there is a need to standardize. So, if most researchers agree on certain issues and disagree on others, it makes sense to fix the points of agreement. This way, even if the more ambitious research efforts should fail, there will be at least partial positive outcomes.

Once a standard has been established, many more groups and companies will adopt it, instead of waiting to see which of the alternative research lines will be successful in the end. The nature of the Semantic Web is such that companies and single users must build tools, add content, and use that content. We cannot wait until the full Semantic Web vision materializes — it may take another ten years for it to be realized to its full extent (as envisioned today, of course).

In building one layer of the Semantic Web on top of another, two principles should be followed:

- Downward compatibility. Agents fully aware of a layer should also be able to interpret and use information written at lower levels. For example, agents aware of the semantics of OWL can take full advantage of information written in RDF and RDF Schema.

- Upward partial understanding. The design should be such that agents fully aware of a layer should be able to take at least partial advantage of information at higher levels. For example, an agent aware only of the RDF and RDF Schema semantics might interpret knowledge written in OWL partly, by disregarding those elements that go beyond RDF and RDF Schema. Of course, there is no requirement for all tools to provide this functionality; the point is that this option should be enabled.

While these ideas are theoretically appealing and have been used as guiding principles for the development of the Semantic Web, their realization in practice turned out to be difficult, and some compromises needed to be made. This will become clear in chapter 4, where the layering of RDF and OWL is discussed.

Figure 1.3 shows the "layer cake" of the Semantic Web (due to Tim Berners-Lee), which describes the main layers of the Semantic Web design and vision.

At the bottom we find *XML*, a language that lets one write structured Web documents with a user-defined vocabulary. XML is particularly suitable for sending documents across the Web.

RDF is a basic data model, like the entity-relationship model, for writing simple statements about Web objects (resources). The RDF data model does not rely on XML, but RDF has an XML-based syntax. Therefore, in figure 1.3, it is located on top of the XML layer.

RDF Schema provides modeling primitives for organizing Web objects into hierarchies. Key primitives are classes and properties, subclass and subproperty relationships, and domain and range restrictions. RDF Schema is based on RDF.

RDF Schema can be viewed as a primitive language for writing ontologies. But there is a need for more powerful *ontology languages* that expand RDF Schema and allow the representations of more complex relationships between Web objects. The *Logic* layer is used to enhance the ontology lan-

Figure 1.3 A layered approach to the Semantic Web

guage further and to allow the writing of application-specific declarative knowledge.

The *Proof layer* involves the actual deductive process as well as the representation of proofs in Web languages (from lower levels) and proof validation.

Finally, the *Trust layer* will emerge through the use of *digital signatures* and other kinds of knowledge, based on recommendations by trusted agents or on rating and certification agencies and consumer bodies. Sometimes "Web of Trust" is used to indicate that trust will be organized in the same distributed and chaotic way as the WWW itself. Being located at the top of the pyramid, trust is a high-level and crucial concept: the Web will only achieve its full potential when users have trust in its operations (security) and in the quality of information provided.

This classical layer stack is currently being debated. Figure 1.4 shows an alternative layer stack that takes recent developments into account. The main differences, compared to the stack in figure 1.3, are the following:

Figure 1.4 An alternative Semantic Web stack

- The ontology layer is instantiated with two alternatives: the current standard Web ontology language, OWL, and a rule-based language. Thus an alternative stream in the development of the Semantic Web appears.

- DLP is the intersection of OWL and Horn logic, and serves as a common foundation.

The Semantic Web architecture is currently being debated and may be subject to refinements and modifications in the future.

1.5 Book Overview

In this book we concentrate on the Semantic Web technologies that have reached a reasonable degree of maturity.

In chapter 2 we discuss XML and related technologies. XML introduces structure to Web documents, thus supporting syntactic interoperability. The structure of a document can be made machine-accessible through DTDs and XML Schema. We also discuss namespaces; accessing and querying XML documents using XPath; and transforming XML documents with XSLT.

In chapter 3 we discuss RDF and RDF Schema. RDF is a language in which we can express statements about objects (resources); it is a standard data model for machine-processable semantics. RDF Schema offers a number of modeling primitives for organizing RDF vocabularies in typed hierarchies.

Chapter 4 discusses OWL, the current proposal for a Web ontology language. It offers more modeling primitives compared to RDF Schema, and it has a clean, formal semantics.

Chapter 5 is devoted to rules, both monotonic and nonmonotonic, in the framework of the Semantic Web. While this layer has not yet been fully defined, the principles to be adopted are quite clear, so it makes sense to present them.

Chapter 6 discusses several application domains and explains the benefits that they will draw from the materialization of the Semantic Web vision.

Chapter 7 describes the development of ontology-based systems for the Web and contains a miniproject that employs much of the technology described in this book.

Finally, chapter 8 discusses briefly a few issues that are currently under debate in the Semantic Web community.

1.6 Summary

- The Semantic Web is an initiative that aims at improving the current state of the World Wide Web.

- The key idea is the use of machine-processable Web information.

- Key technologies include explicit metadata, ontologies, logic and inferencing, and intelligent agents.

- The development of the Semantic Web proceeds in layers.

Suggested Reading

An excellent introductory article, from which, among others, the scenario in section 1.2.5 was adapted.

- T. Berners-Lee, J. Hendler, and O. Lassila. The Semantic Web. *Scientific American* 284 (May 2001): 34–43.

An inspirational book about the history (and the future) of the Web is

- T. Berners-Lee, with M. Fischetti. *Weaving the Web*. San Francisco: Harper, 1999.

Many introductory articles on the Semantic Web are available online. Here we list a few:

- T. Berners-Lee. Semantic Web Road Map. September 1998.
  <http://www.w3.org/DesignIssues/Semantic.html>.

- T. Berners-Lee. Evolvability. March 1998.
  <http://www.w3.org/DesignIssues/Evolution.html>.

- T. Berners-Lee. What the Semantic Web Can Represent. September 1998.
  <http://www.w3.org/DesignIssues/RDFnot.html>.

- E. Dumbill. The Semantic Web: A Primer. November 1, 2000.
  <http://www.xml.com/pub/a/2000/11/01/semanticweb/>.

- F. van Harmelen and D. Fensel. Practical Knowledge Representation for the Web. 1999. <http://www.cs.vu.nl/~frankh/postscript/IJCAI99-III.html>.

- J. Hendler. Agents and the Semantic Web. *IEEE Intelligent Systems* 16 (March-April 2001): 30–37.
  Preprint at <http://www.cs.umd.edu/users/hendler/AgentWeb.html>.

- S. Palmer. The Semantic Web, Taking Form.
  <http://infomesh.net/2001/06/swform/>.

- S. Palmer. The Semantic Web: An Introduction.
  <http://infomesh.net/2001/swintro/>.

- A. Swartz. The Semantic Web in Breadth.
  <http://logicerror.com/semanticWeb-long>.

- A. Swartz and J. Hendler. The Semantic Web: A Network of Content for the Digital City. 2001. <http://blogspace.com/rdf/SwartzHendler.html>.

A collection of educational material related to the semantic web is maintained at REASE (Repository, European Association for Semantic Web Education):

- <http://rease.semanticweb.org/ubp>.

A number of Web sites maintain up-to-date information about the Semantic Web and related topics:

- <http://www.semanticweb.org/>.

- <http://www.w3.org/2001/sw/>.

- <http://www.ontology.org/>.

There is a good selection of research papers providing technical information on issues relating to the Semantic Web:

- D. Fensel, J. Hendler, H. Lieberman, and W. Wahlster, eds. *Spinning the Semantic Web*. Cambridge, Mass.: MIT Press, 2003.

- J. Davies, D. Fensel, and F. van Harmelen, eds. *Towards the Semantic Web: Ontology-Driven Knowledge Management*. New York: Wiley, 2002.

- The conference series of the *International Semantic Web Conference*. See <http://www.semanticweb.org/>.

Issues related to the Semantic Web architecture are discussed in the following article:

- I. Horrocks, B. Parsia, P. Patel-Schneider and J. Hendler. Semantic Web Architecture: Stack or Two Towers? In *Proceedings of the 3rd Workshop on Principles and Practice of Semantic Web Reasoning (PPSWR'05)*, LNCS 3703, Springer 2005, 37–41.

Information about semantic wikis is found at

- <http://wiki.ontoworld.org/wiki/Semantic_Wiki_Interest_Group>.

2 *Structured Web Documents: XML*

2.1 Introduction

Today HTML (hypertext markup language) is the standard language in which Web pages are written. HTML, in turn, was derived from SGML (standard generalized markup language), an international standard (ISO 8879) for the definition of device- and system-independent methods of representing information, both human- and machine-readable. Such standards are important because they enable effective communication, thus supporting technological progress and business collaboration. In the WWW area, standards are set by the W3C (World Wide Web Consortium); they are called *recommendations,* in acknowledgment of the fact that in a distributed environment without central authority, standards cannot be enforced.

Languages conforming to SGML are called SGML applications. HTML is such an application; it was developed because SGML was considered far too complex for Internet-related purposes. XML (extensible markup language) is another SGML application, and its development was driven by shortcomings of HTML. We can work out some of the motivations for XML by considering a simple example, a Web page that contains information about a particular book.

```
<h2>Nonmonotonic Reasoning:  Context-Dependent
    Reasoning</h2>
<i>by <b>V. Marek</b> and <b>M. Truszczynski</b></i><br>
Springer 1993<br>
ISBN 0387976892
```

A typical XML representation of the same information might look like this:

```
<book>
  <title>
    Nonmonotonic Reasoning:  Context-Dependent Reasoning
  </title>
  <author>V. Marek</author>
  <author>M. Truszczynski</author>
  <publisher>Springer</publisher>
  <year>1993</year>
  <ISBN>0387976892</ISBN>
</book>
```

Before we turn to differences between the HTML and XML representations, let us observe a few similarities. First, both representations use *tags*, such as <h2> and </year>. Indeed both HTML and XML are *markup languages*: they allow one to write some content and provide information about what role that content plays.

Like HTML, XML is based on tags. These tags may be nested (tags within tags). All tags in XML must be closed (for example, for an opening tag <title> there must be a closing tag </title>), whereas in HTML some tags, such as <br>, may be left open. The enclosed content, together with its opening and closing tags, is referred to as an *element*. (The recent development of XHTML has brought HTML more in line with XML: any valid XHTML document is also a valid XML document, and as a consequence, opening and closing tags in XHTML are balanced.)

A less formal observation is that human users can read both HTML and XML representations quite easily. Both languages were designed to be easily understandable and usable by humans. But how about machines? Imagine an intelligent agent trying to retrieve the names of the authors of the book in the previous example. Suppose the HTML page could be located with a Web search (something that is not at all clear; the limitations of current search engines are well documented). There is no *explicit* information as to who the authors are. A reasonable guess would be that the authors' names appear immediately after the title or immediately follow the word *by*. But there is no guarantee that these conventions are always followed. And even if they were, are there two authors, "V. Marek" and "M. Truszczynski", or just one, called "V. Marek and M. Truszczynski"? Clearly, more text processing is needed to answer this question, processing that is open to errors.

The problems arise from the fact that the HTML document does not contain structural information, that is, information about pieces of the document and their relationships. In contrast, the XML document is far more easily accessible to machines because every piece of information is described. Moreover, some forms of their *relations* are also defined through the nesting structure. For example, the <author> tags appear within the <book> tags, so they describe properties of the particular book. A machine processing the XML document would be able to deduce that the author element refers to the enclosing book element, rather than having to infer this fact from proximity considerations, as in HTML. An additional advantage is that XML allows the definition of constraints on values (for example, that a year must be a number of four digits, that the number must be less than 3,000). *XML allows the representation of information that is also machine-accessible.*

Of course, we must admit that the HTML representation provides more than the XML representation: the formatting of the document is also described. However, this feature is not a strength but a weakness of HTML: it *must* specify the formatting; in fact, the main use of an HTML document is to display information (apart from linking to other documents). On the other hand, *XML separates content from formatting.* The same information can be displayed in different ways without requiring multiple copies of the same content; moreover, the content may be used for purposes other than display.

Let us now consider another example, a famous law of physics. Consider the HTML text

```
<h2>Relationship force-mass</h2>
<i>F = M x a</i>
```

and the XML representation

```
<equation>
  <meaning>Relationship force-mass</meaning>
  <leftside>F</leftside>
  <rightside>M x a</rightside>
</equation>
```

If we compare the HTML document to the previous HTML document, we notice that both use basically the same tags. That is not surprising, since they are *predefined*. In contrast, the second XML document uses completely different tags from the first XML document. This observation is related to the intended use of representations. HTML representations are intended to display information, so the set of tags is fixed: lists, bold, color, and so on. In XML we may use information in various ways, and it is up to the user to define a vocabulary suitable for the application. Therefore, *XML is a metalanguage for markup: it does not have a fixed set of tags but allows users to define tags of their own.*

Just as people cannot communicate effectively if they don't use a common language, applications on the WWW must agree on common vocabularies if they need to communicate and collaborate. Communities and business sectors are in the process of defining their specialized vocabularies, creating XML applications (or extensions; thus the term *extensible* in the name of XML). Such XML applications have been defined in various domains, for example, mathematics (MathML), bioinformatics (BSML), human resources (HRML), astronomy (AML), news (NewsML), and investment (IRML).

Also, the W3C has defined various languages on top of XML, such as SVG and SMIL. This approach has also been taken for RDF (see chapter 3).

It should be noted that XML can serve as a *uniform data exchange format* between applications. In fact, XML's use as a data exchange format between applications nowadays far outstrips its originally intended use as document markup language. Companies often need to retrieve information from their customers and business partners, and update their corporate databases accordingly. If there is not an agreed common standard like XML, then specialized processing and querying software must be developed for each partner separately, leading to technical overhead; moreover, the software must be updated every time a partner decides to change its own database format.

Chapter Overview

This chapter presents the main features of XML and associated languages. It is organized as follows:

- Section 2.2 describes the XML language in more detail, and section 2.3 describes the structuring of XML documents.

- In relational databases the structure of tables must be defined. Similarly, the structure of an XML document must be defined. This can be done by writing a DTD (Document Type Definition), the older approach, or an XML schema, the modern approach that will gradually replace DTDs.

- Section 2.4 describes namespaces, which support the modularization of DTDs and XML schemas.

- Section 2.5 is devoted to the accessing and querying of XML documents, using XPath.

- Finally, section 2.6 shows how XML documents can be transformed to be displayed (or for other purposes) using XSL and XSLT.

2.2 The XML Language

An *XML document* consists of a prolog, a number of elements, and an optional epilog (not discussed here).

2.2.1 Prolog

The prolog consists of an XML declaration and an optional reference to external structuring documents. Here is an example of an *XML declaration*:

```
<?xml version="1.0" encoding="UTF-16"?>
```

It specifies that the current document is an XML document, and defines the version and the character encoding used in the particular system (such as UTF-8, UTF-16, and ISO 8859-1). The character encoding is not mandatory, but its specification is considered good practice. Sometimes we also specify whether the document is self-contained, that is, whether it does not refer to external structuring documents:

```
<?xml version="1.0" encoding="UTF-16" standalone="no"?>
```

A reference to external structuring documents looks like this:

```
<!DOCTYPE book SYSTEM "book.dtd">
```

Here the structuring information is found in a local file called book.dtd. Instead, the reference might be a URL. If only a locally recognized name or only a URL is used, then the label SYSTEM is used. If, however, one wishes to give both a local name and a URL, then the label PUBLIC should be used instead.

2.2.2 Elements

XML elements represent the "things" the XML document talks about, such as books, authors, and publishers. They compose the main concept of XML documents. An element consists of an *opening tag*, its *content*, and a *closing tag*. For example,

```
<lecturer>David Billington</lecturer>
```

Tag names can be chosen almost freely; there are very few restrictions. The most important ones are that the first character must be a letter, an underscore, or a colon; and that no name may begin with the string "xml" in any combination of cases (such as "Xml" and "xML").

The content may be text, or other elements, or nothing. For example,

```
<lecturer>
  <name>David Billington</name>
  <phone>+61-7-3875 507</phone>
</lecturer>
```

If there is no content, then the element is called *empty*. An empty element like

```
<lecturer></lecturer>
```

can be abbreviated as

```
<lecturer/>
```

2.2.3   Attributes

An empty element is not necessarily meaningless, because it may have some properties in terms of *attributes*. An attribute is a name-value pair inside the opening tag of an element:

```
<lecturer name="David Billington" phone="+61-7-3875 507"/>
```

Here is an example of attributes for a nonempty element:

```
<order orderNo="23456" customer="John Smith"
       date="October 15, 2002">
  <item itemNo="a528" quantity="1"/>
  <item itemNo="c817" quantity="3"/>
</order>
```

The same information could have been written as follows, replacing attributes by nested elements:

```
<order>
  <orderNo>23456</orderNo>
  <customer>John Smith</customer>
  <date>October 15, 2002</date>
  <item>
    <itemNo>a528</itemNo>
    <quantity>1</quantity>
  </item>
```

```
<item>
  <itemNo>c817</itemNo>
  <quantity>3</quantity>
</item>
</order>
```

When to use elements and when attributes is often a matter of taste. However, note that attributes cannot be nested.

2.2.4   Comments

A comment is a piece of text that is to be ignored by the parser. It has the form

```
<!-- This is a comment -->
```

2.2.5   Processing Instructions (PIs)

PIs provide a mechanism for passing information to an application about how to handle elements. The general form is

```
<?target instruction?>
```

For example,

```
<?stylesheet type="text/css" href="mystyle.css"?>
```

PIs offer procedural possibilities in an otherwise declarative environment.

2.2.6   Well-Formed XML Documents

An XML document is well-formed if it is syntactically correct. The following are some syntactic rules:

- There is only one outermost element in the document (called the *root element*).

- Each element contains an opening and a corresponding closing tag.

- Tags may not overlap, as in
  `<author><name>Lee Hong</author></name>`.

- Attributes within an element have unique names.

- Element and tag names must be permissible.

2.2.7   Tree Model of XML Documents

It is possible to represent well-formed XML documents as trees; thus trees provide a formal data model for XML. This representation is often instructive. As an example, consider the following document:

```
<?xml version="1.0" encoding="UTF-16"?>
<!DOCTYPE email SYSTEM "email.dtd">
<email>
  <head>
    <from name="Michael Maher"
          address="michaelmaher@cs.gu.edu.au"/>
    <to   name="Grigoris Antoniou"
          address="grigoris@cs.unibremen.de"/>
    <subject>Where is your draft?</subject>
  </head>
  <body>
  Grigoris, where is the draft of the paper
  you promised me last week?
  </body>
</email>
```

Figure 2.1 shows the tree representation of this XML document. It is an ordered labeled tree:

- There is exactly one root.

- There are no cycles.

- Each node, other than the root, has exactly one parent.

- Each node has a label.

- The order of elements is important.

However, whereas the order of elements is important, the order of attributes is not. So, the following two elements are equivalent:

```
<person lastname="Woo" firstname="Jason"/>
<person firstname="Jason" lastname="Woo"/>
```

This aspect is not represented properly in the tree. In general, we would require a more refined tree concept; for example, we should also differentiate between the different types of nodes (element node, attribute node, etc.).

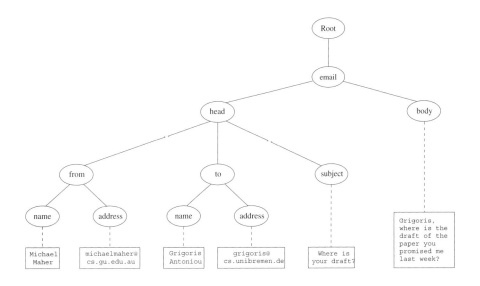

Figure 2.1   Tree representation of an XML document

However, here we use graphs as illustrations, so we do not go into further detail.

Figure 2.1 also shows the difference between the *root* (representing the XML document), and the *root element*, in our case the `email` element. This distinction will play a role when we discuss addressing and querying XML documents in section 2.5.

2.3   Structuring

An XML document is well-formed if it respects certain syntactic rules. However, those rules say nothing specific about the structure of the document. Now, imagine two applications that try to communicate, and that they wish to use the same vocabulary. For this purpose it is necessary to define all the element and attribute names that may be used. Moreover, the structure should also be defined: what values an attribute may take, which elements may or must occur within other elements, and so on.

In the presence of such structuring information we have an enhanced possibility of document validation. We say that an XML document is *valid* if it is well-formed, uses structuring information, and respects that structuring information.

There are two ways of defining the structure of XML documents: DTDs, the older and more restricted way, and XML Schema, which offers extended possibilities, mainly for the definition of data types.

2.3.1   DTDs

External and Internal DTDs

The components of a DTD can be defined in a separate file (*external DTD*) or within the XML document itself (*internal DTD*). Usually it is better to use external DTDs, because their definitions can be used across several documents; otherwise duplication is inevitable, and the maintenance of consistency over time becomes difficult.

Elements

Consider the element

```
<lecturer>
  <name>David Billington</name>
  <phone>+61-7-3875 507</phone>
</lecturer>
```

from the previous section. A DTD for this element type[1] looks like this:

```
<!ELEMENT lecturer (name,phone)>
<!ELEMENT name (#PCDATA)>
<!ELEMENT phone (#PCDATA)>
```

The meaning of this DTD is as follows:

- The element types `lecturer`, `name`, and `phone` may be used in the document.

- A `lecturer` element contains a `name` element and a `phone` element, in that order.

---

1. The distinction between the element type `lecturer` and a particular element of this type, such as `David Billington`, should be clear. All particular elements of type `lecturer` (referred to as `lecturer` elements) share the same structure, which is defined here.

- A `name` element and a `phone` element may have any content. In DTDs, `#PCDATA` is the only atomic type for elements.

We express that a `lecturer` element contains either a `name` element or a `phone` element as follows:

```
<!ELEMENT lecturer (name|phone)>
```

It gets more difficult when we wish to specify that a `lecturer` element contains a `name` element and a `phone` element *in any order*. We can only use the trick

```
<!ELEMENT lecturer ((name,phone)|(phone,name))>
```

However, this approach suffers from practical limitations (imagine ten elements in any order).

Attributes

Consider the element

```
<order orderNo="23456" customer="John Smith"
       date="October 15, 2002">
  <item itemNo="a528" quantity="1"/>
  <item itemNo="c817" quantity="3"/>
</order>
```

from the previous section. A DTD for it looks like this:

```
<!ELEMENT order (item+)>
<!ATTLIST order
  orderNo   ID    #REQUIRED
  customer  CDATA #REQUIRED
  date      CDATA #REQUIRED>
<!ELEMENT item EMPTY>
<!ATTLIST item
  itemNo    ID    #REQUIRED
  quantity  CDATA #REQUIRED
  comments  CDATA #IMPLIED>
```

Compared to the previous example, a new aspect is that the `item` element type is defined to be empty. Another new aspect is the appearance of + after `item` in the definition of the `order` element type. It is one of the *cardinality operators*:

?:   appears zero times or once.

⋆:   appears zero or more times.

+:   appears one or more times.

No cardinality operator means exactly once.

In addition to defining elements, we have to define attributes. This is done in an *attribute list*. The first component is the name of the element type to which the list applies, followed by a list of triplets of attribute name, attribute type, and value type. An *attribute* name is a name that may be used in an XML document using a DTD.

Attribute Types

Attribute types are similar to predefined data types, but the selection is very limited. The most important attribute types are

- CDATA, a string (sequence of characters),

- ID, a name that is unique across the entire XML document,

- IDREF, a reference to another element with an ID attribute carrying the same value as the IDREF attribute,

- IDREFS, a series of IDREFs,

- $(v_1|\ldots|v_n)$, an enumeration of all possible values.

The selection is not satisfactory. For example, dates and numbers cannot be specified; they have to be interpreted as strings (CDATA); thus their specific structure cannot be enforced.

Value Types

There are four value types:

- #REQUIRED. The attribute must appear in every occurrence of the element type in the XML document. In the previous example, itemNo and quantity must always appear within an item element.

- #IMPLIED. The appearance of the attribute is optional. In the example, comments are optional.

- #FIXED "value". Every element must have this attribute, which has always the value given after #FIXED in the DTD. A value given in an XML document is meaningless because it is overridden by the fixed value.

- "value". This specifies the default value for the attribute. If a specific value appears in the XML document, it overrides the default value. For example, the default encoding of the e-mail system may be "mime", but "binhex" will be used if specified explicitly by the user.

Referencing

Here is an example for the use of IDREF and IDREFS. First we give a DTD:

```
<!ELEMENT family (person*)>
<!ELEMENT person (name)>
<!ELEMENT name (#PCDATA)>
<!ATTLIST person
  id        ID       #REQUIRED
  mother    IDREF    #IMPLIED
  father    IDREF    #IMPLIED
  children  IDREFS   #IMPLIED>
```

An XML element that respects this DTD is the following:

```
<family>

  <person id="bob" mother="mary" father="peter">
    <name>Bob Marley</name>
  </person>

  <person id="bridget" mother="mary">
    <name>Bridget Jones</name>
  </person>

  <person id="mary" children="bob bridget">
    <name>Mary Poppins</name>
  </person>

  <person id="peter" children="bob">
    <name>Peter Marley</name>
  </person>

</family>
```

Readers should study the references between `persons`.

XML Entities

An XML entity can play several roles, such as a placeholder for repeatable characters (a type of shorthand), a section of external data (e.g., XML or other), or as a part of a declaration for elements. A typical use of internal entities, and the one used in subsequent chapters of this book, is similar to constants in a programming language. For example, suppose that a document has several copyright notices that refer to the current year. Then it makes sense to declare an entity

```
<!ENTITY thisyear "2007">
```

Then, at each place the current year needs to be included, we can use the entity reference `&thisyear;` instead. That way, updating the year value to "2008" for the whole document will only mean changing the entity declaration.

A Concluding Example

As a final example we give a DTD for the `email` element from section 2.2.7:

```
<!ELEMENT email (head,body)>
<!ELEMENT head (from,to+,cc*,subject)>
<!ELEMENT from EMPTY>
<!ATTLIST from
  name     CDATA     #IMPLIED
  address  CDATA     #REQUIRED>
<!ELEMENT to EMPTY>
<!ATTLIST to
  name     CDATA     #IMPLIED
  address  CDATA     #REQUIRED>
<!ELEMENT cc EMPTY>
<!ATTLIST cc
  name     CDATA     #IMPLIED
  address  CDATA     #REQUIRED>
<!ELEMENT subject (#PCDATA)>
<!ELEMENT body (text,attachment*)>
<!ELEMENT text (#PCDATA)>
<!ELEMENT attachment EMPTY>
<!ATTLIST attachment
```

```
encoding (mime|binhex) "mime"
file      CDATA     #REQUIRED>
```

We go through some interesting parts of this DTD:

- A `head` element contains a `from` element, at least one `to` element, zero or more `cc` elements, and a `subject` element, in that order.

- In `from`, `to`, and `cc` elements the `name` attribute is not required; the `address` attribute, on the other hand, is always required.

- A `body` element contains a `text` element, possibly followed by a number of `attachment` elements.

- The `encoding` attribute of an `attachment` element must have either the value "`mime`" or "`binhex`", the former being the default value.

We conclude with two more remarks on DTDs. First, a DTD can be interpreted as an Extended Backus-Naur Form (EBNF). For example, the declaration

```
<!ELEMENT email (head,body)>
```

is equivalent to the rule

```
email ::= head body
```

which means that an e-mail consists of a head followed by a body. And second, recursive definitions are possible in DTDs. For example,

```
<!ELEMENT bintree ((bintree root bintree)|emptytree)>
```

defines binary trees: a binary tree is the empty tree, or consists of a left subtree, a root, and a right subtree.

2.3.2 XML Schema

XML Schema offers a significantly richer language for defining the structure of XML documents. One of its characteristics is that its syntax is based on XML itself. This design decision provides a significant improvement in readability, but more important, it also allows significant reuse of technology. It is no longer necessary to write separate parsers, editors, pretty printers, and so on, to obtain a separate syntax, as was required for DTDs; any XML will do. An even more important improvement is the possibility of reusing and refining schemas. XML Schema allows one to define new types by extending or restricting already existing ones. In combination with an XML-based syntax, this feature allows one to build schemas from other schemas, thus reducing the workload. Finally, XML Schema provides a sophisticated set of data types that can be used in XML documents (DTDs were limited to strings only).

An XML schema is an element with an opening tag like

```
<xsd:schema
  xmlns:xsd-"http://www.w3.org/2000/10/XMLSchema"
  version="1.0">
```

The element uses the schema of XML Schema found at the W3C Web site. It is, so to speak, the foundation on which new schemas can be built. The prefix xsd denotes the namespace of that schema (more on namespaces in the next section). If the prefix is omitted in the xmlns attribute, then we are using elements from this namespace by default:

```
<schema
  xmlns="http://www.w3.org/2000/10/XMLSchema"
  version="1.0">
```

In the following we omit the xsd prefix.

Now we turn to schema elements. Their most important contents are the definitions of element and attribute types, which are defined using data types.

Element Types

The syntax of element types is

```
<element name="..."/>
```

and they may have a number of optional attributes, such as types,

```
type="..."
```

or cardinality constraints

- minOccurs="x", where x may be any natural number (including zero),

- `maxOccurs="x"`, where x may be any natural number (including zero) or `unbounded`.

`minOccurs` and `maxOccurs` are generalizations of the cardinality operators ?, *, and +, offered by DTDs. When cardinality constraints are not provided explicitly, `minOccurs` and `maxOccurs` have value 1 by default.

Here are a few examples.

```
<element name="email"/>

<element name="head" minOccurs="1" maxOccurs="1"/>

<element name="to" minOccurs="1"/>
```

Attribute Types

The syntax of attribute types is

```
<attribute name="..."/>
```

and they may have a number of optional attributes, such as types,

```
type="..."
```

or existence (corresponds to #OPTIONAL and #IMPLIED in DTDs),

```
use="x", where x may be optional or required or prohibited,
```

or a default value (corresponds to #FIXED and default values in DTDs).

Here are examples:

```
<attribute name="id" type="ID" use="required"/>

<attribute name="speaks" type="Language" use="optional"
    default="en"/>
```

Data Types

We have already recognized the very restricted selection of data types as a key weakness of DTDs. XML Schema provides powerful capabilities for defining data type. First there is a variety of *built-in data types*. Here we list a few:

- Numerical data types, including `integer`, `short`, `Byte`, `long`, `float`, `decimal`

- String data types, including `string`, `ID`, `IDREF`, `CDATA`, `language`

- Date and time data types, including `time`, `date`, `gMonth`, `gYear`

There are also *user-defined data types*, comprising *simple data types*, which cannot use elements or attributes, and *complex data types*, which can use elements and attributes. We discuss complex types first, deferring discussion of simple data types until we talk about restriction. Complex types are defined from already existing data types by defining some attributes (if any) and using

- `sequence`, a sequence of existing data type elements, the appearance of which in a predefined order is important,

- `all`, a collection of elements that must appear but the order of which is not important,

- `choice`, a collection of elements, of which one will be chosen.

Here is an example:

```
<complexType name="lecturerType">
  <sequence>
    <element name="firstname" type="string"
      minOccurs="0" maxOccurs="unbounded"/>
    <element name="lastname" type="string"/>
  </sequence>
  <attribute name="title" type="string" use="optional"/>
</complexType>
```

The meaning is that an element in an XML document that is declared to be of type `lecturerType` may have a `title` attribute; it may also include any number of `firstname` elements and must include exactly one `lastname` element.

Data Type Extension

Already existing data types can be extended by new elements or attributes. As an example, we extend the `lecturer` data type.

```
<complexType name="extendedLecturerType">
  <extension base="lecturerType">
    <sequence>
      <element name="email" type="string"
        minOccurs="0" maxOccurs="1"/>
    </sequence>
    <attribute name="rank" type="string" use="required"/>
  </extension>
</complexType>
```

In this example, `lecturerType` is extended by an `email` element and a `rank` attribute. The resulting data type looks like this:

```
<complexType name="extendedLecturerType">
  <sequence>
    <element name="firstname" type="string"
      minOccurs="0" maxOccurs="unbounded"/>
    <element name="lastname" type="string"/>
    <element name="email" type="string"
      minOccurs="0" maxOccurs="1"/>
  </sequence>
  <attribute name="title" type="string" use="optional"/>
  <attribute name="rank" type="string" use="required"/>
</complexType>
```

A hierarchical relationship exists between the original and the extended type. *Instances of the extended type are also instances of the original type.* They may contain additional information, but neither less information nor information of the wrong type.

Data Type Restriction

An existing data type may also be restricted by adding constraints on certain values. For example, new `type` and `use` attributes may be added, or the numerical constraints of `minOccurs` and `maxOccurs` tightened.

It is important to understand that restriction is *not* the opposite process from extension. Restriction is not achieved by deleting elements or attributes. Therefore, the following hierarchical relationship still holds: *Instances of the restricted type are also instances of the original type.* They satisfy at least the constraints of the original type and some new ones.

As an example, we restrict the `lecturer` data type as follows:

```
<complexType name="restrictedLecturerType">
  <restriction base="lecturerType">
    <sequence>
      <element name="firstname" type="string"
        minOccurs="1" maxOccurs="2"/>
    </sequence>
    <attribute name="title" type="string" use="required"/>
  </restriction>
</complexType>
```

The tightened constraints are shown in boldface. Readers should compare them with the original ones.

Simple data types can also be defined by restricting existing data types. For example, we can define a type `dayOfMonth` that admits values from 1 to 31 as follows:

```
<simpleType name="dayOfMonth">
  <restriction base="integer">
    <minInclusive value="1"/>
    <maxInclusive value="31"/>
  </restriction>
</simpleType>
```

It is also possible to define a data type by listing all the possible values. For example, we can define a data type `dayOfWeek` as follows:

```
<simpleType name="dayOfWeek">
  <restriction base="string">
    <enumeration value="Mon"/>
    <enumeration value="Tue"/>
    <enumeration value="Wed"/>
    <enumeration value="Thu"/>
    <enumeration value="Fri"/>
    <enumeration value="Sat"/>
    <enumeration value="Sun"/>
  </restriction>
</simpleType>
```

A Concluding Example

Here we define an XML schema for `email`, so that it can be compared to the DTD provided on page 38.

```
<element name="email" type="emailType"/>
<complexType name="emailType">
  <sequence>
    <element name="head" type="headType"/>
    <element name="body" type="bodyType"/>
  </sequence>
</complexType>

<complexType name="headType">
  <sequence>
    <element name="from" type="nameAddress"/>
    <element name="to" type="nameAddress"
      minOccurs="1" maxOccurs="unbounded"/>
    <element name="cc" type="nameAddress"
      minOccurs="0" maxOccurs="unbounded"/>
    <element name="subject" type="string"/>
  </sequence>
</complexType>

<complexType name="nameAddress">
  <attribute name="name" type="string" use="optional"/>
  <attribute name="address" type="string" use="required"/>
</complexType>

<complexType name="bodyType">
  <sequence>
    <element name="text" type="string"/>
    <element name="attachment" minOccurs="0"
        maxOccurs="unbounded">
      <complexType>
        <attribute name="encoding" use="optional"
            default="mime">
          <simpleType>
            <restriction base="string">
              <enumeration value="mime"/>
              <enumeration value="binhex"/>
            </restriction>
          </simpleType>
        </attribute>
        <attribute name="file" type="string"
            use="required"/>
      </complexType>
```

```
    </element>
  </sequence>
</complexType>
```

Note that some data types are defined separately and given names, while others are defined within other types and defined anonymously (the types for the `attachment` element and the `encoding` attribute). In general, if a type is only used once, it makes sense to define it anonymously for local use. However, this approach reaches its limitations quickly if nesting becomes too deep.

2.4 Namespaces

One of the main advantages of using XML as a universal (meta) markup language is that information from various sources may be accessed; in technical terms, an XML document may use more than one DTD or schema. But since each structuring document was developed independently, *name clashes* appear inevitable. If DTD A and DTD B define an element type *e* in different ways, a parser that tries to validate an XML document in which an *e* element appears must be told which DTD to use for validation purposes.

The technical solution is simple: disambiguation is achieved by using a different prefix for each DTD or schema. The prefix is separated from the local name by a colon:

```
prefix:name
```

As an example, consider an (imaginary) joint venture of an Australian university, say, Griffith University, and an American university, say, University of Kentucky, to present a unified view for online students. Each university uses its own terminology, and there are differences. For example, lecturers in the United States are not considered regular faculty, whereas in Australia they are (in fact, they correspond to assistant professors in the United States). The following example shows how disambiguation can be achieved.

```
<?xml version="1.0" encoding="UTF-16"?>
<vu:instructors
    xmlns:vu="http://www.vu.com/empDTD"
    xmlns:gu="http://www.gu.au/empDTD"
    xmlns:uky="http://www.uky.edu/empDTD">
  <uky:faculty
    uky:title="assistant professor"
```

```
    uky:name="John Smith"
    uky:department="Computer Science"/>
  <gu:academicStaff
    gu:title="lecturer"
    gu:name="Mate Jones"
    gu:school="Information Technology"/>
 </vu:instructors>
```

So, namespaces are declared within an element and can be used in that element and any of its children (elements and attributes). A namespace declaration has the form:

```
xmlns:prefix="location"
```

where location may be the address of the DTD or schema. If a prefix is not specified, as in

```
xmlns="location"
```

then the location is used by default. For example, the previous example is equivalent to the following document:

```
<?xml version="1.0" encoding="UTF-16"?>
<vu:instructors
    xmlns:vu="http://www.vu.com/empDTD"
    xmlns="http://www.gu.au/empDTD"
    xmlns:uky="http://www.uky.edu/empDTD">
  <uky:faculty
    uky:title="assistant professor"
    uky:name="John Smith"
    uky:department="Computer Science"/>
  <academicStaff
    title="lecturer"
    name="Mate Jones"
    school="Information Technology"/>
 </vu:instructors>
```

2.5 Addressing and Querying XML Documents

In relational databases, parts of a database can be selected and retrieved using query languages such as SQL. The same is true for XML documents, for which there exist a number of proposals for query languages, such as XQL, XML-QL, and XQuery.

The central concept of XML query languages is a *path expression* that specifies how a node, or a set of nodes, in the tree representation of the XML document can be reached. We introduce path expressions in the form of XPath because they can be used for purposes other than querying, namely, for transforming XML documents.

XPath is a language for addressing parts of an XML document. It operates on the tree data model of XML and has a non-XML syntax. The key concepts are path expressions. They can be

- absolute (starting at the root of the tree); syntactically they begin with the symbol /, which refers to the root of the document, situated one level above the root element of the document;

- relative to a context node.

Consider the following XML document:

```
<?xml version="1.0" encoding="UTF-16"?>
<!DOCTYPE library PUBLIC "library.dtd">
<library location="Bremen">
  <author name="Henry Wise">
    <book title="Artificial Intelligence"/>
    <book title="Modern Web Services"/>
    <book title="Theory of Computation"/>
  </author>
  <author name="William Smart">
    <book title="Artificial Intelligence"/>
  </author>
  <author name="Cynthia Singleton">
    <book title="The Semantic Web"/>
    <book title="Browser Technology Revised"/>
  </author>
</library>
```

Its tree representation is shown in figure 2.2.

In the following we illustrate the capabilities of XPath with a few examples of path expressions.

1. Address all `author` elements.

```
/library/author
```

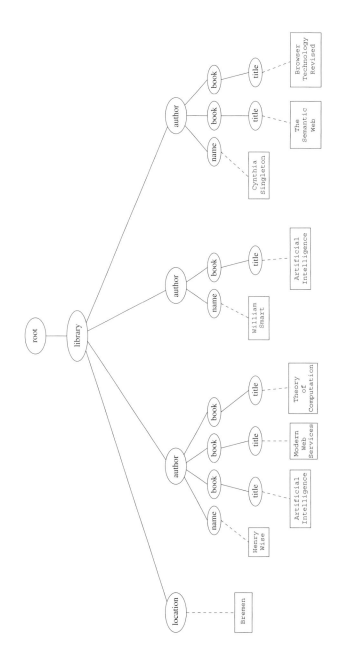

Figure 2.2 Tree representation of a library document

This path expression addresses all `author` elements that are children of the `library` element node, which resides immediately below the root. Using a sequence $/t_1/\ldots/t_n$, where each t_{i+1} is a child node of t_i, we define a path through the tree representation.

2. An alternative solution for the previous example is

   ```
   //author
   ```

   Here `//` says that we should consider all elements in the document and check whether they are of type `author`. In other words, this path expression addresses all `author` elements anywhere in the document. Because of the specific structure of our XML document, this expression and the previous one lead to the same result; however, they may lead to different results, in general.

3. Address the `location` attribute nodes within `library` element nodes.

   ```
   /library/@location
   ```

   The symbol @ is used to denote attribute nodes.

4. Address all `title` attribute nodes within `book` elements anywhere in the document, which have the value "`Artificial Intelligence`" (see figure 2.3).

   ```
   //book/@title=[.="Artificial Intelligence"]
   ```

5. Address all books with title "`Artificial Intelligence`" (see figure 2.4).

   ```
   //book[@title="Artificial Intelligence"]
   ```

We call a test within square brackets a *filter expression*. It restricts the set of addressed nodes.

Note the difference between this expression and the one in query 4. Here we address `book` elements the title of which satisfies a certain condition. In query 4 we collected `title` attribute nodes of `book` elements. A comparison of figures 2.3 and 2.4 illustrates the difference.

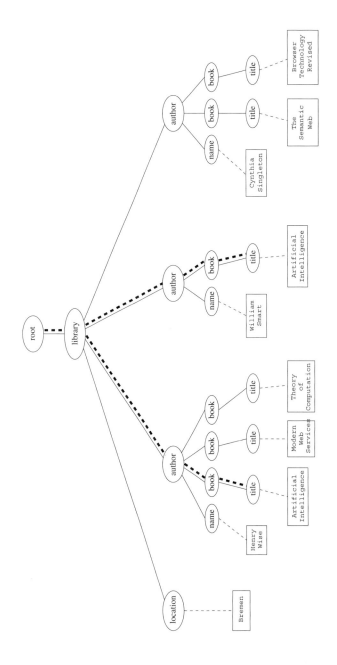

Figure 2.3 Tree representation of query 4

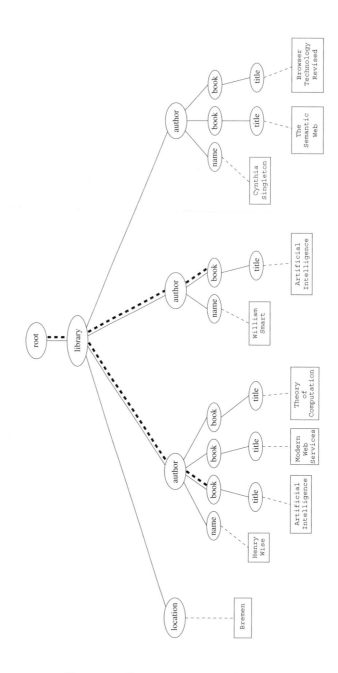

Figure 2.4   Tree representation of query 5

6. Address the first `author` element node in the XML document.

   ```
   //author[1]
   ```

7. Address the last `book` element within the first `author` element node in the document.

   ```
   //author[1]/book[last()]
   ```

8. Address all `book` element nodes without a `title` attribute.

   ```
   //book[not (@title)]
   ```

These examples are meant to give a feeling of the expressive power of path expressions. In general, a path expression consists of a series of steps, separated by slashes. A *step* consists of an axis specifier, a node test, and an optional predicate.

- An *axis specifier* determines the tree relationship between the nodes to be addressed and the context node. Examples are parent, ancestor, child (the default), sibling, attribute node. `//` is such an axis specifier; it denotes descendant or self.

- A *node test* specifies which nodes to address. The most common node tests are element names (which may use namespace information), but there are others. For example, `*` addresses all element nodes, `comment()` all comment nodes, and so on.

- *Predicates* (or *filter expressions*) are optional and are used to refine the set of addressed nodes. For example, the expression `[1]` selects the first node, `[position()=last()]` selects the last node, `[position() mod 2 = 0]` the even nodes, and so on.

We have only presented the abbreviated syntax, XPath actually has a more complicated full syntax. References are found at the end of this chapter.

2.6   Processing

So far we have not provided any information about how XML documents can be displayed. Such information is necessary because unlike HTML documents, XML documents do not contain formatting information. The advantage is that a given XML document can be presented in various ways, when different *style sheets* are applied to it. For example, consider the XML element

```
<author>
  <name>Grigoris Antoniou</name>
  <affiliation>University of Bremen</affiliation>
  <email>ga@tzi.de</email>
</author>
```

The output might look like the following, if a style sheet is used:

Grigoris Antoniou

University of Bremen

ga@tzi.de

Or it might appear as follows, if a different style sheet is used:

Grigoris Antoniou

University of Bremen

ga@tzi.de

Style sheets can be written in various languages, for example, in CSS2 (cascading style sheets level 2). The other possibility is XSL (extensible stylesheet language).

XSL includes both a transformation language (XSLT) and a formatting language. Each of these is, of course, an XML application. XSLT specifies rules with which an input XML document is transformed to another XML document, an HTML document, or plain text. The output document may use the same DTD or schema as the input document, or it may use a completely different vocabulary.

XSLT (XSL transformations) can be used independently of the formatting language. Its ability to move data and metadata from one XML representation to another makes it a most valuable tool for XML-based applications. Generally XSLT is chosen when applications that use different DTDs or schemas need to communicate. XSLT is a tool that can be used for machine-processing of content without any regard to displaying the information for people to read. Despite this fact, in the following we use XSLT only to display XML documents.

One way of defining the presentation of an XML document is to transform it into an HTML document. Here is an example. We define an XSLT document that will be applied to the author example.

```
<?xml version="1.0" encoding="UTF-16"?>
<xsl:stylesheet version="1.0"
    xmlns:xsl="http://www.w3.org/1999/XSL/Transform">

  <xsl:template match="/author">
    <html>
      <head><title>An author< /title></head>
      <body bgcolor="white">
        <b><xsl:value-of select="name"/></b><br></br>
        <xsl:value-of select="affiliation"/><br></br>
        <i><xsl:value-of select="email"/></i>
      </body>
    </html>
  </xsl:template>
</xsl:stylesheet>
```

The output of this style sheet, applied to the previous XML document, produces the following HTML document (which now defines the presentation):

```
<html>
  <head><title>An author< /title></head>
  <body bgcolor="white">
    <b>Grigoris Antoniou</b><br>
    University of Bremen<br>
    <i>ga@tzi.de</i>
  </body>
</html>
```

Let us make a few observations. XSLT documents are XML documents. So XSLT resides on top of XML (that is, it is an XML application). The XSLT document defines a *template*; in this case an HTML document, with some placeholders for content to be inserted (see figure 2.5).

In the previous XSLT document, `xsl:value-of` retrieves the value of an element and copies it into the output document. That is, it places some content into the template.

Now suppose we had an XML document with details of several authors. It would clearly be a waste of effort to treat each `author` element separately. In such cases, a special template is defined for `author` elements, which is used by the main template. We illustrate this approach referring to the following input document:

```
<authors>
```

```
<html>
<head><title>An author</title></head>
<body bgcolor="white">
  <b>...</b><br>
  ...<br>
  <i>...</i>
</body>
</html>
```

Figure 2.5   A template

```
<author>
  <name>Grigoris Antoniou</name>
  <affiliation>University of Bremen</affiliation>
  <email>ga@tzi.de</email>
</author>
<author>
  <name>David Billington</name>
  <affiliation>Griffith University</affiliation>
  <email>david@gu.edu.net</email>
</author>
</authors>
```

We define the following XSLT document:

```
<?xml version="1.0" encoding="UTF-16"?>
<xsl:stylesheet version="1.0"
    xmlns:xsl="http://www.w3.org/1999/XSL/Transform">

  <xsl:template match="/">
    <html>
    <head><title>Authors< /title></head>
    <body bgcolor="white">
      <xsl:apply-templates select="authors"/>
      <!-- Apply templates for AUTHORS children -->
    </body>
    </html>
  </xsl:template>
```

```
    <xsl:template match="authors">
      <xsl:apply-templates select="author"/>
    </xsl:template>

    <xsl:template match="author">
      <h2><xsl:value-of select="name"/></h2>
      Affiliation:<xsl:value-of select="affiliation"/><br>
      Email:  <xsl:value-of select="email"/>
      <p>
    </xsl:template>
  </xsl:stylesheet>
```

The output produced is

```
<html>
<head><title>Authors< /title></head>
<body bgcolor="white">
  <h2>Grigoris Antoniou</h2>
  Affiliation:  University of Bremen<br>
  Email:  ga@tzi.de
  <p>
  <h2>David Billington</h2>
  Affiliation:  Griffith University<br>
  Email:  david@gu.edu.net
  <p>
</body>
</html>
```

The xsl:apply-templates element causes all children of the context node to be matched against the selected path expression. For example, if the current template applies to / (that is, if the current context node is the root), then the element xsl:apply-templates applies to the root element, in this case, the authors element (remember that / is located above the root element). And if the current node is the authors element, then the element xsl:apply-templates select="author" causes the template for the author elements to be applied to all author children of the authors element.

It is good practice to define a template for each element type in the document. Even if no specific processing is applied to certain elements, in our example authors, the xsl:apply-templates element should be used. That way, we work our way from the root to the leaves of the tree, and all templates are indeed applied.

Now we turn our attention to attributes. Suppose we wish to process the element

```
<person firstname="John" lastname="Woo"/>
```

with XSLT. Let us attempt the easiest task imaginable, a transformation of the element to itself. One might be tempted to write

```
<xsl:template match="person">
  <person
    firstname="<xsl:value-of select="@firstname">"
    lastname="<xsl:value-of select="@lastname">"/>
</xsl:template>
```

However, this is not a well-formed XML document because tags are not allowed within the values of attributes. But the intention is clear; we wish to add attribute values into the template. In XSLT, data enclosed in curly brackets take the place of the `xsl:value-of` element. The correct way to define a template for this example is as follows:

```
<xsl:template match="person">
  <person
    firstname="{@firstname}"
    lastname="{@lastname}"/>
</xsl:template>
```

Finally, we give a transformation example from one XML document to another, which does not specify the display. Again we use the `authors` document as input and define an XSLT document as follows:

```
<?xml version="1.0" encoding="UTF-16"?>
<xsl:stylesheet version="1.0"
    xmlns:xsl="http://www.w3.org/1999/XSL/Transform">

  <xsl:template match="/">
    <authors>
      <xsl:apply-templates select="authors"/>
    </authors>
  </xsl:template>


  <xsl:template match="authors">
    <xsl:apply-templates select="author"/>
```

```
  </xsl:template>

  <xsl:template match="author">
    <author>
      <name><xsl:value-of select="name"/></name>
      <contact>
        <institute>
          <xsl:value-of select="affiliation"/>
        </institute>
        <email><xsl:value-of select="email"/></email>
      </contact>
    </author>
  </xsl:template>

</xsl:stylesheet>
```

The tree representation of the output document is shown in figure 2.6 to illustrate the tree transformation character of XSLT.

2.7   Summary

- XML is a metalanguage that allows users to define markup for their documents using tags.

- Nesting of tags introduces structure. The structure of documents can be enforced using schemas or DTDs.

- XML separates content and structure from formatting.

- XML is the de facto standard for the representation of structured information on the Web and supports machine processing of information.

- XML supports the exchange of structured information across different applications through markup, structure, and transformations.

- XML is supported by query languages.

Some points discussed in subsequent chapters include

- The nesting of tags does not have standard meaning.

- The semantics of XML documents is not accessible to machines, only to people.

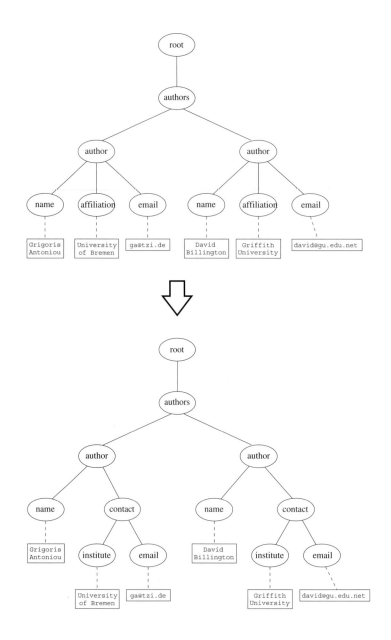

Figure 2.6   XSLT as tree transformation

- Collaboration and exchange are supported if there is an underlying shared understanding of the vocabulary. XML is well-suited for close collaboration, where domain- or community-based vocabularies are used. It is not so well-suited for global communication.

Suggested Reading

Generally the official W3C documents are found at <http://www.w3.org/>. Here we give a few of the most important links, together with some other useful references.

- T. Bray, J. Paoli, C. M. Sperberg-McQueen, E. Maler, and F. Yergeau, eds. Extensible Markup Language (XML) 1.0, 4th ed. W3C Recommendation. September 29, 2006. <http://www.w3.org/TR/REC-xml/>.

- T. Bray, D. Hollander, A. Layman, and R. Tobin, eds. Namespaces in XML 1.0, 2nd ed. W3C Recommendation. August 16, 2006. <http://www.w3.org/TR/REC-xml-names/>.

- J. Clark, and S. DeRose, eds. XML Path Language (XPath) Version 1.0. W3C Recommendation, November 16, 1999. <http://www.w3.org/TR/xpath>.

- A. Berglund, ed. Extensible Stylesheet Language (XSL) Version 1.1. W3C Recommendation. December 5, 2006. <http://www.w3.org/TR/xsl/>.

- J. Clark, ed. XSL Transformations (XSLT) Version 1.0. W3C Recommendation. November 16, 1999. <http://www.w3.org/TR/xslt>.

Recent trends in XML querying may be found at

- <http://www.w3.org/XML/Query/>.

XML has attracted a lot of attention in industry, and many books covering the technicalities in depth exist. Two books for further reading on XML are

- E. R. Harold. *XML 1.1 Bible*, 3rd ed. New York: Wiley 2004.

- W. Willard. *HTML: A Beginner's Guide*, 3rd ed. New York: McGraw Hill (Osborne), 2006.

Several sites have teaching material on XML and related technologies:

- <http://www.xml.com/>, where the following papers may be found:

  - N. Walsh. A Technical Introduction to XML. October 3, 1998.
  - T. Bray. XML Namespaces by Example. January 19, 1999.
  - E. van der Vlist. Using W3C XML Schema. October 17, 2001.
  - G. Holman. What Is XSLT? (I): The Context of XSL Transformations and the XML Path Language. August 16, 2000.

- <http://www.w3schools.com/>.

- <http://www.topxml.com/>.

- <http://www.zvon.org/>.

- <http://www.xslt.com/>.

Exercises and Projects

2.1 In our e-mail example we specified the body of an e-mail to contain exactly one text and a number of attachments. Modify the schema to allow for an arbitrary number of texts and attachments in any order.

2.2 Search the Web for XML applications, with keywords such as "XML DTD" or "XML schema".

2.3 Read the official W3C documents on namespaces, XPath, XSL, and XSLT. Identify some issues that were not covered in this chapter, in particular, the general notation and capabilities of XPath. Write small documents that use these new aspects.

2.4 In this chapter we did not cover links, a crucial ingredient of Web pages. XLink provides linking capabilities that go beyond HTML links. Check out XLink on the official W3C pages. Note that simple links can be created as follows:

```
<mylink xmlns:xlink=http://www.w3.org/1999/xlink"
   xlink:type="simple" xlink:href="target.html">
Click here </mylink>
```

2.5 Discuss the relevance of XSLT for defining *views* on Web sites ("views" hide certain parts of Web sites and display only those parts meant for the particular user's viewing).

2.6   Draw a comparison between document markup using XML and using TeX/LaTeX, also between XML transformations and BibTeX.

For the following projects you are asked to "design a vocabulary". This includes designing a vocabulary, writing a corresponding DTD or schema, writing sample XML documents, and transforming these documents into HTML and viewing them in a Web browser.

2.7   Design a vocabulary to model (parts of) your workplace. For example, if you are at a university, design a vocabulary about courses, teaching staff, rooms, publications, and so on.

2.8   For one of your hobbies, design a vocabulary for exchanging information with others who share your interest.

2.9   Perhaps you read books of certain categories? Design a vocabulary for describing them and communicating about them with other people.

2.10 Are you an investor? Design a vocabulary about available investment options and their properties (for example, risk, return, investor age, investor character).

2.11 Do you like cooking? Design a vocabulary about foods, tastes, and recipes.

2.12 For each of the above vocabularies, consider writing a second XSL style sheet, this time not translating the XML to HTML but instead to a different markup language, such as WML, the markup language for WAP-enabled mobile telephones. Such a style sheet should be geared toward displaying the information on small mobile devices with limited bandwidth and limited screen space. You could use one of the freely available WAP simulators to display the results.

3 *Describing Web Resources: RDF*

3.1 Introduction

XML is a universal metalanguage for defining markup. It provides a uniform framework, and a set of tools like parsers, for interchange of data and metadata between applications. However, XML does not provide any means of talking about the *semantics* (meaning) of data. For example, there is no intended meaning associated with the nesting of tags; it is up to each application to interpret the nesting. Let us illustrate this point using an example. Suppose we want to express the following fact:

> *David Billington is a lecturer of Discrete Mathematics.*

There are various ways of representing this sentence in XML. Three possibilities are

```
<course name="Discrete Mathematics">
  <lecturer>David Billington</lecturer>
</course>

<lecturer name="David Billington">
  <teaches>Discrete Mathematics</teaches>
</lecturer>

<teachingOffering>
  <lecturer>David Billington</lecturer>
  <course>Discrete Mathematics</course>
</teachingOffering>
```

Note that the first two formalizations include essentially an opposite nesting although they represent the same information. So there is no standard way of assigning meaning to tag nesting.

Although often called a "language" (and we commit this sin ourselves in this book), RDF (Resource Description Framework) is essentially a *data model*. Its basic building block is an object-attribute-value triple, called a *statement*. The preceding sentence about Billington is such a statement. Of course, an abstract data model needs a concrete syntax in order to be represented and transmitted, and RDF has been given a syntax in XML. As a result, it inherits the benefits associated with XML. However, it is important to understand that other syntactic representations of RDF, not based on XML, are also possible; XML-based syntax is not a necessary component of the RDF model.

RDF is domain-independent in that no assumptions about a particular domain of use are made. It is up to users to define their own terminology in a schema language called *RDF Schema* (*RDFS*). The name RDF Schema is now widely regarded as an unfortunate choice. It suggests that RDF Schema has a similar relation to RDF as XML Schema has to XML, but in fact this is not the case. XML Schema constrains the *structure* of XML documents, whereas RDF Schema defines the *vocabulary* used in RDF data models. In RDFS we can define the vocabulary, specify which properties apply to which kinds of objects and what values they can take, and describe the relationships between objects. For example, we can write

> *Lecturer* is a subclass of *academic staff member*.

This sentence means that all lecturers are also academic staff members. It is important to understand that there is an intended meaning associated with "is a subclass of". It is not up to the application to interpret this term; its intended meaning must be respected by all RDF processing software. Through fixing the semantics of certain ingredients, RDF/RDFS enables us to model particular domains.

We illustrate the importance of RDF Schema with an example. Consider the following XML elements:

```
<academicStaffMember>Grigoris Antoniou</academicStaffMember>
<professor>Michael Maher</professor>
<course name="Discrete Mathematics">
  <isTaughtBy>David Billington</isTaughtBy>
</course>
```

Suppose we want to collect all academic staff members. A path expression in Xpath might be

```
//academicStaffMember
```

The result is only Grigoris Antoniou. While correct from the XML viewpoint, this answer is *semantically* unsatisfactory. Human readers would have also included Michael Maher and David Billington in the answer because

- all professors are academic staff members (that is, `professor` is a subclass of `academicStaffMember`);

- courses are only taught by academic staff members.

This kind of information makes use of the *semantic model* of the particular domain and cannot be represented in XML or in RDF but is typical of knowledge written in RDF Schema. Thus *RDFS makes semantic information machine-accessible*, in accordance with the Semantic Web vision.

Chapter Overview

Sections 3.2 and 3.3 discuss the basic ideas of RDF and its XML-based syntax, and sections 3.4 and 3.5 introduce the basic concepts and the language of RDF Schema.

Section 3.6 shows the definition of some elements of the namespaces of RDF and RDF Schema. Section 3.7 presents an axiomatic semantics for RDF and RDFS. This semantics uses predicate logic and formalizes the intuitive meaning of the modeling primitives of the languages.

Section 3.8 provides a direct semantics based on inference rules, and section 3.9 is devoted to the querying of RDF/RDFS documents using SPARQL.

3.2 RDF: Basic Ideas

The fundamental concepts of RDF are resources, properties, and statements.

3.2.1 Resources

We can think of a resource as an object, a "thing" we want to talk about. Resources may be authors, books, publishers, places, people, hotels, rooms, search queries, and so on. Every resource has a URI, a Uniform Resource Identifier. A URI can be a URL (Uniform Resource Locator, or Web address) or some other kind of unique identifier; note that an identifier does not necessarily enable *access* to a resource. URI schemes have been defined not only for Web locations but also for such diverse objects as telephone numbers, ISBN numbers, and geographic locations. There has been a long discussion about the nature of URIs, even touching philosophical questions (for example, what is an appropriate unique identifier for a person?), but we will not go into detail here. In general, we assume that a URI is the identifier of a Web resource.

3.2.2 Properties

Properties are a special kind of resources; they describe relations between resources, for example "written by", "age", "title", and so on. Properties in RDF are also identified by URIs (and in practice by URLs). This idea of using URIs to identify "things" and the relations between them is quite important. This choice gives us in one stroke a global, worldwide, unique naming scheme. The use of such a scheme greatly reduces the homonym problem that has plagued distributed data representation until now.

3.2.3 Statements

Statements assert the properties of resources. A statement is an object-attribute-value triple, consisting of a resource, a property, and a value. Values can either be resources or *literals*. Literals are atomic values (strings), the structure of which we do not discuss further.

3.2.4 Three Views of a Statement

An example of a statement is

> *David Billington is the owner of the Web page*
> *http://www.cit.gu.edu.au/~db.*

The simplest way of interpreting this statement is to use the definition and consider the triple

```
(http://www.cit.gu.edu.au/~db,
 http://www.mydomain.org/site-owner, #DavidBillington).
```

We can think of this triple (x, P, y) as a logical formula $P(x, y)$, where the binary predicate P relates the object x to the object y. In fact, *RDF offers only*

Figure 3.1   Graphic representation of a triple

binary predicates (properties). Note that the property "site-owner" and both of the two objects are identified by URLs.

A second view is graph-based. Figure 3.1 shows the graph corresponding to the preceding statement. It is a directed graph with labeled nodes and arcs; the arcs are directed from the resource (the *subject* of the statement) to the value (the *object* of the statement). This kind of graph is known in the Artificial Intelligence community as a *semantic net*.

As we have said, the value of a statement may be a resource. Therefore, it may be linked to other resources. Consider the following triples:

```
(http://www.cit.gu.edu.au/~db,
 http://www.mydomain.org/site-owner,
 #DavidBillington)

(#DavidBillington, http://www.mydomain.org/phone,
 "3875507")

(#DavidBillington, http://www.mydomain.org/uses,
 http://www.cit.gu.edu.au/~arock/defeasible/Defeasible.cgi)

(http://www.cit.gu.edu.au/~arock/defeasible/Defeasible.cgi,
 http://www.mydomain.org/site-owner, ``Andrew Rock'')
```

The graphic representation is found in figure 3.2.

Graphs are a powerful tool for human understanding. But the Semantic Web vision requires machine-accessible and machine-processable representations.

Therefore, there is a third representation possibility based on XML. According to this possibility, an RDF document is represented by an XML element with the tag `rdf:RDF`. The content of this element is a number of *descriptions*, which use `rdf:Description` tags. Every description makes a statement about a resource, which is identified in one of three different ways:

- An `about` attribute, referencing an existing resource

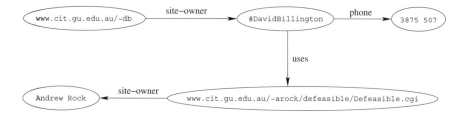

Figure 3.2   A semantic net

- An ID attribute, creating a new resource

- Without a name, creating an anonymous resource

We will discuss the XML-based syntax of RDF in section 3.3; here we just show the representation of our first statement:

```
<?xml version="1.0" encoding="UTF-16"?>
<rdf:RDF
  xmlns:rdf="http://www.w3.org/1999/02/22-rdf-syntax-ns#"
  xmlns:mydomain="http://www.mydomain.org/my-rdf-ns">

 <rdf:Description rdf:about="http://www.cit.gu.edu.au/~db">
  <mydomain:site-owner rdf:resource="#DavidBillington"/>
 </rdf:Description>

</rdf:RDF>
```

The first line specifies that we are using XML. In the following examples we omit this line.

The rdf:Description element makes a statement about the resource http://www.cit.gu.edu.au/~db. Within the description the property is used as a tag, and the content is the value of the property.

The descriptions are given in a certain order; in other words, the XML syntax imposes a *serialization*. The order of descriptions (or resources) is *not* significant according to the abstract model of RDF. This again shows that the graph model is the real data model of RDF and that XML is just a possible serial representation of the graph.

3.2.5   Reification

In RDF it is possible to make statements about statements, such as

> Grigoris believes that David Billington is the creator of the Web page http://www.cit.gu.edu.au/~db.

This kind of statement can be used to describe belief or trust in other statements, which is important in some kinds of applications. The solution is to assign a unique identifier to each statement, which can be used to refer to the statement. RDF allows this using a *reification mechanism* (see section 3.3.6).

The key idea is to introduce an auxiliary object, say, *belief1*, and relate it to each of the three parts of the original statement through the properties *subject*, *predicate*, and *object*. In the preceding example the subject of *belief1* would be *David Billington*, the predicate would be *creator*, and the object *http://www.cit.gu.edu.au/~db*. Note that this rather cumbersome approach is necessary because there are only triples in RDF; therefore we cannot add an identifier directly to a triple (then it would be a quadruple).

3.2.6   Data Types

Consider the telephone number "3875507". A program reading this RDF data model cannot know if the literal "3875507" is to be interpreted as an integer (an object which it would make sense to, say, divide by 17) or as a string, or indeed if it is a integer, whether it is in decimal or hexadecimal representation. A program can only know how to interpret this resource if the application is explicitly given the information that the literal is intended to represent a number, and which number the literal is supposed to represent. The common practice in programming languages or database systems is to provide this kind of information by associating a data type with the literal, in this case, a data type like decimal or integer. In RDF, *typed literals* are used to provide this kind of information.

Using a typed literal, we could describe David Billington's age as being the integer number 27 using the triple

```
(#DavidBillington, http://www.mydomain.org/age,
 "27"^http://www.w3.org/2001/XMLSchema#integer )
```

This example shows two things: the use of the ^^ notation to indicate the type of a literal,[1] and the use of data types that are predefined by XML

---

1. This notation takes a different form in the XML-based syntax described in section 3.3.

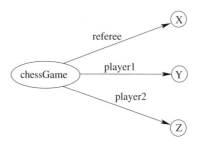

Figure 3.3   Representation of a tertiary predicate

Schema. Strictly speaking, the use of any externally defined data typing scheme is allowed in RDF documents, but in practice the most widely used data typing scheme will be the one by XML Schema. XML Schema predefines a large range of data types, including Booleans, integers, floating-point numbers, times, and dates.

3.2.7   A Critical View of RDF

We have already pointed out that RDF uses only binary properties. This restriction seems quite serious because often we use predicates with more than two arguments. Luckily, such predicates can be simulated by a number of binary predicates. We illustrate this technique for a predicate *referee* with three arguments. The intuitive meaning of *referee(X, Y, Z)* is

X is the referee in a chess game between players Y and Z.

We now introduce a new auxiliary resource *chessGame* and the binary predicates *ref*, *player1*, and *player2*. Then we can represent *referee(X, Y, Z)* as follows:

ref(chessGame, X)

player1(chessGame, Y)

player2(chessGame, Z)

The graphic representation is shown in figure 3.3. Although the solution is sound, the problem remains that the original predicate with three arguments was simpler and more natural.

Another problem with RDF has to do with the handling of properties. As mentioned, properties are special kinds of resources. Therefore, properties themselves can be used as the object in an object-attribute-value triple (statement). While this possibility offers flexibility, it is rather unusual for modeling languages, and can be confusing for modelers.

Also, the reification mechanism is quite powerful and appears misplaced in a simple language like RDF. Making statements about statements introduces a level of complexity that is not necessary for a basic layer of the Semantic Web. Instead, it would have appeared more natural to include it in more powerful layers, which provide richer representational capabilities.

Finally, the XML-based syntax of RDF is well suited for machine processing but is not particularly human-friendly.

In summary, RDF has its idiosyncrasies and is not an optimal modeling language. However, we have to live with the fact that it is already a de facto standard. In the history of technology, often the better technology was not adopted. For example, the video system VHS was probably the technically weakest of the three systems that were available on the market at one time (the others were Beta and Video 2000), not to mention hardware and software standards in personal computing, which were arguably not adopted because of their technical merit.

On the positive side, it is true that RDF has sufficient expressive power (at least as a basis on which more layers can be built). And ultimately the Semantic Web will not be programmed in RDF, but rather with user-friendly tools that will automatically translate higher representations into RDF. Using RDF offers the benefit that information maps unambiguously to a model. And since it is likely that RDF will become a standard, the benefits of drafting data in RDF can be seen as similar to drafting information in HTML in the early days of the Web.

3.3 RDF: XML-Based Syntax

An RDF document consists of an `rdf:RDF` element, the content of which is a number of descriptions. For example, consider the domain of university courses and lecturers at Griffith University in the year 2001.

```
<!DOCTYPE rdf:RDF [
    <!ENTITY xsd  "http://www.w3.org/2001/XMLSchema#">
]>
```

```
<rdf:RDF
  xmlns:rdf="http://www.w3.org/1999/02/22-rdf-syntax-ns#"
  xmlns:xsd="http://www.w3.org/2001/XMLSchema#"
  xmlns:uni="http://www.mydomain.org/uni-ns#">

 <rdf:Description rdf:about="949352">
  <uni:name>Grigoris Antoniou</uni:name>
  <uni:title>Professor</uni:title>
 </rdf:Description>

 <rdf:Description rdf:about="949318">
  <uni:name>David Billington</uni:name>
  <uni:title>Associate Professor</uni:title>
  <uni:age rdf:datatype="&xsd;integer">27</uni:age>
 </rdf:Description>

 <rdf:Description rdf:about="949111">
  <uni:name>Michael Maher</uni:name>
  <uni:title>Professor</uni:title>
 </rdf:Description>

 <rdf:Description rdf:about="CIT1111">
  <uni:courseName>Discrete Mathematics</uni:courseName>
  <uni:isTaughtBy>David Billington</uni:isTaughtBy>
 </rdf:Description>

 <rdf:Description rdf:about="CIT1112">
  <uni:courseName>Concrete Mathematics</uni:courseName>
  <uni:isTaughtBy>Grigoris Antoniou</uni:isTaughtBy>
 </rdf:Description>

 <rdf:Description rdf:about="CIT2112">
  <uni:courseName>Programming III</uni:courseName>
  <uni:isTaughtBy>Michael Maher</uni:isTaughtBy>
 </rdf:Description>

 <rdf:Description rdf:about="CIT3112">
  <uni:courseName>Theory of Computation</uni:courseName>
  <uni:isTaughtBy>David Billington</uni:isTaughtBy>
 </rdf:Description>

 <rdf:Description rdf:about="CIT3116">
```

```
    <uni:courseName>Knowledge Representation</uni:courseName>
    <uni:isTaughtBy>Grigoris Antoniou</uni:isTaughtBy>
   </rdf:Description>
  </rdf:RDF>
```

Let us make a few comments. First, the namespace mechanism of XML is used, but in an expanded way. In XML namespaces are only used for disambiguation purposes. In RDF external namespaces are expected to be RDF documents defining resources, which are then used in the importing RDF document. This mechanism allows the reuse of resources by other people who may decide to insert additional features into these resources. The result is the emergence of large, distributed collections of knowledge.

Second, the `rdf:about` attribute of the element `rdf:Description` is, strictly speaking, equivalent in meaning to that of an ID attribute, but it is often used to suggest that the object about which a statement is made has already been "defined" elsewhere. Formally speaking, a set of RDF statements together simply forms a large graph, relating things to other things through properties, and there is no such thing as "defining" an object in one place and referring to it elsewhere. Nevertheless, in the serialized XML syntax, it is sometimes useful (if only for human readability) to suggest that one location in the XML serialization is the "defining" location, while other locations state "additional" properties about an object that has been "defined" elsewhere.

In fact the preceding example is slightly misleading. If we wanted to be absolutely correct, we should replace all occurrences of course and staff IDs, such as `949352` and `CIT3112`, by references to the external namespace, for example

```
   <rdf:Description
     rdf:about="http://www.mydomain.org/uni-ns/#CIT3112">
```

We have refrained from doing so to improve readability of our initial example because we are primarily interested here in the ideas of RDF. However, readers should be aware that this would be the precise way of writing a correct RDF document.

The content of `rdf:Description` elements are called *property elements*. For example, in the description

```
   <rdf:Description rdf:about="CIT3116">
    <uni:courseName>Knowledge Representation</uni:courseName>
    <uni:isTaughtBy>Grigoris Antoniou</uni:isTaughtBy>
```

```
</rdf:Description>
```

the two elements `uni:courseName` and `uni:isTaughtBy` both define
property-value pairs for `CIT3116`. The preceding description corresponds
to two RDF statements.

Third, the attribute `rdf:datatype="&xsd;integer"` is used to indicate the data type of the value of the age property. Even though the age
property has been defined to have `"&xsd;integer"` as its range, it is still
required to indicate the type of the value of this property each time it is used.
This is to ensure that an RDF processor can assign the correct type of the
property value even if it has not seen the corresponding RDF Schema definition before (a scenario that is quite likely to occur in the unrestricted World
Wide Web).

Finally, the property elements of a description must be read conjunctively.
In the preceding example, the subject is called "Knowledge Representation"
and is taught by Grigoris Antoniou.

3.3.1   The `rdf:resource` Attribute

The preceding example was not satisfactory in one respect: the relationships
between courses and lecturers were not formally defined but existed implicitly through the use of the same name. To a machine, the use of the same
name may just be a coincidence; for example, the David Billington who
teaches CIT3112 may not be the same person as the person with ID 949318
who happens to be called David Billington. What we need instead is a formal specification of the fact that, for example, the teacher of CIT1111 is the
staff member with number 949318, whose name is David Billington. We can
achieve this effect using an `rdf:resource` attribute:

```
<rdf:Description rdf:about="CIT1111">
 <uni:courseName>Discrete Mathematics</uni:courseName>
 <uni:isTaughtBy rdf:resource="949318"/>
</rdf:Description>

<rdf:Description rdf:about="949318">
 <uni:name>David Billington</uni:name>
 <uni:title>Associate Professor</uni:title>
</rdf:Description>
```

We note that in case we had *defined* the resource of the staff member with ID
number 939318 in the RDF document using the `ID` attribute instead of the

about attribute, we would have had to use a # symbol in front of 949318 in
the value of rdf:resource:

```
<rdf:Description rdf:about="CIT1111">
  <uni:courseName>Discrete Mathematics</uni:courseName>
  <uni:isTaughtBy rdf:resource="#949318"/>
</rdf:Description>

<rdf:Description rdf:ID="949318">
  <uni:name>David Billington</uni:name>
  <uni:title>Associate Professor</uni:title>
</rdf:Description>
```

The same is true for externally defined resources: for example, we refer to
the externally defined resource CIT1111 by using

```
http://www.mydomain.org/uni-ns/#CIT1111
```

as the value of rdf:about, where www.mydomain.org/uni-ns/ is the
URI where the definition of CIT1111 is found. In other words, a description with an ID defines a fragment URI, which can be used to reference the
defined description.

3.3.2   Nested Descriptions

Descriptions may be defined within other descriptions. For example, we may
replace the descriptions of the previous example with the following, nested
description:

```
<rdf:Description rdf:about="CIT1111">
 <uni:courseName>Discrete Mathematics</uni:courseName>
 <uni:isTaughtBy>
  <rdf:Description rdf:about="949318">
   <uni:name>David Billington</uni:name>
   <uni:title>Associate Professor</uni:title>
  </rdf:Description>
 </uni:isTaughtBy>
</rdf:Description>
```

Other courses, such as CIT3112, can still refer to the new resource 949318. In
other words, although a description may be defined within another description, its scope is global.

3.3.3   The `rdf:type` Element

In our examples so far, the descriptions fall into two categories: courses and lecturers. This fact is clear to human readers, but has not been formally declared anywhere, so it is not accessible to machines. In RDF it is possible to make such statements using the `rdf:type` element. Here are a couple of descriptions that include typing information.

```
<rdf:Description rdf:about="CIT1111">
<rdf:type rdf:resource="&uni;course"/>
  <uni:courseName>Discrete Mathematics</uni:courseName>
  <uni:isTaughtBy rdf:resource="949318"/>
</rdf:Description>

<rdf:Description rdf:about="949318">
 <rdf:type rdf:resource="&uni;lecturer"/>
 <uni:name>David Billington</uni:name>
 <uni:title>Associate Professor</uni:title>
</rdf:Description>
```

Note that `rdf:type` allows us to introduce some structure to the RDF document. More structuring possibilities are introduced later in this chapter when we discuss RDF Schema.

3.3.4   Abbreviated Syntax

It is possible to abbreviate the syntax of RDF documents. The simplification rules are as follows:

1. Childless property elements within description elements may be replaced by XML attributes, as in XML.

2. For description elements with a typing element we can use the name specified in the `rdf:type` element instead of `rdf:Description`.

For example, the description

```
<rdf:Description rdf:ID="CIT1111">
 <rdf:type rdf:resource="&uni;course"/>
 <uni:courseName>Discrete Mathematics</uni:courseName>
 <uni:isTaughtBy rdf:resource="#949318"/>
</rdf:Description>
```

is (according to rule 1 applied to `uni:courseName`) equivalent to

```
<rdf:Description rdf:ID="CIT1111"
  uni:courseName="Discrete Mathematics">
  <rdf:type rdf:resource="&uni;course"/>
  <uni:isTaughtBy rdf:resource="#949318"/>
</rdf:Description>
```

and also (by rule 2) to

```
<uni:course rdf:ID="CIT1111"
            uni:courseName="Discrete Mathematics">
 <uni:isTaughtBy rdf:resource="#949318"/>
</uni:course>
```

Keep in mind that these three representations are just syntactic variations of the same RDF statement. That is, they are equivalent according to the RDF data model, although they have different XML syntax.

3.3.5   Container Elements

Container elements are used to collect a number of resources or attributes about which we want to make statements *as a whole*. In our example, we may wish to talk about the courses given by a particular lecturer. Three types of containers are available in RDF:

`rdf:Bag`, an unordered container, which may contain multiple occurrences (not true for a set). Typical examples are members of the faculty board and documents in a folder — examples where an order is not imposed.

`rdf:Seq`, an ordered container, which may contain multiple occurrences. Typical examples are the modules of a course, items on an agenda, an alphabetized list of staff members — examples where an order is imposed.

`rdf:Alt`, a set of alternatives. Typical examples are the document home and mirrors, and translations of a document in various languages.

The contents of container elements are elements which are named `rdf:_1`, `rdf:_2`, and so on. Let us reformulate our entire RDF document.

```
<rdf:RDF
  xmlns:rdf="http://www.w3.org/1999/02/22-rdf-syntax-ns#"
  xmlns:uni="http://www.mydomain.org/uni-ns#">
```

```
<uni:lecturer rdf:about="949352"
              uni:name="Grigoris Antoniou"
              uni:title="Professor">
 <uni:coursesTaught>
  <rdf:Bag>
   <rdf:_1 rdf:resource="CIT1112"/>
   <rdf:_2 rdf:resource="CIT3116"/>
  </rdf:Bag>
 </uni:coursesTaught>
</uni:lecturer>

<uni:lecturer rdf:about="949318"
              uni:name="David Billington"
              uni:title="Associate Professor">
 <uni:coursesTaught>
  <rdf:Bag>
   <rdf:_1 rdf:resource="CIT1111"/>
   <rdf:_2 rdf:resource="CIT3112"/>
  </rdf:Bag>
 </uni:coursesTaught>
</uni:lecturer>

<uni:lecturer rdf:about="949111"
              uni:name="Michael Maher"
              uni:title="Professor">
 <uni:coursesTaught rdf:resource="CIT2112"/>
</uni:lecturer>

<uni:course rdf:about="CIT1111"
            uni:courseName="Discrete Mathematics">
 <uni:isTaughtBy rdf:resource="949318"/>
</uni:course>

<uni:course rdf:about="CIT1112"
            uni:courseName="Concrete Mathematics">
 <uni:isTaughtBy rdf:resource="949352"/>
</uni:course>

<uni:course rdf:about="CIT2112"
            uni:courseName="Programming III">
 <uni:isTaughtBy rdf:resource="949111"/>
```

```
  </uni:course>

  <uni:course rdf:about="CIT3112"
             uni:courseName="Theory of Computation">
   <uni:isTaughtBy rdf:resource="949318"/>
  </uni:course>

  <uni:course rdf:about="CIT3116"
             uni:courseName="Knowledge Representation">
   <uni:isTaughtBy rdf:resource="949352"/>
  </uni:course>

</rdf:RDF>
```

Instead of `rdf:_1`, `rdf:_2` …it is possible to write `rdf:li`. We use this syntactic variant in the following example. Suppose the course CIT1111 is taught by either Grigoris Antoniou or David Billington:

```
<uni:course rdf:about="CIT1111"
           uni:courseName="Discrete Mathematics">
 <uni:lecturer>
  <rdf:Alt>
   <rdf:li rdf:resource="949352"/>
   <rdf:li rdf:resource="949318"/>
  </rdf:Alt>
 </uni:lecturer>
</uni:course>
```

The container elements have an optional `ID` attribute, with which the container can be identified and referred to:

```
<uni:lecturer rdf:about="949318"
             uni:name="David Billington"
             uni:title="Associate Professor">
 <uni:coursesTaught>
  <rdf:Bag rdf:ID="DBcourses">
   <rdf:_1 rdf:resource="CIT1111"/>
   <rdf:_2 rdf:resource="CIT3112"/>
  </rdf:Bag>
 </uni:coursesTaught>
</uni:lecturer>
```

A typical application of container elements is the representation of predicates with more than two arguments. We reconsider the example *referee(X, Y,*

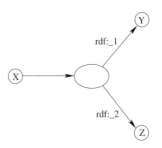

Figure 3.4 Representation of a tertiary predicate

Z), where X is the referee of a chess game between players Y and Z. One solution is to distinguish the referee X from the players Y and Z. The graphic representation is found in figure 3.4. The solution in XML-based syntax looks like this:

```
<referee rdf:about=". . .#X">
 <players>
  <rdf:Bag>
   <rdf:li rdf:resource=". . .#Y"/>
   <rdf:li rdf:resource=". . .#Z"/>
  </rdf:Bag>
 </players>
</referee>
```

Note that `rdf:Bag` defines an anonymous auxiliary resource. We chose to use a bag because we assumed that no distinction between the players is made. If order were important, say the first-named player has White and the second Black, we would use a sequence instead.

A limitation of these containers is that there is no way to close them, to say "these are all the members of the container." This is because, while one graph may describe some of the members, there is no way to exclude the possibility that there is another graph somewhere that describes additional members. RDF provides support for describing groups containing only the specified members, in the form of RDF collections. An RDF collection is a group of things represented as a list structure in the RDF graph. This list structure is constructed using a predefined collection vocabulary consisting of the predefined type `rdf:List`, the predefined properties `rdf:first` and `rdf:rest`, and the predefined resource `rdf:nil`. This allows us to write

```
<rdf:Description rdf:about="CIT2112">
 <uni:isTaughtBy>
  <rdf:List>
   <rdf:first>
    <rdf:Description rdf:about="949111"/>
   </rdf:first>
   <rdf:rest>
    <rdf:List>
     <rdf:first>
      <rdf:Description rdf:about="949352"/>
     </rdf:first>
     <rdf:rest>
      <rdf:List>
       <rdf:first>
        <rdf:Description rdf:about="949318"/>
       </rdf:first>
       <rdf:rest>
        <rdf:Description rdf:about="&rdf;nil"/>
       </rdf:rest>
      </rdf:List>
     </rdf:rest>
    </rdf:List>
   </rdf:rest>
  </rdf:List>
 </uni:isTaughtBy>
</rdf:Description>
```

This states that `CIT2112` is taught by teachers identified as the resources `949111`, `949352`, and `949318`, *and nobody else* (indicated by the terminator symbol `nil`). A shorthand syntax for this has been defined, using the "`Collection`" value for the `rdf:parseType` attribute:

```
<rdf:Description rdf:about="CIT2112">
  <uni:isTaughtBy rdf:parseType="Collection">
    <rdf:Description rdf:about="949111"/>
    <rdf:Description rdf:about="949352"/>
    <rdf:Description rdf:about="949318"/>
  </uni:isTaughtBy>
</rdf:Description>
```

3.3.6   Reification

As we have said, sometimes we wish to make statements about other statements. To do so we must be able to refer to a statement using an identifier. RDF allows such reference through a reification mechanism, which turns a statement into a resource. For example, the description

```
<rdf:Description rdf:about="949352">
 <uni:name>Grigoris Antoniou</uni:name>
</rdf:Description>
```

reifies as

```
<rdf:Statement rdf:about="StatementAbout949352">
 <rdf:subject rdf:resource="949352"/>
 <rdf:predicate rdf:resource="&uni;name"/>
 <rdf:object>Grigoris Antoniou</rdf:object>
</rdf:Statement>
```

Note that `rdf:subject`, `rdf:predicate`, and `rdf:object` allow us to access the parts of a statement.

The ID of the statement can be used to refer to it, as can be done for any description. We can either write an `rdf:Description` if we don't want to talk about it further, or an `rdf:Statement` if we wish to refer to it.

If more than one property element is contained in a description element, the elements correspond to more than one statement. These statements can either be placed in a bag and referred to as an entity, or they can reify separately (see exercise 3.1).

3.4   RDF Schema: Basic Ideas

RDF is a universal language that lets users describe resources using their own vocabularies. RDF does not make assumptions about any particular application domain, nor does it define the semantics of any domain. Is it up to the user to do so in RDF Schema (RDFS).

3.4.1   Classes and Properties

How do we describe a particular domain? Let us consider the domain of courses and lecturers at Griffith University. First we have to specify the "things" we want to talk about. Here we make a first, fundamental distinction. On one hand, we want to talk about particular lecturers, such as David

Billington, and particular courses, such as Discrete Mathematics; we have already done so in RDF. But we also want to talk about courses, first-year courses, lecturers, professors, and so on. What is the difference? In the first case we talk about *individual objects* (resources), in the second we talk about *classes* that define types of objects.

A class can be thought of as a set of elements. Individual objects that belong to a class are referred to as *instances* of that class. We have already defined the relationship between instances and classes in RDF using `rdf:type`.

An important use of classes is to impose restrictions on what can be stated in an RDF document using the schema. In programming languages, *typing* is used to prevent nonsense from being written (such as $A + 1$, where A is an array; we lay down that the arguments of $+$ must be numbers). The same is needed in RDF. After all, we would like to disallow statements such as

Discrete Mathematics is taught by Concrete Mathematics.
Room MZH5760 is taught by David Billington.

The first statement is nonsensical because we want courses to be taught by lecturers only. This imposes a restriction on the values of the property "is taught by". In mathematical terms, we restrict the *range* of the property.

The second statement is nonsensical because only courses can be taught. This imposes a restriction on the objects to which the property can be applied. In mathematical terms, we restrict the *domain* of the property.

3.4.2   Class Hierarchies and Inheritance

Once we have classes we would also like to establish relationships between them. For example, suppose that we have classes for

staff members	assistant professors
academic staff members	administrative staff members
professors	technical support staff members
associate professors	

These classes are not unrelated to each other. For example, every professor is an academic staff member. We say that "professor" is a *subclass* of "academic staff member", or equivalently, that "academic staff member" is a *superclass* of "professor". The subclass relationship defines a hierarchy of classes, as shown in figure 3.5. In general, A is a subclass of B if every instance of A is also an instance of B. There is no requirement in RDF Schema that the classes

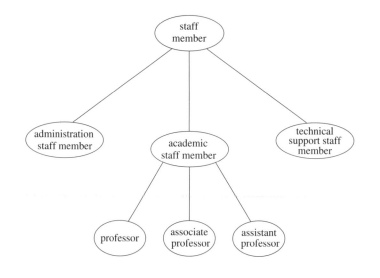

Figure 3.5   A hierarchy of classes

together form a strict hierarchy. In other words, a subclass graph as in figure 3.5 need not be a tree. A class may have multiple superclasses. If a class A is a subclass of both B_1 and B_2, this simply means that every instance of A is both an instance of B_1 and an instance of B_2.

A hierarchical organization of classes has a very important practical significance, which we outline now. Consider the range restriction

Courses must be taught by academic staff members only.

Suppose Michael Maher were defined as a professor. Then, according to the preceding restriction, he is not allowed to teach courses. The reason is that there is no statement specifying that Michael Maher is also an academic staff member. It would be counterintuitive to overcome this difficulty by adding that statement to our description. Instead we would like Michael Maher to *inherit* the ability to teach from the class of academic staff members. Exactly this is done in RDF Schema.

By doing so, RDF Schema *fixes the semantics* of "is a subclass of". Now it is not up to an application to interpret "is a subclass of"; instead its intended meaning must be used by all RDF processing software. By making such semantic definitions RDFS is a (still limited) language for defining the semantics of particular domains. Stated another way, RDF Schema is a primitive *ontology language*.

Classes, inheritance, and properties are, of course, known in other fields of computing, for example, in object-oriented programming. But while there are many similarities, there are differences, too. In object-oriented programming, an object class defines the properties that apply to it. To add new properties to a class means to modify the class.

However, in RDFS, properties are defined globally, that is, they are not encapsulated as attributes in class definitions. It is possible to define new properties that apply to an existing class without changing that class.

On one hand, this is a powerful mechanism with far-reaching consequences: we may use classes defined by others and adapt them to our requirements through new properties. On the other hand, this handling of properties deviates from the standard approach that has emerged in the area of modeling and object-oriented programming. It is another idiosyncratic feature of RDF/RDFS.

3.4.3 Property Hierarchies

We saw that hierarchical relationships between classes can be defined. The same can be done for properties. For example, "is taught by" is a *subproperty* of "involves". If a course c is taught by an academic staff member a, then c also involves a. The converse is not necessarily true. For example, a may be the convener of the course, or a tutor who marks student homework but does not teach c.

In general, P is a subproperty of Q if $Q(x, y)$ whenever $P(x, y)$.

3.4.4 RDF versus RDFS Layers

As a final point, we illustrate the different layers involved in RDF and RDFS using a simple example. Consider the RDF statement

Discrete Mathematics is taught by David Billington.

The schema for this statement may contain classes such as lecturers, academic staff members, staff members, first-year courses, and properties such as is taught by, involves, phone, employee ID. Figure 3.6 illustrates the layers of RDF and RDF Schema for this example. In this figure, blocks are properties, ellipses above the dashed line are classes, and ellipses below the dashed line are instances.

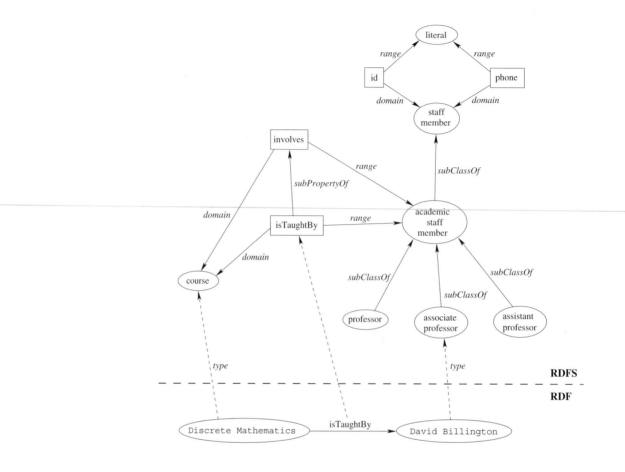

Figure 3.6   RDF and RDFS layers

The schema in figure 3.6 is itself written in a formal language, RDF Schema, that can express its ingredients: `subClassOf`, `Class`, `Property`, `subPropertyOf`, `Resource`, and so on. Next we describe the language of RDF Schema in more detail.

3.5   RDF Schema: The Language

RDF Schema provides modeling primitives for expressing the information described in section 3.4. One decision that must be made is what formal language to use. It should not be surprising that RDF itself will be used: the modeling primitives of RDF Schema are defined using resources and properties. This choice can be justified by looking at figure 3.6. We presented this figure as displaying a class/property hierarchy plus instances, but it is, of course, itself simply a labeled graph that can be encoded in RDF. Remember that RDF allows one to express any statement about any resource, and that anything with a URI can be a resource. So, if we wish to say that the class "lecturer" is a subclass of "academic staff member", we may

1. define the required resources for `lecturer`, `academicStaffMember`, and `subClassOf`;

2. define `subClassOf` to be a property;

3. write the triple (`lecturer`, `subClassOf`, `academicStaffMember`).

All these steps are within the capabilities of RDF. So, an RDFS document (that is, an RDF schema) is just an RDF document, and we use the XML-based syntax of RDF. In particular, all syntactic definitions of section 3.3 must be followed.

Now we define the modeling primitives of RDF Schema.

3.5.1 Core Classes

The core classes are

`rdfs:Resource`, the class of all resources

`rdfs:Class`, the class of all classes

`rdfs:Literal`, the class of all literals (strings)

`rdf:Property`, the class of all properties

`rdf:Statement`, the class of all reified statements

For example, a class `lecturer` can be defined as follows:

```
<rdfs:Class rdf:ID="lecturer">
  ...
</rdfs:Class>
```

3.5.2   Core Properties for Defining Relationships

The core properties for defining relationships are

`rdf:type`, which relates a resource to its class (see section 3.3.3). The resource is declared to be an instance of that class.

`rdfs:subClassOf`, which relates a class to one of its superclasses. All instances of a class are instances of its superclass. Note that a class may be a subclass of more than one class. As an example, the class `femaleProfessor` may be a subclass of both `female` and `professor`.

`rdfs:subPropertyOf`, which relates a property to one of its superproperties.

Here is an example stating that all lecturers are staff members:

```
<rdfs:Class rdf:about="lecturer">
 <rdfs:subClassOf rdf:resource="staffMember"/>
</rdfs:Class>
```

Note that `rdfs:subClassOf` and `rdfs:subPropertyOf` are transitive, by definition. Also, it is interesting that `rdfs:Class` is a subclass of `rdfs:Resource` (every class is a resource), and `rdfs:Resource` is an instance of `rdfs:Class` (`rdfs:Resource` is the class of all resources, so it is a class!). For the same reason, every class is an instance of `rdfs:Class`.

3.5.3   Core Properties for Restricting Properties

The core properties for restricting properties are

`rdfs:domain`, which specifies the domain of a property P and states that any resource that has a given property is an instance of the domain classes.

`rdfs:range`, which specifies the range of a property P and states that the values of a property are instances of the range classes.

Here is an example stating that whenever any resource has a phone number, it is (by inference) a staff member and that its value is a literal:

```
<rdf:Property rdf:ID="phone">
 <rdfs:domain rdf:resource="#staffMember"/>
 <rdfs:range rdf:resource="&rdf;Literal"/>
</rdf:Property>
```

3.5.4 Useful Properties for Reification

The following are some useful properties for reification (see section 3.3.6):

`rdf:subject,` which relates a reified statement to its subject

`rdf:predicate,` which relates a reified statement to its predicate

`rdf:object,` which relates a reified statement to its object

3.5.5 Container Classes

As mentioned in section 3.3.5, the container elements are

`rdf:Bag,` the class of bags,

`rdf:Seq,` the class of sequences,

`rdf:Alt,` the class of alternatives,

`rdfs:Container,` a superclass of all container classes, including the three preceding ones.

3.5.6 Utility Properties

A resource may be defined and described in many places on the Web. The following properties allow us to define links to those addresses:

`rdfs:seeAlso` relates a resource to another resource that explains it.

`rdfs:isDefinedBy` is a subproperty of `rdfs:seeAlso` and relates a resource to the place where its definition, typically an RDF schema, is found.

Often it is useful to provide more information, intended for human readers. This can be done with the following properties:

`rdfs:comment.` Comments, typically longer text, can be associated with a resource.

`rdfs:label.` A human-friendly label (name) is associated with a resource. Among other purposes, it may serve as the name of a node in a graphic representation of the RDF document.

3.5.7   Example: A University

We refer to the courses and lecturers example, and provide a conceptual
model of the domain, that is, an ontology.

```
<rdf:RDF
  xmlns:rdf="http://www.w3.org/1999/02/22-rdf-syntax-ns#"
  xmlns:rdfs="http://www.w3.org/2000/01/rdf-schema#">

 <rdfs:Class rdf:ID="lecturer">
  <rdfs:comment>
   The class of lecturers
   All lecturers are academic staff members.
  </rdfs:comment>
  <rdfs:subClassOf rdf:resource="#academicStaffMember"/>
 </rdfs:Class>

 <rdfs:Class rdf:ID="academicStaffMember">
  <rdfs:comment>
   The class of academic staff members
  </rdfs:comment>
  <rdfs:subClassOf rdf:resource="#staffMember"/>
 </rdfs:Class>

 <rdfs:Class rdf:ID="staffMember">
  <rdfs:comment>The class of staff members</rdfs:comment>
 </rdfs:Class>

 <rdfs:Class rdf:ID="course">
  <rdfs:comment>The class of courses</rdfs:comment>
 </rdfs:Class>

 <rdf:Property rdf:ID="involves">
  <rdfs:comment>
   It relates only courses to lecturers.
  </rdfs:comment>
  <rdfs:domain rdf:resource="#course"/>
  <rdfs:range rdf:resource="#lecturer"/>
 </rdf:Property>

 <rdf:Property rdf:ID="isTaughtBy">
  <rdfs:comment>
   Inherits its domain ("course") and range ("lecturer")
```

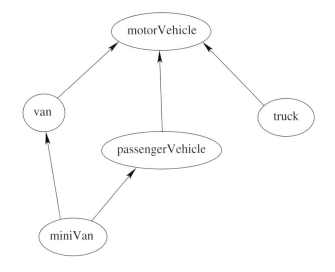

Figure 3.7   Class hierarchy for the motor vehicles example

```
   from its superproperty "involves"
  </rdfs:comment>
  <rdfs:subPropertyOf rdf:resource="#involves"/>
 </rdf:Property>

 <rdf:Property rdf:ID="phone">
  <rdfs:comment>
   It is a property of staff members
   and takes literals as values.
  </rdfs:comment>
  <rdfs:domain rdf:resource="#staffMember"/>
  <rdfs:range rdf:resource="&rdf;Literal"/>
 </rdf:Property>
</rdf:RDF>
```

3.5.8   Example: Motor Vehicles

Here we present a simple ontology of motor vehicles. The class relationships
are shown in figure 3.7.

```
<rdf:RDF
  xmlns:rdf="http://www.w3.org/1999/02/22-rdf-syntax-ns#"
```

```
     xmlns:rdfs="http://www.w3.org/2000/01/rdf-schema#">

     <rdfs:Class rdf:ID="motorVehicle"/>

     <rdfs:Class rdf:ID="van">
      <rdfs:subClassOf rdf:resource="#motorVehicle"/>
     </rdfs:Class>

     <rdfs:Class rdf:ID="truck">
      <rdfs:subClassOf rdf:resource="#motorVehicle"/>
     </rdfs:Class>

     <rdfs:Class rdf:ID="passengerVehicle">
      <rdfs:subClassOf rdf:resource="#motorVehicle"/>
     </rdfs:Class>

     <rdfs:Class rdf:ID="miniVan">
      <rdfs:subClassOf rdf:resource="#passengerVehicle"/>
      <rdfs:subClassOf rdf:resource="#van"/>
     </rdfs:Class>
    </rdf:RDF>
```

3.6   RDF and RDF Schema in RDF Schema

Now that we know the main components of the RDF and RDFS languages, it may be instructive to look at the definitions of RDF and RDFS. These definitions are expressed in the language of RDF Schema. One task is to see how easily they can be read now that the meaning of each component has been clarified.

The following definitions are just part of the full language specification. The remaining parts are found in the namespaces specified in rdf:RDF.

3.6.1   RDF

```
     <?xml version="1.0" encoding="UTF-16"?>
     <rdf:RDF
       xmlns:rdf="http://www.w3.org/1999/02/22-rdf-syntax-ns#"
       xmlns:rdfs="http://www.w3.org/2000/01/rdf-schema#">

      <rdfs:Class rdf:ID="Statement"
       rdfs:comment="The class of triples consisting of a
```

```
                   predicate, a subject and an object
                   (that is, a reified statement)"/>

   <rdfs:Class rdf:ID="Property"
    rdfs:comment="The class of properties"/>

   <rdfs:Class rdf:ID="Bag"
    rdfs:comment="The class of unordered collections"/>

   <rdfs:Class rdf:ID="Seq"
    rdfs:comment="The class of ordered collections"/>

   <rdfs:Class rdf:ID="Alt"
    rdfs:comment="The class of collections of alternatives"/>

   <rdf:Property rdf:ID="predicate"
    rdfs:comment="Identifies the property used in a statement
                  when representing the statement
                  in reified form">
    <rdfs:domain rdf:resource="#Statement"/>
    <rdfs:range rdf:resource="#Property"/>
   </rdf:Property>

   <rdf:Property rdf:ID="subject"
    rdfs:comment="Identifies the resource that a statement is
                  describing when representing the statement
                  in reified form">
    <rdfs:domain rdf:resource="#Statement"/>
   </rdf:Property>

   <rdf:Property rdf:ID="object"
    rdfs:comment="Identifies the object of a statement
                  when representing the statement
                  in reified form"/>

   <rdf:Property rdf:ID="type"
    rdfs:comment="Identifies the class of a resource.
                  The resource is an instance
                  of that class."/>

</rdf:RDF>
```

3.6.2   RDF Schema

```
<rdf:RDF
  xmlns:rdf="http://www.w3.org/1999/02/22-rdf-syntax-ns#"
  xmlns:rdfs="http://www.w3.org/2000/01/rdf-schema#">

 <rdfs:Class rdf:ID="Resource"
  rdfs:comment="The most general class"/>

 <rdfs:Class rdf:ID="comment"
  rdfs:comment="Use this for descriptions">
  <rdfs:domain rdf:resource="#Resource"/>
  <rdfs:range rdf:resource="#Literal"/>
 </rdfs:Class>

 <rdfs:Class rdf:ID="Class"
  rdfs:comment="The concept of classes.
                All classes are resources.">
  <rdfs:subClassOf rdf:resource="#Resource"/>
 </rdfs:Class>

 <rdf:Property rdf:ID="subClassOf">
  <rdfs:domain rdf:resource="#Class"/>
  <rdfs:range rdf:resource="#Class"/>
 </rdf:Property>

 <rdf:Property rdf:ID="subPropertyOf">
  <rdfs:domain rdf:resource="&rdf;Property"/>
  <rdfs:range rdf:resource="&rdf;Property"/>
 </rdf:Property>

</rdf:RDF>
```

The namespaces do *not* provide the full definition of RDF and RDF Schema. Consider, for example, `rdfs:subClassOf`. The namespace specifies only that it applies to classes and has a class as a value. The meaning of being a subclass, namely, that all instances of one class are also instances of its superclass, is not expressed anywhere. In fact, it cannot be expressed in an RDF document. If it could, there would be no need for defining RDF Schema.

We provide a formal semantics in the next section. Of course, RDF parsers and other software tools for RDF (including query processors) must be aware of the full semantics.

3.7 An Axiomatic Semantics for RDF and RDF Schema

In this section we formalize the meaning of the modeling primitives of RDF and RDF Schema. Thus we capture the *semantics* of RDF and RDFS.

The formal language we use is *predicate logic*, universally accepted as the foundation of all (symbolic) knowledge representation. Formulas used in the formalization are referred to as *axioms*.

By describing the semantics of RDF and RDFS in a formal language like logic we make the semantics unambiguous and machine-accessible. Also, we provide a basis for reasoning support by automated reasoners manipulating logical formulas.

3.7.1 The Approach

All language primitives in RDF and RDF Schema are represented by constants: $Resource, Class, Property, subClassOf$, and so on. A few predefined predicates are used as a foundation for expressing relationships between the constants.

An auxiliary theory of lists is used. It has function symbols

nil (empty list),

$cons(x, l)$ (adds an element to the front of the list),

$first(l)$ (returns the first element),

$rest(l)$ (returns the rest of the list),

and predicate symbols

$item(x, l)$ (true iff an element occurs in the list),

$list(l)$ (true iff l is a list).

Lists are used to represent containers in RDF. They are also needed to capture the meaning of certain constructs (such as cardinality constraints) in richer ontology languages.

Most axioms provide typing information. For example,

$$Type(subClassOf, Property)$$

says that $subClassOf$ is a property. We use predicate logic with equality. Variable names begin with ?. All axioms are implicitly universally quantified.

Here we show the definition of most elements of RDF and RDF Schema. The axiomatic semantics of the full languages is found in an online document; see Fikes and McGuinness (2001) in Suggested Reading.

3.7.2 Basic Predicates

The basic predicates are

$PropVal(P, R, V)$, a predicate with three arguments, which is used to represent an RDF statement with resource R, property P, and value V

$Type(R, T)$, short for $PropVal(type, R, T)$, which specifies that the resource R has the type T

$$Type(?r, ?t) \longleftrightarrow PropVal(type, ?r, ?t)$$

3.7.3 RDF

An RDF statement (triple) (R, P, V) is represented as $PropVal(P, R, V)$.

Classes

In our language we have constants $Class, Resource, Property, Literal$. All classes are instances of $Class$, that is, they have the type $Class$:

$$Type(Class, Class)$$
$$Type(Resource, Class)$$
$$Type(Property, Class)$$
$$Type(Literal, Class)$$

$Resource$ is the most general class: every object is a resource. Therefore, every class and every property is a resource:

$$Type(?p, Property) \longrightarrow Type(?p, Resource)$$
$$Type(?c, Class) \longrightarrow Type(?c, Resource)$$

Finally, the predicate in an RDF statement must be a property:

$$PropVal(?p, ?r, ?v) \longrightarrow Type(?p, Property)$$

The *type* Property

type is a property:

$$Type(type, Property)$$

Note that it is equivalent to $PropVal(type, type, Property)$: the type of *type* is *Property*. *type* can be applied to resources and has a class as its value:

$$Type(?r, ?c) \longrightarrow (Type(?r, Resource) \land Type(?c, Class))$$

The Auxiliary *FuncProp* Property

A functional property is a property that is a function: it relates a resource to at most one value. Functional properties are not a concept of RDF but are used in the axiomatization of other primitives.

The constant $FuncProp$ represents the class of all functional properties. P is a functional property if, and only if, it is a property, and there are no x, y_1, and y_2 such that $P(x, y_1)$, $P(x, y_2)$, and $y_1 \neq y_2$.

$$Type(?p, FuncProp) \longleftrightarrow$$
$$(Type(?p, Property) \land \forall ?r \forall ?v1 \forall ?v2$$
$$(PropVal(?p, ?r, ?v1) \land PropVal(?p, ?r, ?v2) \longrightarrow ?v1 = ?v2))$$

Reified Statements

The constant $Statement$ represents the class of all reified statements. All reified statements are resources, and $Statement$ is an instance of $Class$:

$$Type(?s, Statement) \longrightarrow Type(?s, Resource)$$
$$Type(Statement, Class)$$

A reified statement can be decomposed into the three parts of an RDF triple:

$$Type(?st, Statement) \longrightarrow$$
$$\exists ?p \exists ?r \exists ?v (PropVal(Predicate, ?st, ?p) \land$$
$$PropVal(Subject, ?st, ?r) \land PropVal(Object, ?st, ?v))$$

$Subject, Predicate$, and $Object$ are functional properties, that is, every statement has exactly one subject, one predicate, and one object:

$$Type(Subject, FuncProp)$$
$$Type(Predicate, FuncProp)$$
$$Type(Object, FuncProp)$$

Their typing information is

$$PropVal(Subject, ?st, ?r) \longrightarrow$$
$$(Type(?st, Statement) \land Type(?r, Resource))$$
$$PropVal(Predicate, ?st, ?p) \longrightarrow$$
$$(Type(?st, Statement) \land Type(?p, Property))$$
$$PropVal(Object, ?st, ?v) \longrightarrow$$
$$(Type(?st, Statement) \land (Type(?v, Resource) \lor Type(?v, Literal)))$$

The last axiom says, if *Object* appears as the property in an RDF statement, then it must apply to a reified statement and have as value either a resource or a literal.

Containers

All containers are resources:

$$Type(?c, Container) \longrightarrow Type(?c, Resource)$$

Containers are lists:

$$Type(?c, Container) \longrightarrow list(?c)$$

Containers are bags or sequences or alternatives:

$$Type(?c, Container) \longleftrightarrow$$
$$(Type(?c, Bag) \lor Type(?c, Seq) \lor Type(?c, Alt))$$

Bags and sequences are disjoint:

$$\neg(Type(?x, Bag) \land Type(?x, Seq))$$

For every natural number $n > 0$, there is the selector $\_n$, which selects the nth element of a container. It is a functional property

$$Type(\_n, FuncProp)$$

and applies to containers only:

$$PropVal(\_n, ?c, ?o) \longrightarrow Type(?c, Container)$$

3.7.4 RDF Schema

Subclasses and Subproperties

`subClassOf` is a property:

$$Type(subClassOf, Property)$$

If a class C is a subclass of a class C', then all instances of C are also instances of C':

$$PropVal(subClassOf, ?c, ?c') \longleftarrow$$
$$(Type(?c, Class) \wedge Type(?c', Class) \wedge$$
$$\forall?x(Type(?x, ?c) \longrightarrow Type(?x, ?c')))$$

Similarly for `subPropertyOf`: P is a subproperty of P' if $P'(x, y)$ whenever $P(x, y)$:

$$Type(subPropertyOf, Property)$$

$$PropVal(subPropertyOf, ?p, ?p') \longleftrightarrow$$
$$(Type(?p, Property) \wedge Type(?p', Property) \wedge$$
$$\forall?r\forall?v(PropVal(?p, ?r, ?v) \longrightarrow PropVal(?p', ?r, ?v)))$$

Constraints

Every constraint resource is a resource:

$$PropVal(subClassOf, ConstraintResource, Resource)$$

Constraint properties are all properties that are also constraint resources:

$$Type(?cp, ConstraintProperty) \longleftrightarrow$$
$$(Type(?cp, ConstraintResource) \wedge Type(?cp, Property))$$

`domain` and `range` are constraint properties:

$$Type(domain, ConstraintProperty)$$
$$Type(range, ConstraintProperty)$$

`domain` and `range` define the domain, respectively range, of a property. Recall that the domain of a property P is the set of all objects to which P applies. If the domain of P is D, then for every $P(x, y)$, $x \in D$.

$$PropVal(domain, ?p, ?d) \longrightarrow$$

$$\forall ?x \forall ?y (PropVal(?p, ?x, ?y) \longrightarrow Type(?x, ?d))$$

The range of a property P is the set of all values P can take. If the range of P is R, then for every $P(x, y)$, $y \in R$.

$$PropVal(range, ?p, ?r) \longrightarrow$$
$$\forall ?x \forall ?y (PropVal(?p, ?x, ?y) \longrightarrow Type(?y, ?r))$$

Formulas that can be inferred from the precedings ones:

$$PropVal(domain, range, Property)$$

$$PropVal(range, range, Class)$$

$$PropVal(domain, domain, Property)$$

$$PropVal(range, domain, Class)$$

Thus we have formalized the semantics of RDF and RDFS. An agent equipped with this knowledge is able to draw interesting conclusions. For example, given that the domain of *teaches* is *academicStaffMember*, that *academicStaffMember* is a subclass of *staffMembers*, and that *teaches(DB, DiMa)*, the agent can automatically deduce *staffMember(DB)* using the predicate logic semantics or one of the predicate logic proof systems.

3.8   A Direct Inference System for RDF and RDFS

As stated, the axiomatic semantics detailed in section 3.7 can be used for automated reasoning with RDF and RDF Schema. However, it requires a first-order logic proof system to do so. This is a very heavy requirement and also one that is unlikely to scale when millions of statements are involved (e.g., millions of statements of the form $Type(?r, ?c)$).

For this reason, RDF has also been given a semantics (and an inference system that is sound and complete for this semantics) directly in terms of RDF triples instead of restating RDF in terms of first-order logic, as was done in the axiomatic semantics of section 3.7.

This inference system consists of rules of the form

IF   E contains certain triples
THEN   add to E certain additional triples

(where E is an arbitrary set of RDF triples).

Without repeating the entire set of inference rules (which can be found in the official RDF documents), we give here a few basic examples:

IF   E contains the triple $(?x, ?p, ?y)$

THEN   E also contains the triple $(?p, \mathtt{rdf : type}, \mathtt{rdf : property})$

This states that any resource $?p$ that is used in the property position of a triple can be inferred to be a member of the class `rdf:Property`.

A somewhat more interesting example is the following rule:

IF   E contains the triples $(?u, \mathtt{rdfs : subClassOf}, ?v)$

         and $(?v, \mathtt{rdfs : subclassOf}, ?w)$

THEN   E also contains the triple $(?u, \mathtt{rdfs : subClassOf}, ?w)$

which encodes the transitivity of the subclass relation.

Closely related is the rule

IF   E contains the triples $(?x, \mathtt{rdf : type}, ?u)$

         and $(?u, \mathtt{rdfs : subClassOf}, ?v)$

THEN   E also contains the triple $(?x, \mathtt{rdf : type}, ?v)$

which is the essential definition of the meaning of `rdfs:subClassOf`.

A final example often comes as a surprise to people first looking at RDF Schema:

IF   E contains the triples $(?x, ?p, ?y)$

         and $(?p, \mathtt{rdfs : range}, ?u)$

THEN   E also contains the triple $(?y, \mathtt{rdf : type}, ?u)$

This rule states that any resource $?y$ which appears as the value of a property $?p$ can be inferred to be a member of the range of $?p$. This shows that range definitions in RDF Schema are not used to *restrict* the range of a property, but rather to *infer* the membership of the range.

The total set of these closure rules is no larger than a few dozen and can be efficiently implemented without sophisticated theorem-proving technology.

3.9   Querying in SPARQL

In this section we introduce a query language for RDF. Before doing so, we have to say why we need a new query language instead of using an XML query language. The answer is that XML is located at a lower level of abstraction than RDF. This fact would lead to complications if we were querying RDF documents with an XML-based language. Let us illustrate this point.

As we have already seen, there are various ways of syntactically representing an RDF statement in XML. For example, suppose we wish to retrieve the titles of all lecturers. The description of a particular lecturer might look like this:

```
<rdf:Description rdf:about="949318">
 <rdf:type rdf:resource="&uni;lecturer"/>
 <uni:name>David Billington</uni:name>
 <uni:title>Associate Professor</uni:title>
</rdf:Description>
```

An appropriate Xpath query is

```
/rdf:Description[rdf:type=
  "http://www.mydomain.org/uni-ns#lecturer"]/uni:title
```

But we could have written the same description as follows:

```
<uni:lecturer rdf:about="949318">
 <uni:name>David Billington</uni:name>
 <uni:title>Associate Professor</uni:title>
</uni:lecturer>
```

Now the previous XPath query does not work; we have to write

```
//uni:lecturer/uni:title
```

instead. And a third possible representation of the same description is

```
<uni:lecturer rdf:about="949318"
              uni:name="David Billington"
              uni:title="Associate Professor"/>
```

For this syntactic variation, yet another XPath query must be provided:

```
//uni:lecturer/@uni:title
```

Since each description of an individual lecturer may have any of these equivalent forms, we must write different XPath queries.

A better way is, of course, to write queries at the level of RDF. An appropriate query language must understand RDF, that is, it must understand not only the syntax but also the data model of RDF and the semantics of RDF vocabulary.

The SPARQL Query Language[2] is a W3C Candidate Recommendation for querying RDF, and as such is fast becoming the standard query language for this purpose. At the time of writing, almost all major RDF query tools had begun implementing support for the SPARQL query language. Even though other query languages (e.g., SeRQL[3] and RQL[4]) have existed longer and have a more mature implementation base and more expressive feature set, they typically are supported by only one or two tools, hindering interoperability. We therefore concentrate here on the SPARQL query language.

3.9.1 Basic Queries

The SPARQL query language is based on matching graph patterns. The simplest graph pattern is the triple pattern, which is like an RDF triple but with the possibility of a variable instead of an RDF term in the subject, predicate, or object positions. Combining triple patterns gives a basic graph pattern, where an exact match to a graph is needed to fulfill a pattern.

As a simple example, consider the following query:

```
PREFIX rdf: <http://www.w3.org/1999/02/22-rdf-syntax-ns#>
PREFIX rdfs: <http://www.w3.org/2000/01/rdf-schema#>
SELECT ?c
WHERE
{
    ?c rdf:type rdfs:Class .
}
```

This query retrieves all triple patterns where the property is `rdf:type` and the object is `rdfs:Class`. In other words, this query, when executed, will retrieve all classes.

Note that like the namespace mechanism used for writing RDF in XML, SPARQL allows us to define prefixes for namespaces and use these in the query pattern, to make queries shorter and easier to read. In the rest of this chapter, we omit the declaration of the `rdf` and `rdfs` prefixes for brevity.

To get all instances of a particular class, for example, `course`, we write:

```
PREFIX uni: <http://www.mydomain.org/uni-ns#>
SELECT ?i
WHERE
```

---

2. <http://www.w3.org/TR/rdf-sparql-query/>.
3. <http://www.openrdf.org/doc/SeRQLmanual.html>.
4. <http://athena.ics.forth.gr:9090/RDF/RQL/>.

```
{
  ?i rdf:type uni:course .
}
```

SPARQL makes no explicit commitment to support RDFS semantics. Therefore, the result of this query depends on whether the system answering the query supports RDFS semantics. If it does, then the result of this query will include all instances of the subclasses of `course` as well. If it does not support RDFS semantics, it will only retrieve those instances that are explicitly of type `course`.

3.9.2 Using `select-from-where`

As in SQL, SPARQL queries have a SELECT-FROM-WHERE structure:

SELECT specifies the *projection*: the number and order of retrieved data.

FROM is used to specify the source being queried. This clause is optional; when it is not specified, we can simply assume we are querying the knowledge base of a particular system.

WHERE imposes constraints on possible solutions in the form of graph pattern templates and boolean constraints.

For example, to retrieve all phone numbers of staff members, we can write

```
SELECT ?x ?y
WHERE
{
  ?x uni:phone ?y .
}
```

Here ?x and ?y are variables, and ?x uni:phone ?y represents a resource-property-value triple pattern.

We can create more elaborate graph patterns to get more complex information from our queries. For example, to retrieve all lecturers and their phone numbers, we can write

```
SELECT ?x ?y
WHERE
{
    ?x rdf:type uni:Lecturer ;
       uni:phone ?y .
}
```

Here the clause `?x rdf:type uni:Lecturer` collects all instances of the class `Lecturer`, as discussed, and binds the result to the variable `?x`. The second part collects all triples with predicate `phone`. But there is an *implicit join* here, in that we restrict the second pattern only to those triples whose subject is in the variable `?x`. Note that in this case we use a syntax shortcut as well: a semicolon indicates that the following triple pattern shares its subject with the previous one. Thus the above query is equivalent to writing

```
SELECT ?x ?y
WHERE
{
    ?x rdf:type uni:Lecturer .
    ?x uni:phone ?y .
}
```

We demonstrate an *explicit join* by a query that retrieves the name of all courses taught by the lecturer with ID 949352.

```
SELECT ?n
WHERE
{
    ?x rdf:type uni:Course ;
        uni:isTaughtBy :949352 .
    ?c uni:name ?n .
    FILTER (?c = ?x).
}
```

In SPARQL we use a `FILTER` condition to indicate a boolean constraint. In this case the constraint is the explicit join of the variables `?c` and `?x` by using an equality (=) operator.

3.9.3   Optional Patterns

The graph patterns we have seen so far are mandatory patterns. Either the knowledge base matches the complete pattern, in which case an answer is returned, or it doesn't, in which case the query does not produce a result. However, in many cases we may wish to be more flexible. Consider, for example, the following RDF excerpt:

```
<uni:lecturer rdf:about="949352">
 <uni:name>Grigoris Antoniou</uni:name>
</uni:lecturer>
```

```
<uni:professor rdf:about="949318">
 <uni:name>David Billington</uni:name>
 <uni:email>david@work.example.org</uni:email>
</uni:professor>
```

This fragment contains information on two lecturers. For one lecturer it only lists the name; for the other it also lists the e-mail address. Now we want to query for all lecturers and their e-mail addresses:

```
SELECT ?name ?email
WHERE
{ ?x rdf:type uni:Lecturer ;
     uni:name ?name ;
     uni:email ?email .
}
```

The result of this query would be

?name	?email
David Billington	david@work.example.org

So, despite the fact that Grigoris Antoniou is listed as a lecturer, the query does not return his name. The query pattern does not match because he has no e-mail address.

As a solution we can adapt the query to use an optional pattern:

```
SELECT ?name ?email
WHERE
{ ?x rdf:type uni:Lecturer ;
     uni:name ?name .
   OPTIONAL { ?x  uni:email ?email }
}
```

The meaning is roughly "give us all the names of lecturers, and *if known* also their e-mail addresses" and the result looks like this:

?name	?email
Grigoris Antoniou	
David Billington	david@work.example.org

This covers the basics of the SPARQL query language. For a full overview of the SPARQL language and an explanation of more advanced features, such as named graphs, we recommend reading the SPARQL specification.[5]

_____

5. <http://www.w3.org/TR/rdf-sparql-query/>.

3.10 Summary

- RDF provides a foundation for representing and processing metadata.

- RDF has a graph-based data model. Its key concepts are resource, property, and statement. A statement is a resource-property-value triple.

- RDF has an XML-based syntax to support syntactic interoperability. XML and RDF complement each other because RDF supports semantic interoperability.

- RDF has a decentralized philosophy and allows incremental building of knowledge, and its sharing and reuse.

- RDF is domain-independent. RDF Schema provides a mechanism for describing specific domains.

- RDF Schema is a primitive ontology language. It offers certain modeling primitives with fixed meaning. Key concepts of RDF Schema are class, subclass relations, property, subproperty relations, and domain and range restrictions.

- There exist query languages for RDF and RDFS, including SPARQL.

Some points that will be discussed in the next chapter:

- RDF Schema is quite primitive as a modeling language for the Web. Many desirable modeling primitives are missing.

- Therefore we need an ontology layer on top of RDF/RDFS.

Suggested Reading

The following are some official online documents:

- G. Klyne and J. Carroll, eds. Resource Description Framework (RDF): Concepts and Abstract Syntax. W3C Recommendation. February 10, 2004.
<http://www.w3.org/TR/rdf-concepts/>.

- D. Brickley and R.V. Guha, eds. RDF Vocabulary Description Language 1.0: RDF Schema. W3C Recommendation. February 10, 2004.
<http://www.w3.org/TR/rdf-schema/>.

- P. Hayes, ed. RDF Semantics. W3C Recommendation. February 10, 2004.
  <http://www.w3.org/TR/rdf-mt/>.

- D. Beckett, ed. RDF/XML Syntax Specification (Revised). W3C Recommendation. February 10, 2004.
  <http://www.w3.org/TR/rdf-syntax-grammar/>.

- F. Manola and E. Miller, eds. RDF Primer. W3C Recommendation. February 10, 2004.
  <http://www.w3.org/TR/rdf-primer/>.

- R. Fikes and D. McGuinness. An Axiomatic Semantics for RDF, RDF Schema and DAML+OIL. March 2001.
  <http://www.daml.org/2001/03/axiomatic-semantics.html>.

- E. Prud'hommeaux and A. Seaborne, eds. SPARQL Query Language for RDF. W3C Candidate Recommendation. June 14, 2007.
  <http://www.w3.org/TR/rdf-sparql-query/>.

Here are some further useful readings:

- S. Decker et al. The Semantic Web: The Roles of XML and RDF. *IEEE Internet Computing* 15,3 (2000): 63–74.

- D. Dodds et al. *Professional XML Meta Data*. Birmingham, U.K.: Wrox Press, 2001.

- J. Hjelm. *Creating the Semantic Web with RDF*. New York: Wiley, 2001.

- G. Karvounarakis, A. Maganaraki, S. Alexaki, V. Christophides, D. Plexousakis, M. Scholl, K. Tolle. Querying the Semantic Web with RQL. *Computer Networks and ISDN Systems Journal* 42,5 (2003): 617–640.

- M. Nic. RDF Tutorial - Part I: Basic Syntax and Containers.
  <http://www.zvon.org/xxl/RDFTutorial/General/book.html>.

- L. Dodds. Introducing SPARQL: Querying the Semantic Web. November 16, 2005.
  <http://www.xml.com/lpt/a/1628>.

An extensive list of tools and other resources is maintained at

- <http://http://planetrdf.com/guide//>.

- <http://www.w3.org/RDF>.

Exercises and Projects

3.1 Read the RDFS namespace, and try to understand the elements that were not presented in this chapter.

3.2 Read the SPARQL Tutorial by Leigh Dodds (see Suggested Reading), focusing on points not discussed here.

3.3 The RDFS specification allows more than one domain to be defined for a property and uses the intersection of these domains. Discuss the pros and cons of taking the union versus taking the intersection of domains.

3.4 In an older version of the RDFS specification, `rdfs:subClassOf` was not allowed to have cycles. Try to imagine situations where a cyclic class relationship would be beneficial. (*Hint:* Think of equivalence between classes.)

3.5 Discuss the difference between the following statements, and draw graphs to illustrate the difference:

> X supports the proposal; Y supports the proposal; Z supports the proposal. The group of X, Y, and Z supports the proposal.

3.6 Compare `rdfs:subClassOf` with type extensions in XML Schema.

3.7 Consider the formal specification of `rdf:_n` in the axiomatic semantics. Does it capture the intended meaning of `rdf:_n` as the selector of the nth element of a collection? If not, suggest a full axiomatization.

3.8 Prove the inferred formulas at the end of section 3.7 using the previous axioms.

3.9 Discuss why RDF and RDFS do not allow logical contradictions. Any RDF/S document is consistent; thus it has at least one model.

3.10 Try to map the relational database model on RDF.

3.11 Compare entity-relationship modeling to RDF.

3.12 Model part of a library in RDF Schema: books, authors, publishers, years, copies, dates, and so on. Then write some statements in RDF, and query them using SPARQL.

3.13   Write an ontology about geography: cities, countries, capitals, borders, states, and so on.

3.14   In chapter 2 you were asked to consider various domains and develop appropriate vocabularies for them. Try to model these domains by defining suitable classes and properties, and a conceptual model. Then write sample statements in RDF.

In the following you are asked to think about limitations of RDFS. Specifically, what should actually be expressed, and can it be represented in RDF Schema? These limitations will be relevant in chapter 4, where we present a richer modeling language.

3.15   Consider the classes of males and females. Name a relationship between them that should be included in an ontology.

3.16   Consider the classes of persons, males, and females. Name a relationship between all three that should be included in an ontology. Which part of this relationship can be expressed in RDF Schema?

3.17   Suppose we declare Bob and Peter to be the father of Mary. Obviously there is a semantic error here. How should the semantic model make this error impossible?

3.18   What relationship exists between "is child of" and "is parent of"?

3.19   Consider the property *eats* with domain *animal* and range *animal or plant*. Suppose we define a new class *vegetarian*. Name a desirable restriction on *eats* for this class. Do you think that this restriction can be expressed in RDF Schema by using `rdfs:range`?

3.20   Evaluate some SPARQL queries against the RDF repositories that are available at <http://sesame.aduna.biz/>.

3.21   Construct an RDF Schema vocabulary on a topic of your choice, and use the FRODO RDFSViz visualization tool[6] to construct a class and property diagram for your vocabulary.

---

6. <http://www.dfki.uni-kl.de/frodo/RDFSViz/>.

4 *Web Ontology Language: OWL*

4.1   Introduction

The expressivity of RDF and RDF Schema that we described in the previous chapter is deliberately very limited. RDF is (roughly) limited to binary ground predicates, and RDF Schema is (roughly) limited to a subclass hierarchy and a property hierarchy, with domain and range definitions of these properties.

However, the Web Ontology Working Group of W3C[1] identified a number of characteristic use cases for the Semantic Web that would require much more expressiveness than RDF and RDF Schema offer.

A number of research groups in both the United States and Europe had already identified the need for a more powerful ontology modeling language. This led to a joint initiative to define a richer language, called DAML+OIL[2] (the name is a join of the names of the U.S. proposal DAML-ONT,[3] and the European language OIL[4]).

DAML+OIL in turn was taken as the starting point for the W3C Web Ontology Working Group in defining OWL, the language that is aimed to be the standardized and broadly accepted ontology language of the Semantic Web.

In this chapter, we first describe the motivation for OWL in terms of its requirements, and its resulting nontrivial relation with RDF Schema. We then describe the various language elements of OWL in some detail.

---

1. <http://www.w3.org/2001/sw/WebOnt/>.
2. <http://www.daml.org/2001/03/daml+oil-index.html>.
3. <http://www.daml.org/2000/10/daml-ont.html>.
4. <http://www.ontoknowledge.org/oil/>.

Chapter Overview

Section 4.2 describes the motivation for OWL in terms of its requirements and its resulting nontrivial relation with RDF Schema; section 4.3 describes three OWL sublanguages. Section 4.4 describes the various language elements in some detail, and section 4.5 specifies which features may be used in which sublanguage. Several examples are given in section 4.6. A description of OWL in terms of itself appears in section 4.7. Section 4.8 looks at future extensions of ontology languages.

4.2   OWL and RDF/RDFS

4.2.1   Requirements for Ontology Languages

Ontology languages allow users to write explicit, formal conceptualizations of domain models. The main requirements are a well-defined syntax, efficient reasoning support, a formal semantics, sufficient expressive power and convenience of expression.

The importance of a *well-defined syntax* is clear and known from the area of programming languages; it is a necessary condition for machine processing of information. All the languages we have presented so far have a well-defined syntax. DAML+OIL and OWL build upon RDF and RDFS and have the same kind of syntax.

Of course, it is questionable whether the XML-based RDF syntax is very user-friendly; there are alternatives better suited to human users (for example, see the OIL syntax). However, this drawback is not very significant because ultimately users will be developing their own ontologies using authoring tools, or more generally, *ontology development tools*, instead of writing them directly in DAML+OIL or OWL.

A *formal semantics* describes the meaning of knowledge precisely. *Precisely* here means that the semantics does not refer to subjective intuitions, nor is it open to different interpretations by different people (or machines). The importance of a formal semantics is well-established in the domain of mathematical logic, for instance.

One use of a formal semantics is to allow people to reason about the knowledge. For ontological knowledge, we may reason about the following:

- Class membership. If x is an instance of a class C, and C is a subclass of D, then we can infer that x is an instance of D.

- Equivalence of classes. If class A is equivalent to class B, and class B is equivalent to class C, then A is equivalent to C, too.

- Consistency. Suppose we have declared x to be an instance of the class A and that A is a subclass of $B \cap C$, A is a subclass of D, and B and D are disjoint. Then we have an inconsistency because A should be empty but has the instance x. This is an indication of an error in the ontology.

- Classification. If we have declared that certain property-value pairs are a sufficient condition for membership in a class A, then if an individual x satisfies such conditions, we can conclude that x must be an instance of A.

Semantics is a prerequisite for *reasoning support*. Derivations such as the preceding ones can be made mechanically instead of being made by hand. Reasoning support is important because it allows one to

- check the consistency of the ontology and the knowledge,

- check for unintended relationships between classes,

- automatically classify instances in classes.

Automated reasoning support allows one to check many more cases than could be checked manually. Checks like the precedings ones are valuable for designing large ontologies, where multiple authors are involved, and for integrating and sharing ontologies from various sources.

A formal semantics and reasoning support are usually provided by mapping an ontology language to a known logical formalism, and by using automated reasoners that already exist for those formalisms. OWL is (partially) mapped on a description logic, and makes use of existing reasoners such as FaCT and RACER. Description logics are a subset of predicate logic for which efficient reasoning support is possible.

4.2.2   Limitations of the Expressive Power of RDF Schema

RDF and RDFS allow the representation of *some* ontological knowledge. The main modeling primitives of RDF/RDFS concern the organization of vocabularies in typed hierarchies: subclass and subproperty relationships, domain and range restrictions, and instances of classes. However, a number of other features are missing. Here we list a few:

- Local scope of properties. `rdfs:range` defines the range of a property, say `eats`, for all classes. Thus in RDF Schema we cannot declare range restrictions that apply to some classes only. For example, we cannot say that cows eat only plants, while other animals may eat meat, too.

- Disjointness of classes. Sometimes we wish to say that classes are disjoint. For example, `male` and `female` are disjoint. But in RDF Schema we can only state subclass relationships, e.g., `female` is a subclass of `person`.

- Boolean combinations of classes. Sometimes we wish to build new classes by combining other classes using union, intersection, and complement. For example, we may wish to define the class `person` to be the disjoint union of the classes `male` and `female`. RDF Schema does not allow such definitions.

- Cardinality restrictions. Sometimes we wish to place restrictions on how many distinct values a property may or must take. For example, we would like to say that a person has exactly two parents, or that a course is taught by at least one lecturer. Again, such restrictions are impossible to express in RDF Schema.

- Special characteristics of properties. Sometimes it is useful to say that a property is *transitive* (like "greater than"), *unique* (like "is mother of"), or the *inverse* of another property (like "eats" and "is eaten by").

Thus we need an ontology language that is richer than RDF Schema, a language that offers these features and more. In designing such a language one should be aware of the trade-off between expressive power and efficient reasoning support. Generally speaking, the richer the language, the more inefficient the reasoning support becomes, often crossing the border of noncomputability. Thus we need a compromise, a language that can be supported by reasonably efficient reasoners while being sufficiently expressive to express large classes of ontologies and knowledge.

4.2.3   Compatibility of OWL with RDF/RDFS

Ideally, OWL would be an extension of RDF Schema, in the sense that OWL would use the RDF meaning of classes and properties (`rdfs:Class`, `rdfs:subClassOf`, etc.) and would add language primitives to support the richer expressiveness required. Such an extension of RDF Schema would also be consistent with the layered architecture of the Semantic Web (see figure 1.3).

Unfortunately, simply extending RDF Schema would work against obtaining expressive power and efficient reasoning. RDF Schema has some very powerful modeling primitives. Constructions such as `rdfs:Class` (the class of all classes) and `rdf:Property` (the class of all properties) are very expressive and would lead to uncontrollable computational properties if the logic were extended with such expressive primitives.

4.3 Three Sublanguages of OWL

The full set of requirements for an ontology language that seem unobtainable: efficient reasoning support and convenience of expression for a language as powerful as a combination of RDF Schema with a full logic.

Indeed, these requirements have prompted W3C's Web Ontology Working Group to define OWL as three different sublanguages, each geared toward fulfilling different aspects of this full set of requirements.

4.3.1 OWL Full

The entire language is called OWL Full and uses all the OWL language primitives. It also allows the combination of these primitives in arbitrary ways with RDF and RDF Schema. This includes the possibility (also present in RDF) of changing the meaning of the predefined (RDF or OWL) primitives by applying the language primitives to each other. For example, in OWL Full, we could impose a cardinality constraint on the class of all classes, essentially limiting the number of classes that can be described in any ontology.

The advantage of OWL Full is that it is fully upward-compatible with RDF, both syntactically and semantically: any legal RDF document is also a legal OWL Full document, and any valid RDF/RDF Schema conclusion is also a valid OWL Full conclusion. The disadvantage of OWL Full is that the language has become so powerful as to be undecidable, dashing any hope of complete (or efficient) reasoning support.

4.3.2 OWL DL

In order to regain computational efficiency, OWL DL (short for Description Logic) is a sublanguage of OWL Full that restricts how the constructors from OWL and RDF may be used. Essentially application of OWL's constructors to each other is disallowed, thus ensuring that the language corresponds to a well-studied description logic.

The advantage of this is that it permits efficient reasoning support. The disadvantage is that we lose full compatibility with RDF. An RDF document will in general have to be extended in some ways and restricted in others before it is a legal OWL DL document. Every legal OWL DL document is a legal RDF document.

4.3.3   OWL Lite

An even further restriction limits OWL DL to a subset of the language constructors. For example, OWL Lite excludes enumerated classes, disjointness statements, and arbitrary cardinality.

The advantage of this is a language that is both easier to grasp (for users) and easier to implement (for tool builders). The disadvantage is, of course, a restricted expressivity.

Ontology developers adopting OWL should consider which sublanguage best suits their needs. The choice between OWL Lite and OWL DL depends on the extent to which users require the more expressive constructs provided by OWL DL. The choice between OWL DL and OWL Full mainly depends on the extent to which users require the metamodeling facilities of RDF Schema (e.g., defining classes of classes, or attaching properties to classes). When using OWL Full as compared to OWL DL, reasoning support is less predictable because complete OWL Full implementations will be impossible.

There are strict notions of upward compatibility between these three sublanguages:

- Every legal OWL Lite ontology is a legal OWL DL ontology.

- Every legal OWL DL ontology is a legal OWL Full ontology.

- Every valid OWL Lite conclusion is a valid OWL DL conclusion.

- Every valid OWL DL conclusion is a valid OWL Full conclusion.

OWL still uses RDF and RDF Schema to a large extent:

- All varieties of OWL use RDF for their syntax.

- Instances are declared as in RDF, using RDF descriptions and typing information.

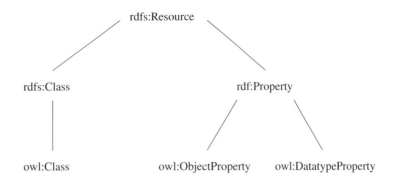

Figure 4.1 Subclass relationships between OWL and RDF/RDFS

- OWL constructors like `owl:Class`, and `owl:DatatypeProperty`, and `owl:ObjectProperty` are specializations of their RDF counterparts.

Figure 4.1 shows the subclass relationships between some modeling primitives of OWL and RDF/RDFS.

One of the main motivations behind the layered architecture of the Semantic Web (see figure 1.3) is a hope for downward compatibility with corresponding reuse of software across the various layers. However, the advantage of full downward compatibility for OWL (any OWL-aware processor will also provide correct interpretations of any RDF Schema document) is only achieved for OWL Full, at the cost of computational intractability.

4.4 Description of the OWL Language

4.4.1 Syntax

OWL builds on RDF and RDF Schema and uses RDF's XML-based syntax. Since this is the primary syntax for OWL, we use it here, but RDF/XML does not provide a very readable syntax. Because of this, other syntactic forms for OWL have also been defined:

- An XML-based syntax[5] that does not follow the RDF conventions and is thus more easily read by human users.

─────────
5. Defined in <http://www.w3.org/TR/owl-xmlsyntax/>.

- An abstract syntax, used in the language specification document[6], that is much more compact and readable then either the XML syntax or the RDF/XML syntax. Appendix A lists all the RDF/XML code in this chapter in this abstract syntax.

- A graphic syntax based on the conventions of UML (Unified Modeling Language), which is widely used and is thus an easy way for people to become familiar with OWL.

4.4.2   Header

OWL documents are usually called *OWL ontologies* and are RDF documents. The root element of an OWL ontology is an `rdf:RDF` element, which also specifies a number of namespaces:

```
<rdf:RDF
    xmlns:owl ="http://www.w3.org/2002/07/owl#"
    xmlns:rdf ="http://www.w3.org/1999/02/22-rdf-syntax-ns#"
    xmlns:rdfs="http://www.w3.org/2000/01/rdf-schema#"
    xmlns:xsd ="http://www.w3.org/2001/XMLSchema#">
```

An OWL ontology may start with a collection of assertions for housekeeping purposes. These assertions are grouped under an `owl:Ontology` element, which contains comments, version control, and inclusion of other ontologies. For example

```
<owl:Ontology rdf:about="">
  <rdfs:comment>An example OWL ontology</rdfs:comment>
  <owl:priorVersion
        rdf:resource="http://www.mydomain.org/uni-ns-old"/>
  <owl:imports
        rdf:resource="http://www.mydomain.org/persons"/>
  <rdfs:label>University Ontology</rdfs:label>
</owl:Ontology>
```

Only one of these assertions has any consequences for the logical meaning of the ontology: `owl:imports`, which lists other ontologies whose content is assumed to be part of the current ontology. Note that while namespaces are used for disambiguation, imported ontologies provide definitions that can

---

6. <http://www.w3.org/TR/owl-semantics/>.

be used. Usually there will be an import element for each namespace used, but it is possible to import additional ontologies, for example, ontologies that provide definitions without introducing any new names.

Also note that `owl:imports` is a transitive property: if ontology A imports ontology B, and ontology B imports ontology C, then ontology A also imports ontology C.

4.4.3 Class Elements

Classes are defined using an `owl:Class` element.[7] For example, we can define a class `associateProfessor` as follows:

```
<owl:Class rdf:ID="associateProfessor">
  <rdfs:subClassOf rdf:resource="#academicStaffMember"/>
</owl:Class>
```

We can also say that this class is disjoint from the `assistantProfessor` and `professor` classes using `owl:disjointWith` elements. These elements can be included in the preceding definition, or added by referring to the ID using `rdf:about`. This mechanism is inherited from RDF.

```
<owl:Class rdf:about="#associateProfessor">
  <owl:disjointWith rdf:resource="#professor"/>
  <owl:disjointWith rdf:resource="#assistantProfessor"/>
</owl:Class>
```

Equivalence of classes can be defined using an `owl:equivalentClass` element:

```
<owl:Class rdf:ID="faculty">
  <owl:equivalentClass rdf:resource="#academicStaffMember"/>
</owl:Class>
```

Finally, there are two predefined classes, `owl:Thing` and `owl:Nothing`. The former is the most general class, which contains everything (everything is a thing), and the latter is the empty class. Thus every class is a subclass of `owl:Thing` and a superclass of `owl:Nothing`.

---

7. `owl:Class` is a subclass of `rdfs:Class`.

4.4.4 Property Elements

In OWL there are two kinds of properties:

- Object properties, which relate objects to other objects. Examples are `isTaughtBy` and `supervises`.

- Data type properties, which relate objects to data type values. Examples are `phone`, `title`, and `age`. OWL does not have any predefined data types, nor does it provide special definition facilities. Instead, it allows one to use XML Schema data types, thus making use of the layered architecture of the Semantic Web.

Here is an example of a data type property:

```
<owl:DatatypeProperty rdf:ID="age">
  <rdfs:range rdf:resource="http://www.w3.org/2001/XMLSchema
  #nonNegativeInteger"/>
</owl:DatatypeProperty>
```

User-defined data types will usually be collected in an XML schema and then used in an OWL ontology.

Here is an example of an object property:

```
<owl:ObjectProperty rdf:ID="isTaughtBy">
  <rdfs:domain rdf:resource="#course"/>
  <rdfs:range rdf:resource="#academicStaffMember"/>
  <rdfs:subPropertyOf rdf:resource="#involves"/>
</owl:ObjectProperty>
```

More than one domain and range may be declared. In this case the intersection of the domains, respectively ranges, is taken.

OWL allows us to relate inverse properties. A typical example is the pair `isTaughtBy` and `teaches`:

```
<owl:ObjectProperty rdf:ID="teaches">
  <rdfs:range rdf:resource="#course"/>
  <rdfs:domain rdf:resource="#academicStaffMember"/>
  <owl:inverseOf rdf:resource="#isTaughtBy"/>
</owl:ObjectProperty>
```

Figure 4.2 illustrates the relationship between a property and its inverse. Actually, domain and range can be inherited from the inverse property (interchange domain with range).

Figure 4.2 Inverse properties

Equivalence of properties can be defined through the use of the element `owl:equivalentProperty`.

```
<owl:ObjectProperty rdf:ID="lecturesIn">
  <owl:equivalentProperty rdf:resource="#teaches"/>
</owl:ObjectProperty>
```

4.4.5   Property Restrictions

With `rdfs:subClassOf` we can specify a class C to be subclass of another class C'; then every instance of C is also an instance of C'.

Suppose we wish to declare instead that the class C satisfies certain conditions, that is, all instances of C satisfy the conditions. This is equivalent to saying that C is subclass of a class C', where C' collects all objects that satisfy the conditions. That is exactly how it is done in OWL. Note that, in general, C' can remain anonymous.

The following element requires first-year courses to be taught by professors only (according to a questionable view, older and more senior academics are better at teaching):

```
<owl:Class rdf:about="#firstYearCourse">
  <rdfs:subClassOf>
    <owl:Restriction>
      <owl:onProperty rdf:resource="#isTaughtBy"/>
      <owl:allValuesFrom rdf:resource="#Professor"/>
    </owl:Restriction>
  </rdfs:subClassOf>
</owl:Class>
```

`owl:allValuesFrom` is used to specify the class of possible values the property specified by `owl:onProperty` can take (in other words, all values of the property must come from this class). In our example, only professors are allowed as values of the property `isTaughtBy`.

We can declare that mathematics courses are taught by David Billington as follows:

```
<owl:Class rdf:about="#mathCourse">
  <rdfs:subClassOf>
    <owl:Restriction>
      <owl:onProperty rdf:resource="#isTaughtBy"/>
      <owl:hasValue rdf:resource="#949318"/>
    </owl:Restriction>
  </rdfs:subClassOf>
</owl:Class>
```

`owl:hasValue` states a specific value that the property specified by `owl:onProperty` must have.

And we can declare that all academic staff members must teach at least one undergraduate course:

```
<owl:Class rdf:about="#academicStaffMember">
  <rdfs:subClassOf>
    <owl:Restriction>
      <owl:onProperty rdf:resource="#teaches"/>
      <owl:someValuesFrom
          rdf:resource="#undergraduateCourse"/>
    </owl:Restriction>
  </rdfs:subClassOf>
</owl:Class>
```

Let us compare `owl:allValuesFrom` and `owl:someValuesFrom`. The example using the former requires *every* person who teaches an instance of the class, a first-year subject, to be a professor. In terms of logic, we have a *universal quantification*.

The example using the latter requires that *there exists* an undergraduate course taught by an instance of the class, an academic staff member. It is still possible that the same academic teaches postgraduate courses in addition. In terms of logic, we have an *existential quantification*.

In general, an `owl:Restriction` element contains an `owl:onProperty` element and one or more restriction declarations. One type of restriction declaration defines restrictions on the kinds of values the property can take: `owl:allValuesFrom`, `owl:hasValue`, and `owl:someValuesFrom`. Another type defines cardinality restrictions. For example, we can require every course to be taught by at least someone:

```
<owl:Class rdf:about="#course">
 <rdfs:subClassOf>
  <owl:Restriction>
   <owl:onProperty rdf:resource="#isTaughtBy"/>
   <owl:minCardinality
     rdf:datatype="&xsd;nonNegativeInteger">
     1
   </owl:minCardinality>
  </owl:Restriction>
 </rdfs:subClassOf>
</owl:Class>
```

Notice that we had to specify that the literal "1" is to be interpreted as `nonNegativeInteger` (instead of, say, a string), and that we used the `xsd` namespace declaration made in the header element to refer to the XML Schema document.

Or we might specify that, for practical reasons, a department must have at least ten and at most thirty members:

```
<owl:Class rdf:about="#department">
 <rdfs:subClassOf>
  <owl:Restriction>
   <owl:onProperty rdf:resource="#hasMember"/>
    <owl:minCardinality
     rdf:datatype="&xsd;nonNegativeInteger">
     10
   </owl:minCardinality>
  </owl:Restriction>
 </rdfs:subClassOf>
 <rdfs:subClassOf>
  <owl:Restriction>
   <owl:onProperty rdf:resource="#hasMember"/>
    <owl:maxCardinality
     rdf:datatype="&xsd;nonNegativeInteger">
     30
   </owl:maxCardinality>
  </owl:Restriction>
 </rdfs:subClassOf>
</owl:Class>
```

It is possible to specify a precise number, for example, a Ph.D. student must have exactly two supervisors. This can be achieved by using the same number in `owl:minCardinality` and `owl:maxCardinality`. For convenience, OWL offers also `owl:cardinality`.

We conclude by noting that `owl:Restriction` defines an anonymous class which has no ID, is not defined by `owl:Class`, and has only local scope: it can only be used in the one place where the restriction appears. When we talk about classes, keep in mind the twofold meaning: classes defined by `owl:Class` with an ID, and local anonymous classes as collections of objects that satisfy certain restriction conditions, or as combinations of other classes. The latter are sometimes called *class expressions*.

4.4.6   Special Properties

Some properties of property elements can be defined directly:

`owl:TransitiveProperty` defines a transitive property, such as "has better grade than", "is taller than", or "is ancestor of".

`owl:SymmetricProperty` defines a symmetric property, such as "has same grade as" or "is sibling of".

`owl:FunctionalProperty` defines a property that has at most one value for each object, such as "age", "height", or "directSupervisor".

`owl:InverseFunctionalProperty` defines a property for which two different objects cannot have the same value, for example, the property "isTheSocialSecurityNumberfor" (a social security number is assigned to one person only).

An example of the syntactic forms for these is

```
<owl:ObjectProperty rdf:ID="hasSameGradeAs">
  <rdf:type rdf:resource="&owl;TransitiveProperty" />
  <rdf:type rdf:resource="&owl;SymmetricProperty" />
  <rdfs:domain rdf:resource="#student" />
  <rdfs:range rdf:resource="#student" />
</owl:ObjectProperty>
```

4.4.7 Boolean Combinations

It is possible to talk about Boolean combinations (union, intersection, complement) of classes (be they defined by `owl:Class` or by class expressions). For example, we can say that courses and staff members are disjoint:

```
<owl:Class rdf:about="#course">
  <rdfs:subClassOf>
    <owl:Class>
      <owl:complementOf rdf:resource="#staffMember"/>
    </owl:Class>
  </rdfs:subClassOf>
</owl:Class>
```

This says that every course is an instance of the complement of staff members, that is, no course is a staff member. Note that this statement could also have been expressed using `owl:disjointWith`.

The union of classes is built using `owl:unionOf`:

```
<owl:Class rdf:ID="peopleAtUni">
  <owl:unionOf rdf:parseType="Collection">
    <owl:Class rdf:about="#staffMember"/>
    <owl:Class rdf:about="#student"/>
  </owl:unionOf>
</owl:Class>
```

This does not say that the new class is a subclass of the union, but rather that the new class is *equal* to the union. In other words, we have stated an *equivalence of classes*. Also, we did not specify that the two classes must be disjoint: it is possible for a staff member to also be a student.

Intersection is stated with `owl:intersectionOf`:

```
<owl:Class rdf:ID="facultyInCS">
  <owl:intersectionOf rdf:parseType="Collection">
    <owl:Class rdf:about="#faculty"/>
    <owl:Restriction>
      <owl:onProperty rdf:resource="#belongsTo"/>
      <owl:hasValue rdf:resource="#CSDepartment"/>
    </owl:Restriction>
  </owl:intersectionOf>
</owl:Class>
```

Note that we have built the intersection of two classes, one of which was defined anonymously: the class of all objects belonging to the CS department. This class is intersected with `faculty` to give us the faculty in the CS department.

Boolean combinations can be nested arbitrarily. The following example defines administrative staff to be those staff members that are neither faculty nor technical support staff:

```
<owl:Class rdf:ID="adminStaff">
 <owl:intersectionOf rdf:parseType="Collection">
  <owl:Class rdf:about="#staffMember"/>
  <owl:Class>
   <owl:complementOf>
    <owl:Class>
     <owl:unionOf rdf:parseType="Collection">
      <owl:Class rdf:about="#faculty"/>
      <owl:Class rdf:about="#techSupportStaff"/>
     </owl:unionOf>
    </owl:Class>
   </owl:complementOf>
  </owl:Class>
 </owl:intersectionOf>
</owl:Class>
```

4.4.8   Enumerations

An enumeration is an `owl:oneOf` element, used to define a class by listing all its elements:

```
<owl:Class rdf:ID="weekdays">
 <owl:oneOf rdf:parseType="Collection">
  <owl:Thing rdf:about="#Monday"/>
  <owl:Thing rdf:about="#Tuesday"/>
  <owl:Thing rdf:about="#Wednesday"/>
  <owl:Thing rdf:about="#Thursday"/>
  <owl:Thing rdf:about="#Friday"/>
  <owl:Thing rdf:about="#Saturday"/>
  <owl:Thing rdf:about="#Sunday"/>
 </owl:oneOf>
</owl:Class>
```

4.4.9   Instances

Instances of classes are declared as in RDF:

```
<rdf:Description rdf:ID="949352">
 <rdf:type rdf:resource="#academicStaffMember"/>
</rdf:Description>
```

or equivalently

```
<academicStaffMember rdf:ID="949352"/>
```

We can also provide further details, such as

```
<academicStaffMember rdf:ID="949352">
 <uni:age rdf:datatype="&xsd;integer">39</uni:age>
</academicStaffMember>
```

Unlike typical database systems, OWL does not adopt the *unique-names assumption*; just because two instances have a different name or ID does not imply that they are different individuals. For example, if we state that each course is taught by at most one staff member

```
<owl:ObjectProperty rdf:ID="isTaughtBy">
 <rdf:type rdf:resource="&owl;FunctionalProperty" />
</owl:ObjectProperty>
```

and we subsequently state that a given course is taught by two staff members

```
<course rdf:ID="CIT1111">
 <isTaughtBy rdf:resource="#949318"/>
 <isTaughtBy rdf:resource="#949352"/>
</course>
```

this does *not* cause an OWL reasoner to flag an error. After all, the system could validly infer that the resources "949318" and "949352" are apparently equal. To ensure that different individuals are indeed recognized as such, we must explicitly assert their inequality:

```
<lecturer rdf:ID="949318">
 <owl:differentFrom rdf:resource="#949352"/>
</lecturer>
```

Because such inequality statements occur frequently, and the required number of such statements would explode if we wanted to state the inequality of a large number of individuals, OWL provides a shorthand notation to assert the pairwise inequality of all individuals in a given list:

```
<owl:AllDifferent>
 <owl:distinctMembers rdf:parseType="Collection">
  <lecturer rdf:about="#949318"/>
  <lecturer rdf:about="#949352"/>
  <lecturer rdf:about="#949111"/>
 </owl:distinctMembers>
</owl:AllDifferent>
```

Note that `owl:distinctMembers` can only be used in combination with `owl:allDifferent`.

4.4.10   Data Types

Although XML Schema provides a mechanism to construct user-defined data types (e.g., the data type of `adultAge` as all integers greater than 18, or the data type of all strings starting with a number), such derived data types cannot be used in OWL. In fact, not even all of the many built-in XML Schema data types can be used in OWL. The OWL reference document lists all the XML Schema data types that can be used, but these include the most frequently used types such as string, integer, Boolean, time, and date.

4.4.11   Versioning Information

We have already seen the `owl:priorVersion` statement as part of the header information to indicate earlier versions of the current ontology. This information has no formal model-theoretic semantics but can be exploited by human readers and programs alike for the purposes of ontology management.

Besides `owl:priorVersion`, OWL has three more statements to indicate further informal versioning information. None of these carry any formal meaning.

`owl:versionInfo` generally contains a string giving information about the current version, for example RCS/CVS keywords.

`owl:backwardCompatibleWith` contains a reference to another ontology. This identifies the specified ontology as a prior version of the containing ontology and further indicates that it is backward-compatible with it. In particular, this indicates that all identifiers from the previous version have the same intended interpretations in the new version. Thus, it is a hint to document authors that they can safely change their documents to commit to the new version (by simply updating namespace declarations and `owl:imports` statements to refer to the URL of the new version).

`owl:incompatibleWith,` on the other hand, indicates that the containing ontology is a later version of the referenced ontology but is not backward-compatible with it. Essentially, this is for use by ontology authors who want to be explicit that documents cannot upgrade to use the new version without checking whether changes are required.

4.5 Layering of OWL

Now that we have discussed all the language constructors of OWL, we can completely specify which features of the language may be used in which sublanguage (OWL Full, OWL DL, or OWL Lite).

4.5.1 OWL Full

In OWL Full, all the language constructors may be used in any combination as long as the result is legal RDF.

4.5.2 OWL DL

In order to exploit the formal underpinnings and computational tractability of Description Logics, the following constraints must be obeyed in an OWL DL ontology:

- Vocabulary partitioning. Any resource is allowed to be only a class, a data type, a data type property, an object property, an individual, a data value, or part of the built-in vocabulary, and not more than one of these. This means that, for example, a class cannot at the same time be an individual, or that a property cannot have some values from a data type and some values from a class (this would make it both a data type property and an object property).

- Explicit typing. Not only must all resources be partitioned (as prescribed in the previous constraint) but this partitioning must be stated explicitly. For example, if an ontology contains the following:

```
<owl:Class rdf:ID="C1">
  <rdfs:subClassOf rdf:about="#C2" />
</owl:Class>
```

this already entails that `C2` is a class (by virtue of the range specification of `rdfs:subClassOf`). Nevertheless, an OWL DL ontology must *explicitly* state this information:

```
<owl:Class rdf:ID="C2"/>
```

- Property separation. By virtue of the first constraint, the set of object properties and data type properties are disjoint. This implies that the following can never be specified for data type properties:
  `owl:inverseOf`,
  `owl:FunctionalProperty`,
  `owl:InverseFunctionalProperty`, and
  `owl:SymmetricProperty`.

- No transitive cardinality restrictions. No cardinality restrictions may be placed on transitive properties (or their superproperties, which are of course also transitive, by implication).

- Restricted anonymous classes. Anonymous classes are only allowed to occur as the domain and range of either `owl:equivalentClass` or `owl:disjointWith`, and as the range (but not the domain) of `rdfs:subClassOf`.

4.5.3 OWL Lite

An OWL Lite ontology must be an OWL DL ontology and must further satisfy the following constraints:

- The constructors `owl:oneOf`, `owl:disjointWith`, `owl:unionOf`, `owl:complementOf`, and `owl:hasValue` are not allowed.

- Cardinality statements (minimal, maximal, and exact cardinality) can only be made on the values 0 or 1 and no longer on arbitrary non-negative integers.

- `owl:equivalentClass` statements can no longer be made between anonymous classes but only between class identifiers.

4.5.4 OWL DLP

As explained, OWL is based on Description Logic. Since this is a fragment of first-order logic, it inherits many of the properties of that logic. In particular, it inherits the open-world assumption and the non-unique-name assumption. We explain both of those here, their consequences for ontology design and application, and why they are controversial. This has led to the definition of an interesting sublanguage of OWL DL, named OWL DLP. OWL DLP is not part of the official W3C OWL species layering but is nevertheless sufficiently interesting to deserve some discussion here.

The *open-world assumption* says that we cannot conclude some statement x to be false simply because we cannot show x to be true. After all, our axioms may be simply noncommittal on the status of x. In other words, we may not deduce falsity from the absence of truth. The opposite assumption (closed-world, CWA) would allow deriving falsity from the inability to derive truth.

Here's a simple example where this matters:

Question: "Did it rain in Tokyo yesterday?"
Answer: "I don't know that it rained, but that's not enough reason to conclude that it didn't rain."

Clearly, for this question, the open-world assumption is appropriate. However, consider the following:

Question: "Was there a big earthquake disaster in Tokyo yesterday?"
Answer: "I don't know that there was, but if there had been such a disaster, I'd have heard about it. Therefore I conclude that there wasn't such a disaster."

Apparently, for this question, the closed-world assumption is appropriate and allows us to draw the reasonable conclusion that the open-world assumption would have blocked. So, the fact that OWL is strictly committed to the open-world assumption is in some applications not the right choice.

The *unique-name assumption* (UNA) says that when two individuals are known by different names, they are in fact different individuals. Again, this is an assumption that sometimes works well and sometimes doesn't. When talking about something like product codes in a catalog, it makes sense to assume that when two products are known by different codes, they are indeed different products. But when talking about people in our social environment, it often happens that we only later find out that two people with different identifiers (e.g., "Prof. van Harmelen" and "Frank") are in fact the same person. OWL does not make the unique-name assumption, although it is possible to explicitly assert of a set of identifiers that they are all unique (using `owl:allDifferent`).

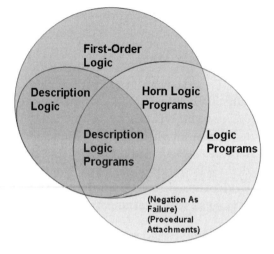

Figure 4.3   relation of OWL DLP to other languages

Traditionally, systems such as databases and logic-programming systems have tended to support closed worlds and unique names, whereas knowledge representation systems and theorem provers support open worlds and non-unique names. Ontologies are sometimes in need of one and sometimes in need of the other. Consequently, discussions can be found in the literature and on the WWW about whether OWL should be more like a knowledge representation system or more like a database system. This debate was nicely resolved by Volz and Horrocks (see the Grosof, Horrocks, Volz and Decker item in the further readings), who identified a fragment of OWL called DLP (Description Logic Programming). This fragment is the largest fragment on which the choice for CWA and UNA does not matter, see figure 4.3. That is, OWL DLP is weak enough so that the differences between the choices don't show up. The advantage of this is that people or applications that wish to make different choices on these assumptions can still exchange ontologies in OWL DLP without harm. Of course, as soon as they go outside OWL DLP, they will notice that they draw different conclusions from the same statements. In other words, they will notice that they disagree on the semantics.

Fortunately, DLP is still large enough to enable useful representation and reasoning tasks. It allows the use of such OWL constructors as class and property equivalence; equality and inequality between individuals; in-

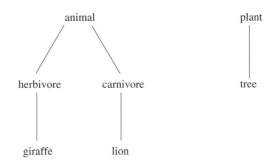

Figure 4.4 Classes and subclasses of the African wildlife ontology

verse, transitive, symmetric and functional properties; and the intersection of classes. It excludes, however, constructors such as intersection and arbitrary cardinality constraints.

These constructors not only allow useful expressivity for many practical cases, while guaranteeing correct interchange between OWL reasoners independent of CWA and UNA, but also allow for translation into efficiently implementable reasoning techniques based on databases and logic programs. More on this topic is discussed in section 5.5.

4.6 Examples

4.6.1 An African Wildlife Ontology

This example shows an ontology that describes African wildlife. Figure 4.4 shows the basic classes and their subclass relationships. Note that the subclass information is only part of the information included in the ontology. The entire graph is much larger. Figure 4.5 shows the graphic representation of the statement that branches are parts of trees.

The ontology includes comments written using `rdfs:comment`.

```
<rdf:RDF
  xmlns:rdf="http://www.w3.org/1999/02/22-rdf-syntax-ns#"
  xmlns:rdfs="http://www.w3.org/2000/01/rdf-schema#"
  xmlns:owl ="http://www.w3.org/2002/07/owl#">

<owl:Ontology rdf:about="xml:base"/>
```

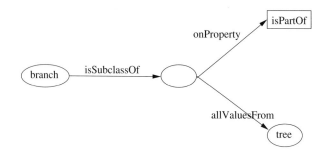

Figure 4.5 Branches are parts of trees

```
<owl:Class rdf:ID="animal">
 <rdfs:comment>Animals form a class.</rdfs:comment>
</owl:Class>

<owl:Class rdf:ID="plant">
 <rdfs:comment>
  Plants form a class disjoint from animals.
 </rdfs:comment>
 <owl:disjointWith rdf:resource="#animal"/>
</owl:Class>

<owl:Class rdf:ID="tree">
 <rdfs:comment>Trees are a type of plant.</rdfs:comment>
 <rdfs:subClassOf rdf:resource="#plant"/>
</owl:Class>

<owl:Class rdf:ID="branch">
 <rdfs:comment>Branches are parts of trees.</rdfs:comment>
 <rdfs:subClassOf>
  <owl:Restriction>
   <owl:onProperty rdf:resource="#is_part_of"/>
   <owl:allValuesFrom rdf:resource="#tree"/>
  </owl:Restriction>
 </rdfs:subClassOf>
</owl:Class>

<owl:Class rdf:ID="leaf">
<rdfs:comment>Leaves are parts of branches.</rdfs:comment>
```

```
  <rdfs:subClassOf>
   <owl:Restriction>
    <owl:onProperty rdf:resource="#is_part_of"/>
    <owl:allValuesFrom rdf:resource="#branch"/>
   </owl:Restriction>
  </rdfs:subClassOf>
</owl:Class>

<owl:Class rdf:ID="herbivore">
 <rdfs:comment>
  Herbivores are exactly those animals that eat only plants
  or parts of plants.
 </rdfs:comment>
 <owl:intersectionOf rdf:parseType="Collection">
  <owl:Class rdf:about="#animal"/>
  <owl:Restriction>
   <owl:onProperty rdf:resource="#eats"/>
   <owl:allValuesFrom>
    <owl:Class>
     <owl:unionOf rdf:parseType="Collection">
      <owl:Class rdf:about="#plant"/>
      <owl:Restriction>
       <owl:onProperty rdf:resource="#is_part_of"/>
       <owl:allValuesFrom rdf:resource="#plant"/>
      </owl:Restriction>
     </owl:unionOf>
    </owl:Class>
   </owl:allValuesFrom>
  </owl:Restriction>
 </owl:intersectionOf>
</owl:Class>

<owl:Class rdf:ID="carnivore">
 <rdfs:comment>
  Carnivores are exactly those animals that eat animals.
 </rdfs:comment>
 <owl:intersectionOf rdf:parseType="Collection">
  <owl:Class rdf:about="#animal"/>
  <owl:Restriction>
   <owl:onProperty rdf:resource="#eats"/>
   <owl:someValuesFrom rdf:resource="#animal"/>
  </owl:Restriction>
```

```
  </owl:intersectionOf>
</owl:Class>

<owl:Class rdf:ID="giraffe">
 <rdfs:comment>
  Giraffes are herbivores, and they eat only leaves.
 </rdfs:comment>
 <rdfs:subClassOf rdf:resource="#herbivore"/>
 <rdfs:subClassOf>
  <owl:Restriction>
   <owl:onProperty rdf:resource="#eats"/>
   <owl:allValuesFrom rdf:resource="#leaf"/>
  </owl:Restriction>
 </rdfs:subClassOf>
</owl:Class>

<owl:Class rdf:ID="lion">
 <rdfs:comment>
  Lions are animals that eat only herbivores.
 </rdfs:comment>
 <rdfs:subClassOf rdf:resource="#carnivore"/>
 <rdfs:subClassOf>
  <owl:Restriction>
   <owl:onProperty rdf:resource="#eats"/>
   <owl:allValuesFrom rdf:resource="#herbivore"/>
  </owl:Restriction>
 </rdfs:subClassOf>
</owl:Class>

<owl:Class rdf:ID="tasty_plant">
 <rdfs:comment>
  Tasty plants are plants that are eaten
  both by herbivores and carnivores.
 </rdfs:comment>
 <rdfs:subClassOf rdf:resource="#plant"/>
 <rdfs:subClassOf>
  <owl:Restriction>
   <owl:onProperty rdf:resource="#eaten_by"/>
   <owl:someValuesFrom>
     <owl:Class rdf:about="#herbivore"/>
   </owl:someValuesFrom>
  </owl:Restriction>
```

```
   </rdfs:subClassOf>
   <rdfs:subClassOf>
    <owl:Restriction>
     <owl:onProperty rdf:resource="#eaten_by"/>
     <owl:someValuesFrom>
       <owl:Class rdf:about="#carnivore"/>
     </owl:someValuesFrom>
    </owl:Restriction>
   </rdfs:subClassOf>
  </owl:Class>

  <owl:TransitiveProperty rdf:ID="is_part_of"/>

  <owl:ObjectProperty rdf:ID="eats">
   <rdfs:domain rdf:resource="#animal"/>
  </owl:ObjectProperty>

  <owl:ObjectProperty rdf:ID="eaten_by">
   <owl:inverseOf rdf:resource="#eats"/>
  </owl:ObjectProperty>

  </rdf:RDF>
```

4.6.2 A Printer Ontology

Classes and subclass relationships in this example are shown in figure 4.6.

```
<!DOCTYPE owl [
    <!ENTITY xsd  "http://www.w3.org/2001/XMLSchema#" >
]>

<rdf:RDF
  xmlns:rdf="http://www.w3.org/1999/02/22-rdf-syntax-ns#"
  xmlns:rdfs="http://www.w3.org/2000/01/rdf-schema#"
  xmlns:xsd="http://www.w3.org/2001/XMLSchema#"
  xmlns:owl ="http://www.w3.org/2002/07/owl#"
  xmlns="http://www.cs.vu.nl/~frankh/spool/printer.owl#">

<owl:Ontology rdf:about="">
 <owl:versionInfo>
  My example version 1.2, 17 October 2002
```

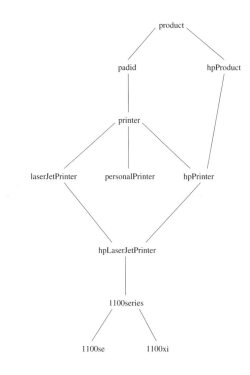

Figure 4.6   Classes and subclasses of the printer ontology

```
  </owl:versionInfo>
</owl:Ontology>

<owl:Class rdf:ID="product">
 <rdfs:comment>Products form a class.</rdfs:comment>
</owl:Class>

<owl:Class rdf:ID="padid">
 <rdfs:comment>
  Printing and digital imaging devices
  form a subclass of products.
 </rdfs:comment>
 <rdfs:label>Device</rdfs:label>
 <rdfs:subClassOf rdf:resource="#product"/>
</owl:Class>
```

```
<owl:Class rdf:ID="hpProduct">
 <rdfs:comment>
  HP products are exactly those products
  that are manufactured by Hewlett Packard.
 </rdfs:comment>
 <owl:intersectionOf rdf:parseType="Collection">
  <owl:Class rdf:about="#product"/>
  <owl:Restriction>
   <owl:onProperty rdf:resource="#manufactured_by"/>
   <owl:hasValue rdf:datatype="&xsd;string">
     Hewlett Packard
   </owl:hasValue>
  </owl:Restriction>
 </owl:intersectionOf>
</owl:Class>

<owl:Class rdf:ID="printer">
 <rdfs:comment>
  Printers are printing and digital imaging devices.
 </rdfs:comment>
 <rdfs:subClassOf rdf:resource="#padid"/>
</owl:Class>

<owl:Class rdf:ID="personalPrinter">
 <rdfs:comment>
  Printers for personal use form a subclass of printers.
 </rdfs:comment>
 <rdfs:subClassOf rdf:resource="#printer"/>
</owl:Class>

<owl:Class rdf:ID="hpPrinter">
 <rdfs:comment>
  HP printers are  HP products and printers.
 </rdfs:comment>
 <rdfs:subClassOf rdf:resource="#printer"/>
 <rdfs:subClassOf rdf:resource="#hpProduct"/>
</owl:Class>

<owl:Class rdf:ID="laserJetPrinter">
 <rdfs:comment>
  Laser jet printers are exactly those
  printers that use laser jet printing technology.
```

```
   </rdfs:comment>
   <owl:intersectionOf rdf:parseType="Collection">
    <owl:Class rdf:about="#printer"/>
    <owl:Restriction>
     <owl:onProperty rdf:resource="#printingTechnology"/>
     <owl:hasValue rdf:datatype="&xsd;string">
      laser jet
     </owl:hasValue>
    </owl:Restriction>
   </owl:intersectionOf>
  </owl:Class>

  <owl:Class rdf:ID="hpLaserJetPrinter">
   <rdfs:comment>
    HP laser jet printers are HP products
    and laser jet printers.
   </rdfs:comment>
   <rdfs:subClassOf rdf:resource="#laserJetPrinter"/>
   <rdfs:subClassOf rdf:resource="#hpPrinter"/>
  </owl:Class>

  <owl:Class rdf:ID="1100series">
   <rdfs:comment>
    1100series printers are HP laser jet printers with
    8ppm printing speed and 600dpi printing resolution.
   </rdfs:comment>
   <rdfs:subClassOf rdf:resource="#hpLaserJetPrinter"/>
   <rdfs:subClassOf>
    <owl:Restriction>
     <owl:onProperty rdf:resource="#printingSpeed"/>
     <owl:hasValue rdf:datatype="&xsd;string">
      8ppm
     </owl:hasValue>
    </owl:Restriction>
   </rdfs:subClassOf>
   <rdfs:subClassOf>
    <owl:Restriction>
     <owl:onProperty rdf:resource="#printingResolution"/>
     <owl:hasValue rdf:datatype="&xsd;string">
      600dpi
     </owl:hasValue>
    </owl:Restriction>
```

```
  </rdfs:subClassOf>
 </owl:Class>

 <owl:Class rdf:ID="1100se">
  <rdfs:comment>
    1100se printers belong to the 1100 series and cost $450.
  </rdfs:comment>
  <rdfs:subClassOf rdf:resource="#1100series"/>
  <rdfs:subClassOf>
   <owl:Restriction>
    <owl:onProperty rdf:resource="#price"/>
    <owl:hasValue rdf:datatype="&xsd;integer">
     450
    </owl:hasValue>
   </owl:Restriction>
  </rdfs:subClassOf>
 </owl:Class>

 <owl:Class rdf:ID="1100xi">
  <rdfs:comment>
    1100xi printers belong to the 1100 series and cost $350.
  </rdfs:comment>
  <rdfs:subClassOf rdf:resource="#1100series"/>
  <rdfs:subClassOf>
   <owl:Restriction>
    <owl:onProperty rdf:resource="#price"/>
    <owl:hasValue rdf:datatype="&xsd;integer">
     350
    </owl:hasValue>
   </owl:Restriction>
  </rdfs:subClassOf>
 </owl:Class>

 <owl:DatatypeProperty rdf:ID="manufactured_by">
  <rdfs:domain rdf:resource="#product"/>
  <rdfs:range rdf:resource="&xsd;string"/>
 </owl:DatatypeProperty>

 <owl:DatatypeProperty rdf:ID="price">
  <rdfs:domain rdf:resource="#product"/>
  <rdfs:range rdf:resource="&xsd;nonNegativeInteger"/>
 </owl:DatatypeProperty>
```

```
<owl:DatatypeProperty rdf:ID="printingTechnology">
 <rdfs:domain rdf:resource="#printer"/>
 <rdfs:range rdf:resource="&xsd;string"/>
</owl:DatatypeProperty>

<owl:DatatypeProperty rdf:ID="printingResolution">
 <rdfs:domain rdf:resource="#printer"/>
 <rdfs:range rdf:resource="&xsd;string"/>
</owl:DatatypeProperty>

<owl:DatatypeProperty rdf:ID="printingSpeed">
 <rdfs:domain rdf:resource="#printer"/>
 <rdfs:range rdf:resource="&xsd;string"/>
</owl:DatatypeProperty>

</rdf:RDF>
```

This ontology demonstrates that siblings in a hierarchy tree need not be disjoint. For example, a personal printer may be an HP printer or a LaserJet printer, although the three classes involved are subclasses of the class of all printers.

4.7   OWL in OWL

Here we present a part of the definition of OWL in terms of itself. The full description is found on the Web (see Suggested Reading). In our presentation we comment on some aspects of OWL that have not been discussed so far.

4.7.1   Namespaces

```
<?xml version="1.0"?>
<!DOCTYPE owl [
 <!ENTITY rdf "http://www.w3.org/1999/02/22-rdf-syntax-ns#">
 <!ENTITY rdfs "http://www.w3.org/2000/01/rdf-schema#">
 <!ENTITY xsd "http://www.w3.org/2001/XMLSchema#">
 <!ENTITY owl "http://www.w3.org/2002/07/owl#"> ]>
<rdf:RDF
  xml:base  ="http://www.w3.org/2002/07/owl"
  xmlns     ="&owl;"
```

```
xmlns:owl ="&owl;"
xmlns:rdf ="&rdf;"
xmlns:rdfs="&rdfs;"
xmlns:dc  ="http://purl.org/dc/elements/1.1/">
```

The URI of the current document (the OWL definition) is defined as the default namespace. Therefore, the prefix `owl:` will not be used in the following. Also, note the use of XML entity definitions, which allows us to abbreviate URLs appearing in attribute values.

4.7.2 Classes of Classes (Metaclasses)

The class of all OWL classes is itself a subclass of the class of all RDF Schema classes:

```
<rdfs:Class rdf:ID="Class">
  <rdfs:label>Class</rdfs:label>
  <rdfs:comment>The class of all OWL classes</rdfs:comment>
  <rdfs:subClassOf rdf:resource="&rdfs;Class"/>
</rdfs:Class>
```

`Thing` is the most general object class in OWL, and `Nothing` the most specific, that is, the empty object class. The following relationships hold:

$$Thing = Nothing \cup Nothing^c$$
$$Nothing = Thing^c = Nothing^c \cap Nothing^{cc} = \emptyset$$

```
<Class rdf:ID="Thing">
  <rdfs:label>Thing</rdfs:label>
  <unionOf rdf:parseType="Collection">
    <Class rdf:about="#Nothing"/>
    <Class>
      <complementOf rdf:resource="#Nothing"/>
    </Class>
  </unionOf>
</Class>

<Class rdf:ID="Nothing">
  <rdfs:label>Nothing</rdfs:label>
  <complementOf rdf:resource="#Thing"/>
</Class>
```

4.7.3   Class Equivalence

Class equivalence, expressed by `owl:EquivalentClass`, implies a sub-class relationship and is always stated between two classes. This is analogous for `owl:EquivalentProperty`. Disjointness statements can only be stated between classes.

```
<rdf:Property rdf:ID="EquivalentClass">
  <rdfs:label>EquivalentClass</rdfs:label>
  <rdfs:subPropertyOf rdf:resource="&rdfs;subClassOf"/>
  <rdfs:domain rdf:resource="#Class"/>
  <rdfs:range rdf:resource="#Class"/>
</rdf:Property>

<rdf:Property rdf:ID="EquivalentProperty">
  <rdfs:label>EquivalentProperty</rdfs:label>
  <rdfs:subPropertyOf rdf:resource="&rdfs;subPropertyOf"/>
</rdf:Property>

<rdf:Property rdf:ID="disjointWith">
  <rdfs:label>disjointWith</rdfs:label>
  <rdfs:domain rdf:resource="#Class"/>
  <rdfs:range rdf:resource="#Class"/>
</rdf:Property>
```

Equality and inequality can be stated between arbitrary things; in OWL Full this statement can also be applied to classes. `owl:sameAs` is simply a synonym for `owl:sameIndividualAs`.

```
<rdf:Property rdf:ID="sameIndividualAs">
  <rdfs:label>sameIndividualAs</rdfs:label>
  <rdfs:domain rdf:resource="#Thing"/>
  <rdfs:range rdf:resource="#Thing"/>
</rdf:Property>

<rdf:Property rdf:ID="differentFrom">
  <rdfs:label>differentFrom</rdfs:label>
  <rdfs:domain rdf:resource="#Thing"/>
  <rdfs:range rdf:resource="#Thing"/>
</rdf:Property>

<rdf:Property rdf:ID="sameAs">
  <rdfs:label>sameAs</rdfs:label>
```

```
    <EquivalentProperty rdf:resource="#sameIndividualAs"/>
  </rdf:Property>
```

`owl:distinctMembers` can only be used for `owl:AllDifferent`:

```
  <rdfs:Class rdf:ID="AllDifferent">
    <rdfs:label>AllDifferent</rdfs:label>
  </rdfs:Class>

  <rdf:Property rdf:ID="distinctMembers">
    <rdfs:label>distinctMembers</rdfs:label>
    <rdfs:domain rdf:resource="#AllDifferent"/>
    <rdfs:range rdf:resource="&rdf;List"/>
  </rdf:Property>
```

4.7.4   Building Classes from Other Classes

`owl:unionOf` builds a class from a list (assumed to be a list of other class expressions).

```
  <rdf:Property rdf:ID="unionOf">
    <rdfs:label>unionOf</rdfs:label>
    <rdfs:domain rdf:resource="#Class"/>
    <rdfs:range rdf:resource="&rdf;List"/>
  </rdf:Property>
```

`owl:intersectionOf` and `owl:oneOf` also build classes from a list, although for these constructs the list is assumed to be a list of individuals. `owl:complementOf` defines a class in terms of a single other class.

```
  <rdf:Property rdf:ID="complementOf">
    <rdfs:label>complementOf</rdfs:label>
    <rdfs:domain rdf:resource="#Class"/>
    <rdfs:range rdf:resource="#Class"/>
  </rdf:Property>
```

4.7.5   Restricting Properties of Classes

Restrictions in OWL define the class of those objects that satisfy some attached conditions.

```
  <rdfs:Class rdf:ID="Restriction">
    <rdfs:label>Restriction</rdfs:label>
```

```
   <rdfs:subClassOf rdf:resource="#Class"/>
</rdfs:Class>
```

All the following properties are only allowed to occur within a restriction definition; that is, their domain is owl:Restriction, but they differ with respect to their range:

```
<rdf:Property rdf:ID="onProperty">
  <rdfs:label>onProperty</rdfs:label>
  <rdfs:domain rdf:resource="#Restriction"/>
  <rdfs:range rdf:resource="&rdf;Property"/>
</rdf:Property>

<rdf:Property rdf:ID="allValuesFrom">
  <rdfs:label>allValuesFrom</rdfs:label>
  <rdfs:domain rdf:resource="#Restriction"/>
  <rdfs:range rdf:resource="&rdfs;Class"/>
</rdf:Property>

<rdf:Property rdf:ID="hasValue">
  <rdfs:label>hasValue</rdfs:label>
  <rdfs:domain rdf:resource="#Restriction"/>
</rdf:Property>

<rdf:Property rdf:ID="minCardinality">
  <rdfs:label>minCardinality</rdfs:label>
  <rdfs:domain rdf:resource="#Restriction"/>
  <rdfs:range rdf:resource="&xsd;nonNegativeInteger"/>
</rdf:Property>
```

owl:maxCardinality and owl:cardinality are defined analogously to owl:minCardinality, and owl:someValuesFrom is defined analogously to owl:allValuesFrom

It is also worth noting that owl:onProperty allows the restriction on an object or data type property. Therefore, the range of the restricting properties like owl:allValuesFrom is not owl:Class (object classes) but the more general rdfs:Class.

4.7.5.1 Properties

owl:ObjectProperty is a special case of rdf:Property,

```
<rdfs:Class rdf:ID="ObjectProperty">
  <rdfs:label>ObjectProperty</rdfs:label>
  <rdfs:subClassOf rdf:resource="&rdf;Property"/>
</rdfs:Class>
```

and similarly for `owl:DatatypeProperty`.
`owl:TransitiveProperty` can only be applied to object properties,

```
<rdfs:Class rdf:ID="TransitiveProperty">
  <rdfs:label>TransitiveProperty</rdfs:label>
  <rdfs:subClassOf rdf:resource="#ObjectProperty"/>
</rdfs:Class>
```

and similarly for symmetric, functional, and inverse functional properties.
Finally, `owl:inverseOf` relates two object properties:

```
<rdf:Property rdf:ID="inverseOf">
  <rdfs:label>inverseOf</rdfs:label>
  <rdfs:domain rdf:resource="#ObjectProperty"/>
  <rdfs:range rdf:resource="#ObjectProperty"/>
</rdf:Property>
```

Although not stated in the online references, the following would also seem
to be true:

```
<TransitiveProperty rdf:ID="&rdfs;subClassOf"/>
<TransitiveProperty rdf:ID="&rdfs;subProperty/>

<TransitiveProperty rdf:ID="EquivalentClass"/>
<SymmetricProperty  rdf:ID="EquivalentClass"/>

<SymmetricProperty  rdf:ID="disjointWith"/>

<TransitiveProperty rdf:ID="EquivalentProperty"/>
<SymmetricProperty  rdf:ID="EquivalentProperty"/>

<TransitiveProperty rdf:ID="sameIndividualAs"/>
<SymmetricProperty  rdf:ID="sameIndividualAs"/>

<SymmetricProperty  rdf:ID="differentFrom"/>

<SymmetricProperty  rdf:ID="complementOf"/>
<rdf:Property       rdf:about="complementOf">
```

```
    <rdfs:subPropertyOf rdf:resource="disjointWith"/>
  </rdf:Property>

  <rdf:Property      rdf:about="cardinality">
    <rdfs:subPropertyOf rdf:resource="mincardinality"/>
    <rdfs:subPropertyOf rdf:resource="maxcardinality"/>
  </rdf:Property>

  <SymmetricProperty  rdf:ID="inverseOf"/>

  <rdf:Property      rdf:about="inverseOf">
    <inverseOf rdf:resource="inverseOf"/>
  </rdf:Property>
```

Although this captures some of OWL's meaning in OWL, it does not capture the entire semantics, so a separate semantic specification (as given in the OWL standard) remains necessary.

4.8   Future Extensions

Clearly, OWL is not the final word on ontology languages for the Semantic Web. A number of additional features have already been identified in the OWL Requirements Document, and many others are under discussion. In this section, we briefly list a few of these possible extensions and improvements to OWL.

4.8.1   Modules and Imports

Importing ontologies defined by others will be the norm on the Semantic Web. However, the importing facility of OWL is very trivial; it only allows importing of an *entire* ontology, specified by location. Even if one would want to use only a small portion of another ontology, one would be forced to import that entire ontology. Module constructions in programming languages are based on a notion of information hiding. The module promises to provide some functionality to the outside world (the export clause of the module), but the importing module need not concern itself with how this functionality is achieved. It is an open research question what a corresponding notion of information hiding for ontologies would be, and how it could be used as the basis for a good import construction

4.8.2   Defaults

Many practical knowledge representation systems allow inherited values to be overridden by more specific classes in the hierarchy, treating the inherited values as defaults. Although this is widely used in practice, no consensus has been reached on the right formalization for the nonmonotonic behavior of default values.

4.8.3   Closed-World Assumption

The semantics of OWL currently adopts the standard logical model of an open-world assumption: a statement cannot be assumed true on the basis of a failure to prove it. Clearly, on the huge and only partially knowable World Wide Web, this is the correct assumption. Nevertheless, the opposite approach (a closed-world assumption: a statement is true when its negation cannot be proved) is also useful in certain applications. The closed-world assumption is closely tied to the notion of defaults and leads to the same nonmonotonic behavior, a reason for it not to be included in OWL.

4.8.4   Unique-Names Assumption

Typical database applications assume that individuals with different names are indeed different individuals. OWL follows the usual logical paradigm where this is not the case. If two individuals (or classes or properties) have different names, we may still derive by inference that they must be the same. As with the non-closed-world assumption, the non-unique-names assumption is the most plausible one to make on the World Wide Web, but as before, situations exist where the unique-names assumption is useful. More subtly, one may want to indicate portions of the ontology for which the assumption does or does not hold.

4.8.5   Procedural Attachment

A common concept in knowledge representation is to define the meaning of a term not through explicit definitions in the language (as is done in OWL) but by attaching a piece of code to be executed for computing the meaning of the term. Although widely used, this concept does not lend itself very well to integration in a system with a formal semantics, and it has not been included in OWL.

4.8.6   Rules for Property Chaining

As explained previously, for reasons of decidability OWL does not currently allow the composition of properties, but of course in many applications this is a useful operation. Even more generally, one would want to define properties as general rules (Horn or otherwise) over other properties. Such integration of rule-based knowledge representation and DL-style knowledge representation is currently an active area of research. (See chapter 5 for an extensive discussion on this topic).

Some of the issues mentioned here (rules, nonmonotonicity) are addressed in chapter 5.

4.9   Summary

- OWL is the proposed standard for Web ontologies. It allows us to describe the semantics of knowledge in a machine-accessible way.

- OWL builds upon RDF and RDF Schema; XML-based RDF syntax is used; instances are defined using RDF descriptions; and most RDFS modeling primitives are used.

- Formal semantics and reasoning support is provided through the mapping of OWL on logics. Predicate logic and description logics have been used for this purpose.

While OWL is sufficiently rich to be used in practice, extensions are in the making. They will provide further logical features, including rules.

Suggested Reading

Here are the key references for OWL:

- D. McGuinness and F van Harmelen, eds. OWL Web Ontology Language Overview. W3C Recommendation, February 10, 2004.
  <http://www.w3.org/TR/owl-features/>.

- S. Bechhofer, F. van Harmelen, J. Hendler, I. Horrocks, D. McGuinness, P. Patel-Schneider, and L. Stein, OWL Web Ontology Language Reference. W3C Recommendation, February 10, 2004.
  <http://www.w3.org/TR/owl-ref/>.

- M. Smith, C. Welty, and D. McGuinness, eds. OWL Web Ontology Language: Guide. W3C Recommendation, February 10, 2004. <http://www.w3.org/TR/owl-guide/>.

Interesting articles related to DAML+OIL and OIL include the following

- J. Broekstra, M. Klein, S. Decker, D. Fensel, F. van Harmelen, and I. Horrocks, Enabling Knowledge Representation on the Web by Extending RDF Schema. In *Proceedings of the 10th World Wide Web Conference (WWW10)*, 2001, 467–478. <http://www10.org/cdrom/papers/291/>

- D. Fensel, I. Horrocks, F. van Harmelen, D. McGuinness, and P. Patel-Schneider. OIL: An Ontology Infrastructure for the Semantic Web. *IEEE Intelligent Systems* 16 (March-April 2001): 38–45. <http://www.cs.vu.nl/~frankh/abstracts/IEEE-IS01.html>.

- D. McGuinness. Ontologies Come of Age. In *Spinning the Semantic Web*, ed. D. Fensel, J. Hendler, H. Lieberman, and W. Wahlster. MIT Press, Cambridge, Mass., 2003.

- P. Patel-Schneider, I. Horrocks, and F. van Harmelen. Reviewing the Design of DAML+OIL: An Ontology Language for the Semantic Web. In *Proceedings of the 18th National Conference on Artificial Intelligence (AAAI02)*, 2002. <http://www.cs.vu.nl/~frankh/abstracts/AAAI02.html>.

Here are a few references regarding description logics:

- F. Baader, D. Calvanese, D. McGuinness, D. Nardi, and P. Patel-Schneider, eds. *The Description Logic Handbook: Theory, Implementation and Applications*. Cambridge: Cambridge University Press, 2002.

- E. Franconi. Description Logics Course Information. <http://www.inf.unibz.it/~franconi/dl/course/>.

- I. Horrocks and U. Sattler. Ontology Reasoning in the *SHOQ(D)* Description Logic. In *Proceedings of the 17th International Joint Conference on Artificial Intelligence (IJCAI-01)*, 2001, 199–204.

- I. Horrocks. Tutorial on Description Logic. <http://www.cs.man.ac.uk/~horrocks/Slides/IJCAR-tutorial/Print/>.

- Benjamin Grosof, Ian Horrocks, Raphael Volz, Stefan Decker. Description logic programs: combining logic programs with description logic. In *Proceedings of the 12th international conference on World Wide Web, (WWW03)*, 2003, 48–57.

Web sites with information on the various languages:

- <http://www.w3.org/2001/sw/WebOnt/>. Information on OWL.

- <http://www.daml.org/>. Information on DAML+OIL. See especially the pages /language, /ontologies, and /tools.

- <http://logic.aifb.uni-karlsruhe.de/>. Information on OWL DLP.

The following are a few links related to the general notion of ontologies but quite different in nature from the content of this chapter. Thesauri are simple kinds of informal ontologies.

- <http://www.topicmaps.org/>. Topic maps constitute a simple ontology language in use today.

- <http://dublincore.org/>. The Dublin Core is an example of an ontology used extensively in the digital library domain.

Exercises and Projects

4.1   Read the online specification and the complete namespace of OWL (see Suggested Reading).

4.2   Give three different ways of stating that two classes are disjoint.

4.3   Express the fact that all mathematics courses are taught by David Billington only (no other lecturer may be involved). Also express the fact that the mathematics courses are exactly the courses taught by David Billington. Is the difference clear?

4.4   Strictly speaking, the notion of `SymmetricProperty` was not needed in OWL because it could have been expressed in terms of other language primitives. Explain how this can be done. (*Hint:* Consider the inverse, too.)

4.5   Similar question for `FunctionalProperty`. Show how it can be expressed using other OWL language constructions.

4.6 Determine in general which features of OWL are necessary and which are only convenient but can be simulated by other modeling primitives.

4.7 In the example African wildlife ontology, what problem would emerge if we replaced `owl:allValuesFrom` by `owl:someValuesFrom` in the definition of carnivores? (*Hint*: Consider the definition of tasty plants.)

4.8 State the relationship between the concepts `FunctionalProperty`, `InverseFunctionalProperty`, and `Inverseof`.

4.9 Explain why it was necessary to declare `owl:Class` as a subclass of `rdfs:Class`.

4.10 In chapter 3 we presented an axiomatic semantics for RDF. A similar axiomatic semantics can be developed for OWL. Define the axiomatic semantics of `intersectionOf`.

4.11 Define the axiomatic semantics of `inverseOf`.

4.12 In this exercise you are asked to develop an axiomatic semantics for cardinality restrictions.

   (a) Define `noRepeatsList`. L is a "no repeats list" if there is not an element that occurs in L more than once. The concept is not part of the OWL language but will be used to count the elements for cardinality restrictions.

   (b) Define `minCardinality` and `maxCardinality` as properties with domain `Restriction` and range `NonNegativeInteger`.

   (c) Give an axiom that captures the meaning of `minCardinality`: If $onProperty(R, P)$ and $minCardinality(R, n)$ then x is an instance of R if, and only if, there is a "no repeats list" L of length $\geq n$, such that $P(x, y)$ for all $y \in L$.

   (d) Express the meaning of `maxCardinality` in a similar way.

4.13 Look at some ontologies at <http://www.daml.org/ontologies>.

4.14 Write your own ontologies in OWL.

4.15 OIL is a predecessor of OWL. Read the pages about the OIL language and some of the example ontologies. Compare the OIL language to the OWL language, paying attention both to commonalities and differences.

4.16 Compare the online documents on OWL to those for DAML+OIL.

4.17 Rewrite some examples from the DAML+OIL documents using OWL terminology.

4.18 Try to think of features that are still missing in OWL. *Hint:* Think of projects and persons involved. What should be true for each project, and what for each person (to be valuable to their company)? Can you express these conditions in OWL?

5 *Logic and Inference: Rules*

5.1 Introduction

From an abstract viewpoint, the subjects of the previous chapters were related to the *representation of knowledge*: knowledge about the content of Web resources, and knowledge about the concepts of a domain of discourse and their relationships (ontology).

Knowledge representation had been studied long before the emergence of the World Wide Web, in the area of artificial intelligence and, before that, in philosophy. In fact, it can be traced back to ancient Greece; Aristotle is considered to be the father of logic. Logic is still the foundation of knowledge representation, particularly in the form of *predicate logic* (also known as *first-order logic*). Here we list a few reasons for the popularity and importance of logic:

- It provides a high-level language in which knowledge can be expressed in a transparent way. And it has a high expressive power.

- It has a well-understood formal semantics, which assigns an unambiguous meaning to logical statements.

- There is precise notion of logical consequence, which determines whether a statement follows semantically from a set of other statements (premises). In fact, the primary original motivation of logic was the study of objective laws of logical consequence.

- There exist proof systems that can automatically derive statements syntactically from a set of premises.

- There exist proof systems for which semantic logical consequence coincides with syntactic derivation within the proof system. Proof systems

157

should be sound (all derived statements follow semantically from the premises) and complete (all logical consequences of the premises can be derived in the proof system).

- Predicate logic is unique in the sense that sound and complete proof systems do exist. More expressive logics (higher-order logics) do not have such proof systems.

- Because of the existence of proof systems, it is possible to trace the proof that leads to a logical consequence. In this sense, the logic can provide explanations for answers.

The languages of RDF and OWL (Lite and DL) can be viewed as specializations of predicate logic. The correspondence was illustrated by the axiomatic semantics in the form of logical axioms.

One justification for the existence of such specialized languages is that they provide a syntax that fits well with the intended use (in our case, Web languages based on tags). The other major justification is that they define reasonable subsets of logic. As mentioned in section 4.1, there is a trade-off between the expressive power and the computational complexity of certain logics: the more expressive the language, the less efficient (in the worst case) the corresponding proof systems. As we stated, OWL Lite and OWL DL correspond roughly to a description logic, a subset of predicate logic for which efficient proof systems exist.

Another subset of predicate logic with efficient proof systems comprises the so-called *rule systems* (also known as *Horn logic* or *definite logic programs*). A rule has the form

$$A_1, \ldots A_n \rightarrow B$$

where A_i and B are atomic formulas. In fact, there are two intuitive ways of reading such a rule:

1. If $A_1, \ldots, A_n$ are known to be true, then B is also true. Rules with this interpretation are referred to as *deductive rules*.

2. If the conditions $A_1, \ldots, A_n$ are true, then carry out the action B. Rules with this interpretation are referred to as *reactive rules*.

Both views have important applications. However, in this chapter we take the deductive approach. We study the language and possible queries that one can ask, as well as appropriate answers. Also we outline the working of a proof mechanism that can return such answers.

It is interesting to note that description logics and Horn logic are orthogonal in the sense that neither of them is a subset of the other. For example, it is impossible to express the relation $uncleOf(X, Y)$. This relation requires the ability to constrain the value of the property $brotherOf$ of one term (X) to be the value of the property $childOf$ of another term (Y). Stated another way, the property $brotherOf$ applied to X must produce a result that is also a value of $childOf$ when applied to Y. This "joining" of predicates is beyond the expressive capabilities of OWL. On the other hand, this piece of knowledge can easily be represented using rules:

$$brother(X, Y), childOf(Z, Y) \rightarrow uncle(X, Z)$$

On the other hand, rules cannot (in the general case) assert (a) negation/complement of classes; (b) disjunctive information, for instance, that a person is either a man or a woman; (c) existential quantification, for instance, that all persons have a father. In contrast, OWL is able to express complement and union of classes and certain forms of existential quantification.

Then we turn our attention to another kind of rules. We give a simple example. Suppose an online vendor wants to give a special discount if it is a customer's birthday. An easy way to represent this application with rules is as follows:

$R1$: If birthday, then special discount.

$R2$: If not birthday, then not special discount.

This solution works properly in case the birthday is known. But imagine a customer who refuses to provide his birthday because of privacy concerns. In such a case, the preceding rules cannot be applied because their premises are not known. To capture this situation we need to write something like

$R1$: If birthday, then special discount.

$R2'$: If birthday is not known, then not special discount.

However, the premise of rule $R2'$ is not within the expressive power of predicate logic. Thus we need a new kind of rule system. We note that the solution with rules $R1$ and $R2$ works in case we have complete information about the situation (for example, either birthday or not birthday). The new kind of rule system will find application in cases where the available information is incomplete.

Predicate logic and its special cases are monotonic in the following sense. If a conclusion can be drawn, it remains valid even if new knowledge becomes available. But if rule $R2'$ is applied to derive "not special discount," then this conclusion may become invalid if the customer's birthday becomes known at a later stage and it happens to coincide with the purchase date. Thus we talk of *nonmonotonic rules* to distinguish them from monotonic rules (which are a special case of predicate logic). In this chapter we discuss both monotonic and nonmonotonic rules.

Our final concern is the exchange of rules across different applications. For example, an online store might wish to make its pricing, refund, and privacy policies, which are expressed using rules, accessible to intelligent agents. The Semantic Web approach is to express the knowledge in a machine-accessible way using one of the Web languages we have already discussed. In this chapter we show how rules can be expressed in XML-like languages ("rule markup languages"). Some applications of rule systems are discussed in chapter 6.

Chapter Overview

Readers who are not comfortable with the notation and basic notions of predicate logic are advised to read some introductory chapters of logic books, like those listed at the end of this chapter.

- Section 5.2 provides an example using monotonic rules (that is, of the subset of predicate logic called Horn logic).

- Sections 5.3 and 5.4 describe the syntax and semantics of Horn logic.

- Sections 5.5 and 5.6 describe DLP and SWRL, two approaches to combining rules with description logics (OWL DL).

- Section 5.7 describes the syntax of nonmonotonic rules, and section 5.8 presents an example of nonmonotonic rules.

- Finally, section 5.9 briefly describes RuleML, a major standardization activity for rule markup on the Web.

5.2 Example of Monotonic Rules: Family Relationships

Imagine a database of facts about some family relationships. Suppose that the database contains facts about the following *base predicates*:

$mother(X, Y)$	X is the mother of Y
$father(X, Y)$	X is the father of Y
$male(X)$	X is male
$female(X)$	X is female

Then we can infer further relationships using appropriate rules. First, we can define a predicate *parent*: a parent is either a father or a mother.

$$mother(X, Y) \rightarrow parent(X, Y)$$
$$father(X, Y) \rightarrow parent(X, Y)$$

Then we can define a brother to be a male person sharing a parent:

$$male(X), parent(P, X), parent(P, Y), notSame(X, Y) \rightarrow$$
$$brother(X, Y)$$

The predicate *notSame* denotes inequality; we assume that such facts are kept in a database. Of course, every practical logical system offers convenient ways of expressing equality and inequality, but we chose the abstract solution to keep the discussion general.

Similarly, *sister* is defined as follows:

$$female(X), parent(P, X), parent(P, Y), notSame(X, Y) \rightarrow$$
$$sister(X, Y)$$

An uncle is a brother of a parent:

$$brother(X, P), parent(P, Y) \rightarrow uncle(X, Y)$$

A grandmother is the mother of a parent:

$$mother(X, P), parent(P, Y) \rightarrow grandmother(X, Y)$$

An ancestor is either a parent or an ancestor of a parent:

$$parent(X, Y) \rightarrow ancestor(X, Y)$$
$$ancestor(X, P), parent(P, Y) \rightarrow ancestor(X, Y)$$

5.3   Monotonic Rules: Syntax

Let us consider a simple rule stating that all loyal customers aged over 60 are entitled to a special discount:

$$loyalCustomer(X), age(X) > 60 \rightarrow discount(X)$$

We distinguish some ingredients of rules:

- *variables*, which are placeholders for values: X

- *constants*, which denote fixed values: 60

- *predicates*, which relate objects: $loyalCustomer, >$

- *function symbols*, which return a value for certain arguments: age

Rules

A rule has the form

$$B_1, \ldots, B_n \rightarrow A$$

where $A, B_1, \ldots, B_n$ are atomic formulas. A is the *head* of the rule, and $B_1, \ldots, B_n$ are the *premises* of the rule. The set $\{B_1, \ldots, B_n\}$ is referred to as the *body* of the rule.

The commas in the rule body are read conjunctively: if B_1 and B_2 and ... and B_n are true, then A is also true (or equivalently, to prove A it is sufficient to prove all $B_1, \ldots, B_n$).

Note that variables may occur in $A, B_1, \ldots, B_n$. For example,

$$loyalCustomer(X), age(X) > 60 \rightarrow discount(X)$$

This rule is applied for *any* customer: if a customer happens to be loyal and over 60, then she gets the discount. In other words, the variable X is implicitly universally quantified (using $\forall X$). In general, all variables occurring in a rule are implicitly universally quantified.

In summary, a rule r

$$B_1, \ldots, B_n \rightarrow A$$

is interpreted as the following formula, denoted by $pl(r)$:

$$\forall X_1 \ldots \forall X_k((B_1 \wedge \ldots \wedge B_n) \rightarrow A)$$

or equivalently,

$$\forall X_1 \ldots \forall X_k(A \vee \neg B_1 \vee \ldots \vee \neg B_n)$$

where $X_1, \ldots, X_k$ are all variables occurring in $A, B_1, \ldots, B_n$.

Facts

A fact is an atomic formula, such as $loyalCustomer(a345678)$; it says that the customer with ID a345678 is loyal. The variables of a fact are implicitly universally quantified.

Logic Programs

A logic program P is a finite set of facts and rules. Its predicate logic translation $pl(P)$ is the set of all predicate logic interpretations of rules and facts in P.

Goals

A goal denotes a query G asked to a logic program. It has the form

$$B_1, \ldots, B_n \rightarrow$$

If $n = 0$ we have the *empty goal* $\square$.

Our next task is to interpret goals in predicate logic. Using the ideas we developed before (interpretations of commas as conjunction, implicit universal quantification), we get the following interpretation:

$$\forall X_1 \ldots \forall X_k(\neg B_1 \vee \ldots \vee \neg B_n)$$

This formula is the same as $pl(r)$, with the only difference that the rule head A is omitted[1].

An equivalent representation in predicate logic is

$$\neg \exists X_1 \ldots \exists X_k(B_1 \wedge \ldots \wedge B_n)$$

---

1. Note that the formula is equivalent to $\forall X_1 \ldots \forall X_k(false \vee \neg B_1 \vee \ldots \vee \neg B_n)$, so a missing rule head can be thought of as a contradiction $false$.

where $X_1, \ldots, X_k$ are all variables occurring in $B_1, \ldots, B_n$. Let us briefly explain this formula. Suppose we know

$p(a)$

and we have the goal

$p(X) \rightarrow$

Actually, we want to know whether there is a value for which p is true. We expect a positive answer because of the fact $p(a)$. Thus $p(X)$ is existentially quantified. But then why do we negate the formula? The explanation is that we use a proof technique from mathematics called *proof by contradiction*. This technique proves that a statement A follows from a statement B by assuming that A is false and deriving a contradiction, when combined with B. Then A *must* follow from B.

In logic programming we prove that a goal can be answered positively by negating the goal and proving that we get a contradiction using the logic program. For example, given the logic program

$p(a)$

and the goal

$\neg \exists X p(X)$

we get a logical contradiction: the second formula says that no element has the property p, but the first formula says that the value of a does have the property p. Thus $\exists X p(X)$ follows from $p(a)$.

5.4   Monotonic Rules: Semantics

Predicate Logic Semantics

One way of answering a query is to use the predicate logic interpretation of rules, facts, and queries, and to make use of the well-known semantics of predicate logic. To be more precise, given a logic program P and a query

$B_1, \ldots, B_n \rightarrow$

with the variables $X_1, \ldots, X_k$, we answer positively if, and only if,

$$pl(P) \models \exists X_1 \ldots \exists X_k(B_1 \wedge \ldots \wedge B_n) \tag{1}$$

or equivalently, if

$$pl(P) \cup \{\neg \exists X_1 \ldots \exists X_k(B_1 \wedge \ldots \wedge B_n)\} \text{ is unsatisfiable} \tag{2}$$

In other words, we give a positive answer if the predicate logic representation of the program P, together with the predicate logic interpretation of the query, is unsatisfiable (a contradiction).

The formal definition of the semantic concepts of predicate logic is found in the literature. Here we just give an informal presentation. The components of the logical language (signature) may have any meaning we like. A predicate logic *model* $\mathcal{A}$ assigns a certain meaning. In particular, it consists of

- a *domain dom*$(\mathcal{A})$, a nonempty set of objects about which the formulas make statements,

- an element from the domain for each constant,

- a concrete function on $dom(\mathcal{A})$ for every function symbol,

- a concrete relation on $dom(\mathcal{A})$ for every predicate.

The meanings of the logical connectives $\neg, \vee, \wedge, \rightarrow, \forall, \exists$ are defined according to their intuitive meaning: not, or, and, implies, for all, there is. This way we define when a formula is true in a model $\mathcal{A}$, denoted as $\mathcal{A} \models \varphi$.

A formula φ *follows* from a set M of formulas if φ is true in all models $\mathcal{A}$ in which M is true (that is, all formulas in M are true in $\mathcal{A}$).

Now we are able to explain (1) and (2). Regardless of how we interpret the constants, predicates, and function symbols occurring in P and the query, once the predicate logic interpretation of P is true, $\exists X_1 \ldots \exists X_k(B_1 \wedge \ldots \wedge B_n)$ must be true, too. That is, there are values for the variables $X_1, \ldots, X_k$ such that all atomic formulas B_i become true.

For example, suppose P is the program

$p(a)$

$p(X) \rightarrow q(X)$

Consider the query

$q(X) \rightarrow$

Clearly, $q(a)$ follows from $pl(P)$. Therefore, $\exists X q(X)$ follows from $pl(P)$, thus $pl(P) \cup \{\neg \exists X q(X)\}$ is unsatisfiable, and we give a positive answer. But if we consider the query

$q(b) \rightarrow$

then we must give a negative answer because $q(b)$ does not follow from $pl(P)$.

Least Herbrand Model Semantics

The other kind of semantics for logic programs, least Herbrand model semantics, requires more technical treatment, and is described in standard logic textbooks (see Suggested Reading).

Ground and Parameterized Witnesses

So far we have focused on yes/no answers to queries. However, such answers are not necessarily optimal. Suppose that we have the fact

$p(a)$

and the query

$p(X) \rightarrow$

The answer yes is correct but not satisfactory. It resembles the joke where you are asked, "Do you know what time it is?" and you look at your watch and answer "yes." In our example, the appropriate answer is a substitution

$\{X/a\}$

which gives an instantiation for X, making the answer positive. The constant a is called a *ground witness*. Given the facts

$p(a)$
$p(b)$

there are two ground witnesses to the same query: a and b. Or equivalently, we should return the substitutions:

$\{X/a\}$
$\{X/b\}$

While valuable, ground witnesses are not always the optimal answer. Consider the logic program

$$add(X, 0, X)$$
$$add(X, Y, Z) \rightarrow add(X, s(Y), s(Z))$$

This program computes addition, if we read s as the "successor function," which returns as value the value of its argument plus 1. The third argument of add computes the sum of its first two arguments. Consider the query

$$add(X, s^8(0), Z) \rightarrow$$

Possible ground witnesses are determined by the substitutions

$$\{X/0, Z/s^8(0)\}$$
$$\{X/s(0), Z/s^9(0)\}$$
$$\{X/s(s(0)), Z/s^{10}(0)\}$$

. . .

However, the *parameterized witness* $Z = s^8(X)$ is the most general way to witness the existential query

$$\exists X \exists Z \; add(X, s^8(0), Z)$$

since it represents the fact that $add(X, s^8(0), Z)$ is true whenever the value of Z equals the value of X plus 8.

The computation of such most general witnesses is the primary aim of a proof system, called SLD resolution, the presentation of which is beyond the scope of this book.

5.5 Description Logic Programs (DLP)

As stated at the beginning of this chapter, Horn logic and description logics are orthogonal. In attempting to achieve their integration in one framework, the simplest approach is to consider the intersection of both logics, that is, the part of one language that can be translated in a semantics-preserving way to the other language, and vice versa. In our particular case, the "intersection" of Horn logic and OWL is called *Description Logic Programs (DLP)*; it is the Horn-definable part of OWL, or stated another way, the OWL-definable part of Horn logic.

Consideration of DLP has certain advantages:

- From the modeler's perspective, there is freedom to use either OWL or rules (and associated tools and methodologies) for modeling purposes, depending on the modeler's experience and preferences.

- From the implementation perspective, either description logic reasoners or deductive rule systems can be used. Thus it is possible to model using one framework, for instance, OWL, and to use a reasoning engine from the other framework, for instance, rules. This feature provides extra flexibility and ensures interoperability with a variety of tools.

- Preliminary experience with using OWL has shown that existing ontologies frequently use very few constructs outside the DLP language.

In the remainder of this section we show how many constructs of RDF Schema and OWL can be expressed in Horn logic (thus they lie within the expressive power of DLP), and also discuss some constructs that in general cannot be expressed.

We begin with RDF and RDF Schema. A triple of the form (a, P, b) in RDF can be expressed as a fact

$$P(a, b)$$

Similarly, an instance declaration of the form $type(a, C)$, stating that a is an instance of class C, can be expressed as

$$C(a)$$

The fact that C is a subclass of D is easily expressed as

$$C(X) \to D(X)$$

and similarly for subproperty. Finally, domain and range restrictions can also be expressed in Horn logic. For example, the following rule states that C is the domain of property P:

$$P(X, Y) \to C(X)$$

Now we turn to OWL. $sameClassAs(C, D)$ can be expressed by the pair of rules

$$C(X) \to D(X)$$
$$D(X) \to C(X)$$

and similarly for $samePropertyAs$. Transitivity of a property P is easily expressed as

$$P(X,Y), P(Y,Z) \rightarrow P(X,Z)$$

Now we turn to Boolean operators. We can state that the intersection of classes C_1 and C_2 is a subclass of D as follows:

$$C_1(X), C_2(X) \rightarrow D(X)$$

In the other direction, we can state that C is a subclass of the intersection of D_1 and D_2 as follows:

$$C(X) \rightarrow D_1(X)$$
$$C(X) \rightarrow D_2(X)$$

For union, we can express that the union of C_1 and C_2 is a subclass of D using the following pair of rules:

$$C_1(X) \rightarrow D(X)$$
$$C_2(X) \rightarrow D(X)$$

However, the opposite direction is outside the expressive power of Horn logic. To express the fact that C is a subclass of the union of D_1 and D_2 would require a disjunction in the head of the corresponding rule, which is not available in Horn logic. Note that there are cases where the translation is possible. For example, when D_1 is a subclass of D_2, then the rule $C(X) \rightarrow D_2(X)$ is sufficient to express that C is a subclass of the union of D_1 and D_2. The point is that there is not a translation that works in all cases.

Finally, we briefly discuss some forms of restriction in OWL. For a property P and a class D, let $allValuesFrom(P, D)$ denote the anonymous class of all x such that y must be an instance of D whenever $P(x, y)$. The OWL statement

$$C \; subClassOf \; allValuesFrom(P, D)$$

can be expressed in Horn logic as follows:

$$C(X), P(X, Y) \rightarrow D(Y)$$

However, the opposite direction cannot in general be expressed.

Now let $someValuesFrom(P, D)$ denote the anonymous class of all x for which there exists at least one y instance of D, such that $P(x, y)$. The OWL statement

$$someValuesFrom(P, D) \ subClassOf \ C$$

can be expressed in Horn logic as follows:

$$P(X, Y), D(Y) \rightarrow C(X)$$

The opposite direction cannot in general be expressed.

Also, cardinality constraints and complement of classes cannot be expressed in Horn logic in the general case.

5.6   Semantic Web Rules Language (SWRL)

SWRL is a proposed Semantic Web language combining OWL DL (and thus OWL Lite) with function-free Horn logic, written in Datalog RuleML (see section 5.9). Thus it allows Horn-like rules to be combined with OWL DL ontologies.

A rule in SWRL has the form

$$B_1, \ldots, B_n \rightarrow A_1, \ldots, A_m$$

where the commas denote conjunction on both sides of the arrow and $A_1, \ldots, A_m, B_1, \ldots, B_n$ can be of the form $C(x)$, $P(x, y)$, $sameAs(x, y)$, or $differentFrom(x, y)$, where C is an OWL description, P is an OWL property, and x, y are Datalog variables, OWL individuals, or OWL data values.

If the head of a rule has more than one atom (if it is a conjunction of atoms without shared variables), the rule can be transformed to an equivalent set of rules with one atom in the head in a straightforward way.

The main complexity of the SWRL language stems from the fact that arbitrary OWL expressions, such as restrictions, can appear in the head or body of a rule. This feature adds significant expressive power to OWL, but at the high price of undecidability; that is, there can be no inference engine that draws exactly the same conclusions as the SWRL semantics.

Compared to DLP, SWRL lies at the other end of the integration of description logics and function-free rules. Where DLP uses a very conservative approach, seeking to combine the advantages of both languages in their common sublanguage, SWRL takes a more maximalist approach and unites their respective expressivities. From a practical perspective, the challenge is to identify sublanguages of SWRL that find the right balance between expressive power and computational tractability. A candidate for such a sublanguage is the extension of OWL DL with *DL-safe rules*, in which every variable must appear in a non-description logic atom in the rule body. See the articles on integrating rules with description logics in Suggested Reading.

5.7 Nonmonotonic Rules: Motivation and Syntax

5.7.1 Informal Discussion

Now we turn our attention to nonmonotonic rule systems. So far, once the premises of a rule were proved, the rule could be applied, and its head could be derived as a conclusion. In nonmonotonic rule systems, a rule may not be applied even if all premises are known because we have to consider contrary reasoning chains. In general, the rules we consider from now on are called *defeasible* because they can be defeated by other rules. To allow conflicts between rules, *negated atomic formulas* may occur in the head and the body of rules. For example, we may write

$$p(X) \rightarrow q(X)$$
$$r(X) \rightarrow \neg q(X)$$

To distinguish between defeasible rules and standard, monotonic rules, we use a different arrow:

$$p(X) \Rightarrow q(X)$$
$$r(X) \Rightarrow \neg q(X)$$

In this example, given also the facts

$$p(a)$$
$$r(a)$$

we conclude neither $q(a)$ nor $\neg q(a)$. It is a typical example of two rules blocking each other. This conflict may be resolved using *priorities among rules*. Suppose we knew somehow that the first rule is stronger than the second; then we could indeed derive $q(a)$.

Priorities arise naturally in practice and may be based on various principles:

• The source of one rule may be more reliable than the source of the second rule, or it may have higher authority. For example, federal law preempts state law. And in business administration, higher management has more authority than middle management.

- One rule may be preferred over another because it is more recent.

- One rule may be preferred over another because it is more specific. A typical example is a general rule with some exceptions; in such cases, the exceptions are stronger than the general rule.

Specificity may often be computed based on the given rules, but the other two principles cannot be determined from the logical formalization. Therefore we abstract from the specific prioritization principle, and assume the existence of an *external priority relation* on the set of rules. To express the relation syntactically, we extend the rule syntax to include a unique label, for example,

$$r_1 : p(X) \Rightarrow q(X)$$
$$r_2 : r(X) \Rightarrow \neg q(X)$$

Then we can write

$$r_1 > r_2$$

to specify that r_1 is stronger than r_2.

We do not impose many conditions on $>$. It is not even required that the rules form a complete ordering. We only require the priority relation to be acyclic. That is, it is impossible to have cycles of the form

$$r_1 > r_2 > \ldots > r_n > r_1$$

Note that priorities are meant to resolve conflicts among *competing rules*. In simple cases two rules are competing only if the head of one rule is the negation of the head of the other. But in applications it is often the case that once a predicate p is derived, some other predicates are excluded from holding. For example, an investment consultant may base his recommendations on three levels of risk that investors are willing to take: low, moderate, and high. Only one risk level per investor is allowed to hold at any given time. Technically, these situations are modeled by maintaining a conflict set $C(L)$ for each literal L. $C(L)$ always contains the negation of L but may contain more literals.

5.7.2   Definition of the Syntax

A *defeasible rule* has the form

$$r : L_1, \ldots, L_n \Rightarrow L$$

where r is the *label*, $\{L_1, \ldots, L_n\}$ the *body* (or *premises*), and L the *head* of the rule. $L, L_1, \ldots, L_n$ are positive or negative literals (a literal is an atomic formula $p(t_1, \ldots, t_m)$ or its negation $\neg p(t_1, \ldots, t_m)$). No function symbols may occur in the rule.[2] Sometimes we denote the head of a rule as $head(r)$, and its body as $body(r)$. Slightly abusing notation, sometimes we use the label r to refer to the whole rule.

A *defeasible logic program* is a triple $(F, R, >)$ consisting of a set F of facts, a finite set R of defeasible rules, and an acyclic binary relation $>$ on R (precisely, a set of pairs $r > r'$ where r and r' are labels of rules in R).

5.8   Example of Nonmonotonic Rules: Brokered Trade

This example shows how rules can be used in an electronic commerce application (which ideally will run on the Semantic Web). Brokered trades take place via an independent third party, the broker. The broker matches the buyer's requirements and the sellers' capabilities, and proposes a transaction when both parties can be satisfied by the trade.

As a concrete application we discuss apartment renting,[3] a common activity that is often tedious and time-consuming. Appropriate Web services can reduce the effort considerably. We begin by presenting the potential renter's requirements.

> Carlos is looking for an apartment of at least 45 sq m with at least two bedrooms. If it is on the third floor or higher, the house must have an elevator. Also, pet animals must be allowed.

> Carlos is willing to pay $300 for a centrally located 45 sq m apartment, and $250 for a similar flat in the suburbs. In addition, he is willing to pay an extra $5 per square meter for a larger apartment, and $2 per square meter for a garden.

> He is unable to pay more than $400 in total. If given the choice, he would go for the cheapest option. His second priority is the presence of a garden; his lowest priority is additional space.

---

2. This restriction is imposed for technical reasons, the discussion of which is beyond the scope of this chapter.
3. In this case the landlord takes the role of the abstract seller.

Formalization of Carlos's Requirements

We use the following predicates to describe properties of apartments:

$size(x, y)$	y is the size of apartment x (in sq m)
$bedrooms(x, y)$	x has y bedrooms
$price(x, y)$	y is the price for x
$floor(x, y)$	x is on the yth floor
$garden(x, y)$	x has a garden of size y
$lift(x)$	there is an elevator in the house of x
$pets(x)$	pets are allowed in x
$central(x)$	x is centrally located

We also make use of the following predicates:

$acceptable(x)$	flat x satisfies Carlos's requirements
$offer(x, y)$	Carlos is willing to pay \$ y for flat x

Now we present Carlos's firm requirements. Any apartment is a priori acceptable.

$r_1 : \Rightarrow acceptable(X)$

However, Y is unacceptable if one of Carlos's requirements is not met.

$r_2 :\ bedrooms(X, Y), Y < 2 \Rightarrow \neg acceptable(X)$

$r_3 :\ size(X, Y), Y < 45 \Rightarrow \neg acceptable(X)$

$r_4 :\ \neg pets(X) \Rightarrow \neg acceptable(X)$

$r_5 :\ floor(X, Y), Y > 2, \neg lift(X) \Rightarrow \neg acceptable(X)$

$r_6 :\ price(X, Y), Y > 400 \Rightarrow \neg acceptable(X)$

Rules r_2-r_6 are exceptions to rule r_1, so we add

$r_2 > r_1,\ r_3 > r_1,\ r_4 > r_1,\ r_5 > r_1,\ r_6 > r_1$

Next we calculate the price Carlos is willing to pay for an apartment.

$r_7 :\ size(X,Y), Y \geq 45, garden(X,Z), central(X) \Rightarrow$
$\quad offer(X, 300\ +\ 2Z + 5(Y - 45))$

$r_8 :\ size(X,Y), Y \geq 45, garden(X,Z), \neg central(X) \Rightarrow$
$\quad offer(X, 250\ +\ 2Z + 5(Y - 45))$

An apartment is only acceptable if the amount Carlos is willing to pay is not less than the price specified by the landlord (we assume no bargaining can take place).

$r_9 :\ offer(X,Y), price(X,Z), Y < Z \Rightarrow \neg acceptable(X)$

$r_9 > r_1$

Representation of Available Apartments

Each available apartment is given a unique name, and its properties are represented as facts. For example, apartment a_1 might be described as follows:

$bedrooms(a_1, 1)$
$size(a_1, 50)$
$central(a_1)$
$floor(a_1, 1)$
$\neg lift(a_1)$
$pets(a_1)$
$garden(a_1, 0)$
$price(a_1, 300)$

The descriptions of the available apartments are summarized in table 5.1. In practice, the flats on offer could be stored in a relational database or, in a Semantic Web setting, in an RDF storage system.

If we match Carlos's requirements and the available apartments, we see that

- flat a_1 is not acceptable because it has one bedroom only (rule r_2);

- flats a_4 and a_6 are unacceptable because pets are not allowed (rule r_4);

- for a_2, Carlos is willing to pay \$300, but the price is higher (rules r_7 and r_9);

- flats a_3, a_5, and a_7 are acceptable (rule r_1).

Flat	Bedrooms	Size	Central	Floor	Lift	Pets	Garden	Price
a_1	1	50	yes	1	no	yes	0	300
a_2	2	45	yes	0	no	yes	0	335
a_3	2	65	no	2	no	yes	0	350
a_4	2	55	no	1	yes	no	15	330
a_5	3	55	yes	0	no	yes	15	350
a_6	2	60	yes	3	no	no	0	370
a_7	3	65	yes	1	no	yes	12	375

Table 5.1   Available Apartments

Selecting an Apartment

So far, we have identified the apartments acceptable to Carlos. This selection is valuable in itself because it reduces the focus to relevant flats, which may then be physically inspected. But it is also possible to reduce the number further, even down to a single apartment, by taking further preferences into account. Carlos's preferences are based on price, garden size, and size, in that order. We represent them as follows:

$r_{10}:$ $acceptable(X) \Rightarrow cheapest(X)$

$r_{11}:$ $acceptable(X), price(X, Z), acceptable(Y), price(Y, W),$
    $W < Z \Rightarrow \neg cheapest(X)$

$r_{12}:$ $cheapest(X) \Rightarrow largestGarden(X)$

$r_{13}:$ $cheapest(X), gardenSize(X, Z), cheapest(Y),$
    $gardenSize(Y, W), W > Z \Rightarrow \neg largestGarden(X)$

$r_{14}:$ $largestGarden(X) \Rightarrow rent(X)$

$r_{15}:$ $largestGarden(X), size(X, Z), largestGarden(Y),$
    $size(Y, W), W > Z \Rightarrow \neg rent(X)$

   $r_{11} > r_{10}, \ r_{13} > r_{12}, \ r_{15} > r_{14}$

Rule r_{10} says that every acceptable apartment is cheapest by default. However, if there is an acceptable apartment cheaper than X, rule r_{11} (which is stronger than r_{10}) fires and concludes that X is not cheapest.

Rule Ingredient	RuleML
fact	Asserted Atom
rule	Asserted Implies
head	head
body	body
atom	Atom
conjunction	And
predicate	Rel
constant	Ind
variable	Var

Figure 5.1 RuleML vocabulary

Similarly, rules r_{12} and r_{13} select the apartments with the largest garden among the cheapest apartments. And of these, rules r_{14} and r_{15} select the proposed apartments to be rented, based on apartment size.

In our example, apartments a_3 and a_5 are cheapest. Of these a_5 has the largest garden. Note that in this case the apartment size criterion does not play a role: r_{14} fires only for a_5, and rule r_{15} is not applicable. Thus a selection has been made, and Carlos will soon move in.

5.9 Rule Markup Language (RuleML)

In accordance with the Semantic Web vision, it is necessary to make knowledge in the form of rules machine-accessible. We outline an encoding of monotonic rules in XML.

RuleML is an important standardization effort for markup of rules on the Web. It is actually not one language but a family of rule markup languages, corresponding to different kinds of rule languages: derivation rules, integrity constraints, reaction rules, and so on. The kernel of the RuleML family is Datalog, which is function-free Horn logic.

The RuleML family provides descriptions of rule markup languages in XML, in the form of XML schemas (and DTDs for earlier versions). The representation of rule ingredients is straightforward. Figure 5.1 describes the key vocabulary of Datalog RuleML.

The expression of rules using the RuleML vocabulary is straightforward.

For example, the rule *"The discount for a customer buying a product is 7.5 percent if the customer is premium and the product is luxury."* is represented as follows.

```
<Implies>
    <head>
        <Atom>
            <Rel>discount</Rel>
            <Var>customer</Var>
            <Var>product</Var>
            <Ind>7.5 percent</Ind>
        </Atom>
    </head>
    <body>
        <And>
            <Atom>
                <Rel>premium</Rel>
                <Var>customer</Var>
            </Atom>
            <Atom>
                <Rel>luxury</Rel>
                <Var>product</Var>
            </Atom>
        </And>
    </body>
</Implies>
```

The language SWRL, introduced in section 5.6, is an extension of RuleML, and its use is straightforward. As an example, we show the representation of the rule

$$brother(X, Y), childOf(Z, Y) \rightarrow uncle(X, Z)$$

in the XML syntax of SWRL.

```
<ruleml:Implies>
    <ruleml:head>
        <swrlx:individualPropertyAtom swrlx:property="uncle">
            <ruleml:Var>X</ruleml:Var>
            <ruleml:Var>Z</ruleml:Var>
        </swrlx:individualPropertyAtom>
    </ruleml:head>
    <ruleml:body>
        <ruleml:And>
```

```
            <swrlx:individualPropertyAtom swrlx:property="brother">
                <ruleml:Var>X</ruleml:Var>
                <ruleml:Var>Y</ruleml:Var>
            </swrlx:individualPropertyAtom>
            <swrlx:individualPropertyAtom swrlx:property="childOf">
                <ruleml:Var>Z</ruleml:Var>
                <ruleml:Var>Y</ruleml:Var>
            </swrlx:individualPropertyAtom>
        </ruleml:And>
    </ruleml:body>
</ruleml:Implies>
```

5.10 Summary

- Horn logic is a subset of predicate logic that allows efficient reasoning. It forms a subset orthogonal to description logics. Horn logic is the basis of monotonic rules.

- DLP and SWRL are two important ways of combining OWL with Horn rules. DLP is essentially the intersection of OWL and Horn logic, whereas SWRL is a much richer language.

- Nonmonotonic rules are useful in situations where the available information is incomplete. They are rules that may be overridden by contrary evidence (other rules).

- Priorities are used to resolve some conflicts between nonmonotonic rules.

- The representation of rules in XML-like languages, such as RuleML, is straightforward.

Suggested Reading

Horn logic is a standard topic in logic. More information can be found in relevant textbooks, such as the following:

- E. Burke and E. Foxley. *Logic and Its Applications*. Upper Saddle River, N.J.: Prentice Hall, 1996.

- M. A. Covington, D. Nute, and A. Vellino. *Prolog Programming in Depth*, 2nd ed. Upper Saddle River, N.J.: Prentice Hall, 1997.

- A. Nerode and R. A. Shore. *Logic for Applications*. New York: Springer, 1997.

- U. Nilsson and J. Maluszynski. *Logic, Programming and Prolog*, 2nd ed. New York: Wiley, 1995.

- N. Nissanke. *Introductory Logic and Sets for Computer Scientists*. Boston: Addison-Wesley, 1998.

Nonmonotonic rules are a quite new topic. Information can be found in the second textbook above, and in the following articles:

- G. Antoniou, D. Billington, G. Governatori, and M. J. Maher. Representation Results for Defeasible Logic. *ACM Transactions on Computational Logic* 2 (April 2001): 255–287.

- N. Bassiliades, G. Antoniou, and I. Vlahavas. A Defeasible Logic Reasoner for the Semantic Web. *International Journal on Semantic Web and Information Systems* 2,1 (2006): 1–41.

- T. Eiter, T. Lukasiewicz, R. Schindlauer, and H. Tompits. Combining Answer Set Programming with Description Logics for the Semantic Web. In *Proceedings of the 9th International Conference on Principles of Knowledge Representation and Reasoning (KR'04)*, AAAI Press 2004, 141–151.

- D. Nute. Defeasible Logic. In *Handbook of Logic in Artificial Intelligence and Logic Programming Vol. 3*, ed. D. M. Gabbay, C. J. Hogger, and J. A. Robinson. New York: Oxford University Press, 1994.

Information about DLP is found at

- <http://logic.aifb.uni-karlsruhe.de/>.

Information about SWRL is found at

- <http://www.w3.org/Submission/SWRL/>.

Other important works on integrating rules with description logics are

- R. Rosati. On the Decidability and Complexity of Integrating Ontologies and Rules. *Journal of Web Semantics* 3,1 (2005): 61–73. <http://www.websemanticsjournal.org/ps/pub/2005-4>.

- I. Horrocks, P. Patel-Schneider, S. Bechhofer, and D. Tsarkov. OWL Rules: A Proposal and Prototype Implementation. *Journal of Web Semantics* 3,1 (2005): 23–40.
  <http://www.websemanticsjournal.org/ps/pub/2005-2>.

- B. Motik, U. Sattler, and R. Studer. Query Answering for OWL-DL with Rules. *Journal of Web Semantics* 3,1 (2005): 41–60.
  <http://www.websemanticsjournal.org/ps/pub/2005-3>.

General information about markup languages for rules and their use in the Semantic Web can be found at the RuleML Web site:

- <http://www.ruleml.org/>.

TRIPLE is an inference system designed for the Semantic Web. Details can be found at

- <http://triple.semanticweb.org/>.

Exercises and Projects

5.1 We refer to the example in section 5.2. Define the predicates `aunt`, `grandfather`, `sibling`, and `descendant`.

5.2 Consider a graph with nodes and directed edges, and let an edge from node a to node b be represented by a fact $edge(a, b)$. Define a binary predicate *path* that is true for nodes c and d if, and only if, there is a path from c to d in the graph.

5.3 Propose a combination of nonmonotonic rules with ontologies. In particular, propose an integration such that

    (a) an ontology is used to derive some facts,

    (b) defeasible rules may use facts from (a),

    (c) the predicates of rule heads do not occur in the ontology (that is, rules may only use, but not derive, new ontological knowledge).

The following projects use rule technology. It is assumed that readers have some knowledge and experience with basic Semantic Web technologies. If not, it may be best to work on more basic projects first (see chapter 7).

Semantic Brokering

5.4 This basic project can be done by two people in two or three weeks. The aim is to implement an application similar to the apartment renting example in section 5.8. The following tasks should be carried out:

(a) Select a topic in which a brokering activity is to be carried out. Here brokering refers to the matching of offerings and requirements.

(b) Build an RDFS ontology for the domain.

(c) Populate the ontology with offerings, expressed in RDF.

(d) Express the selection criteria using nonmonotonic rules.

(e) Run your rules with the RDF/RDFS information using an engine such as DR-DEVICE[4] or DR-Prolog.[5] To do so, you will need to express the rules in the format prescribed by these systems.

5.5 This advanced project can be carried out bby two or three people over the course of a term. The aim is to implement a brokering scenario in a multi-agent environment. Apart from carrying out the steps described in project 5.4, project participants need, among others, to:

(a) Develop a basic understanding of brokering in multi-agent environments by studying some relevant literature:

K. Sycara, S. Widoff, M. Klusch, and J. Lu. Larks: Dynamic Matchmaking among Heterogeneous Software Agents in Cyberspace. *Autonomous Agents and Multi-Agent Systems* 5, 2 (2002): 173–203.
G. Antoniou, T. Skylogiannis, A. Bikakis, and N. Bassiliades. A Deductive Semantic Brokering System. In *Proceedings of the 9th International Conference on Knowledge-Based Intelligent Information and Engineering Systems*. LNCS 3682, Springer 2005, 746–752.

(b) Choose and familiarize yourselves with a multi-agent system. We have had good experience with JADE [6].

(c) Decide on the precise messages to be exchanged between agents.

(d) Find out how to call remotely the inference engine to be used.

---

4. <http://iskp.csd.auth.gr/systems/dr-device.html>.
5. <http://www.csd.uoc.gr/~bikakis/DR-Prolog/>.
6. <http://jade.tilab.com/>.

Proof Layer

The aim of these projects is to realize a proof layer, the vision of which was briefly outlined in chapter 1. Note that there is not one proof layer, but rather a proof layer for each selected Semantic Web reasoning system (logic). Still, some considerations are common to all such systems. Two possible logical systems for which one could implement a proof layer are

- a simple monotonic rules language, such as Datalog (Horn logic without function symbols), for which the reasoning tool Mandarax[7] could be used;

- a nonmonotonic rules language, as discussed in this chapter, for which DR-DEVICE[8] or DR-Prolog[9] could be used.

5.6 This basic project can be done by two or three people in about two months. The aim is to develop an interactive system that provides explanation to the user. Important aspects to be addressed include the following:

   (a) Decide how to extract relevant information from the overall proof trace. You could consult the automated reasoning and logic programming literature for ideas.

   (b) Define levels of granularity for representing proofs. Should whole proofs be shown, or only metasteps? These could then be refined if the user questions a certain step.

   (c) Ultimately, the "leaves" of a proof will be RDF facts, or rules, or inference conditions used.

5.7 Four or five people can carry out this advanced project over the course of a term. The aim is to implement a proof layer in a multi-agent environment, that is, requests and proof parts will be exchanged between agents. Additional aspects to be considered include the following:

   (a) Choose and familiarize yourselves with a multi-agent system. We have had good experience with JADE[10].

   (b) Represent proofs in an XML language, ideally extending RuleML.

   (c) Decide on the precise messages to be exchanged between agents.

---

7. <http://mandarax.sourceforge.net/>.
8. <http://iskp.csd.auth.gr/systems/dr-device.html>.
9. <http://www.csd.uoc.gr/~bikakis/DR-Prolog/>.
10. <http://jade.tilab.com/>.

6 *Applications*

6.1 Introduction

In this chapter we describe a number of applications in which the technologies described in this book have been or could be put to use. We have aimed to describe realistic scenarios only; if the scenarios are not already implemented, they are at least being seriously considered by major industrial firms in different sectors.

The descriptions in this chapter give a general overview of the kinds of uses to which Semantic Web technology can be applied. These include horizontal information products, data integration, skill-finding, a think tank portal, e-learning, web services, multimedia collection indexing, on-line procurement, and device interoperability.

Chapter Overview

This chapter gives a general overview of the kinds of uses to which Semantic Web technology can be applied. These include information publishing (section 6.2), data integration (sections 6.3 — 6.5), knowledge management (sections 6.6 — 6.7), e-learning (section 6.8), web-services (section 6.9), multimedia collection indexing, on-line procurement and device interoperability (section 6.10).

6.2 Horizontal Information Products at Elsevier

6.2.1 The Setting

Elsevier is a leading scientific publisher. Its products, like those of many of its competitors, are organized mainly along traditional lines: subscriptions to journals. Online availability of these journals has until now not really changed the organization of the product line. Although individual papers are available online, this is only in the form in which they appeared in the journal, and collections of articles are organized according to the journal in which they appeared. Customers of Elsevier can take subscriptions to online content, but again these subscriptions are organized according to the traditional product lines: journals or bundles of journals.

6.2.2   The Problem

These traditional journals can be described as vertical products. The products are split up into a number of separate columns (e.g., biology, chemistry, medicine), and each product covers one such column (or more likely part of one such column). However, with the rapid developments in the various sciences (information sciences, life sciences, physical sciences), the traditional division into separate sciences covered by distinct journals is no longer satisfactory. Customers of Elsevier are instead interested in covering certain topic areas that spread across the traditional disciplines. A pharmaceutical company wants to buy from Elsevier all the information it has about, say, Alzheimer's disease, regardless of whether this comes from a biology journal, a medical journal, or a chemistry journal. Thus, the demand is rather for horizontal products: all the information Elsevier has about a given topic, sliced across all the separate traditional disciplines and journal boundaries.

Currently, it is difficult for large publishers like Elsevier to offer such horizontal products. The information published by Elsevier is locked inside the separate journals, each with its own indexing system, organized according to different physical, syntactic, and semantic standards. Barriers of physical and syntactic heterogeneity can be solved. Elsevier has translated much of its content to an XML format that allows cross-journal querying. However, the semantic problem remains largely unsolved. Of course, it is possible to search across multiple journals for articles containing the same keywords, but given the extensive homonym and synonym problems within and between the various disciplines, this is unlikely to provide satisfactory results. What is needed is a way to search the various journals on a coherent set of concepts against which all of these journals are indexed.

Figure 6.1   Querying across data sources at Elsevier

6.2.3   The Contribution of Semantic Web Technology

Ontologies and thesauri, which can be seen as very lightweight ontologies, have proved to be a key technology for effective information access because they help to overcome some of the problems of free-text search by relating and grouping relevant terms in a specific domain as well as providing a controlled vocabulary for indexing information. A number of thesauri have been developed in different domains of expertise. Examples from the area of medical information include MeSH[1] and Elsevier's life science thesaurus EMTREE.[2] These thesauri are already used to access information sources like MBASE[3] or Science Direct; however, currently there are no links between the different information sources and the specific thesauri used to index and query these sources.

Elsevier is experimenting with the possibility of providing access to multiple information sources in the area of the life sciences through a single interface, using EMTREE as the single underlying ontology against which all the vertical information sources are indexed (see figure 6.1).

Semantic Web technology plays multiple roles in this architecture. First, RDF is used as an interoperability format between heterogeneous data sources. Second, an ontology (in this case, EMTREE) is itself represented in RDF (even though this is by no means its native format). Each of the sepa-

---

1. <http://www.nlm.nih.gov/mesh>.
2. 42,000 indexing terms, 175,000 synonyms.
3. <http://www.embase.com/>; 4000 journals, 8 million records.

rate data sources is mapped onto this unifying ontology, which is then used as the single point of entry for all of these data sources.

This problem is not unique to Elsevier. The entire scientific publishing industry is currently struggling with these problems. Actually, Elsevier is one of the leaders in trying to adapt its contents to new styles of delivery and organization.

6.2.4   The Results

As part of its experiments, Elsevier has sponsored the DOPE project (Drug Ontology Project for Elsevier), where the EMTREE thesaurus was used to index approximately 10 million medical abstracts from MedLine as well as approximately 500,000 full text articles from Elsevier's own collections. This was done with concept extraction software from Collexis[4]. The architecture from figure 6.1 was implemented using the Sesame RDF storage and querying engine[5], and a search and browse interface was constructed using Aduna's ClusterMap software[6]. This yielded an interface as shown in figure 6.2.

In this interface, the EMTREE ontology was used in a number of ways:

1. It is used to disambiguate the original free-text user query: does the search term "AIDS" stand for "Acquired Immune Deficiency Syndrome" or is it the plural of "aid" (as in "first aid")?

2. It is then used to categorize the results, as shown in the left column of figure 6.2: each entry in that column is in fact a category from the EMTREE ontology in its proper hierarchical position.

3. These same categories are used to produce a visual clustering of the search results, as shown in the right-hand pane of figure 6.2.

4. Finally, when a search produces too many or too few results, the hierarchical structure of EMTREE can be used to narrow or widen the search query in a meaningful way.

---

4. <http://www.collexis.com/>.
5. <http://www.openrdf.org/>.
6. <http://www.aduna-software.com/>.

Figure 6.2   DOPE search and browse interface

6.3   **Openacademia:** Distributed Publication Management

6.3.1   The Setting

Information about scientific publications is often maintained by individual researchers. Reference management software such as EndNote and Bib-TeX helps researchers to maintain personal collections of bibliographic references. Typically, these are references to a researcher's own publications and also those that have been read and cited by the researcher in her own work. Most researchers and research groups also have to maintain a Web page about publications for interested peers from other institutes. Often personal reference management and the maintenance of Web pages are isolated efforts. The author of a new publication adds the reference to his own collection and updates his Web page and possibly that of his research group. Then the newly added reference simply waits until other researchers discover it.

6.3.2   The Problem

Ideally, maintaining personal references and Web pages about publications should not require redundant efforts. One could achieve this by directly using individual bibliographical records generate personal Web pages and joined publication lists for Web pages at the group or institutional level.

For this to happen, several problems need to be solved. First, information from different files and possibly in different formats has to be collected and integrated — not only bibliographic information but also information about membership of research groups and contact details. Second, duplicate information should be detected and merged. It is very likely that the same author name appears in different files with different spellings, and that the same publication is referenced by different people in different forms. Finally, it should be possible to query for specific selections of the bibliographic entries and represent them in customized layouts.

6.3.3   The Contribution of Semantic Web Technology

Openacademia[7] is a web-based application that can do these tasks. All tasks in openacademia are performed on RDF representations of the data, and only standard ontologies are used to describe the meaning of the data. Moreover, W3C standards are used for the transformation and presentation of the information.

Functionality

Before discussing the details of the system, we first describe its functionality. The most immediate service of openacademia is to enable generating an HTML representation of a personal collection of publications and publishing it on the Web. This requires filling out a single form on the openacademia Web site, which generates the code (one line of JavaScript!) that needs to be inserted into the body of the home page. The code inserts the publication list in the page dynamically, and thus there is no need to update the page separately if the underlying collection changes. The appearance of the publication list can be customized by style sheets. A variety of them is available in the system. An XSL style sheet specifies the pieces of information that should be included (e.g., whether an abstract is shown in the presentation), and CSS style sheets determine the layout.

---

7. <http://www.openacademia.org/>.

One can also generate an RSS feed from the collection. RSS is a simple XML-based data format that allows users to subscribe to frequently updated content. RSS feeds can be viewed and organized through RSS readers or automatically included as new content on another Web site. Adding such an RSS feed to a home page allows visitors to subscribe to the publication list. Whenever a new publication is added, the subscribers of the feed will be notified of this change through their reader (*information push*). Modern browsers such as Mozilla Firefox have builtin RSS readers that allow subscribing to RSS feeds attached to Web pages. The RSS feeds of openacademia are RDF-based and can also be consumed by any RDF-aware software such as the Piggy Bank browser extension.[8] Piggy Bank allows users to collect RDF statements linked to Web pages while browsing through the Web and to save them for later use.

Research groups can install their own openacademia server. Members of the research group can submit their publications by creating a FOAF profile[9] that points to the location of their publication collection. Openacademia thus enables the creation of a unified group publication list its posting it to a Web site similarly to personal lists. Groups can have their RSS feeds as well.

There is also an AJAX-based interface[10] for browsing and searching the publication collection (see figure 6.3) which builds queries and displays the results. This interface offers a number of visualizations. For example, the important keywords in the titles of publications matching the current query can be viewed as a *tag cloud*[11], where the size of the tags shows the importance of the keywords. It is also possible to browse the co-authorship networks of researchers. If the underlying data source includes FOAF data, the researchers' photos are shown (with links to their home pages). Another interactive visualization shows publications along a time line that can be scrolled using a mouse (see Figure 6.4).[12]

---

8. <http://simile.mit.edu/wiki/Piggy_Bank/>.
9. FOAF (Friend of a Friend; <http://www.foaf-project.org/>) is an RDF vocabulary for describing people, the links between them, and the things they create and do.
10. Ajax (Asynchronous JavaScript and XML) is a Web development technique for creating interactive Web applications. The intent is to make Web pages feel more responsive by exchanging small amounts of data with the server behind the scenes, so that the entire web page does not have to be reloaded each time the user requests a change. *(Wikipedia).*
11. <http://en.wikipedia.org/wiki/Tag_cloud>.
12. This time-based visualization uses the Timeline widget developed by the SIMILE project, <http://simile.mit.edu/timeline/>.

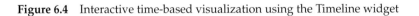

Figure 6.3   AJAX-based query interface of openacademia

Figure 6.4   Interactive time-based visualization using the Timeline widget

Information Sources

Openacademia uses the RDF-based FOAF format as a schema for information about persons and groups. To have their information included in openacademia researchers need to have a FOAF profile that contains at least their name and a link to a file with their publications. Anyone who does not have a FOAF profile can fill out a form at the openacademia Web site to generate it.

To be able to make selections on groups, information about group membership is required. This can also be specified in a FOAF file. Alternatively, it can be generated from a database. For example, at the Vrije Universiteit Amsterdam an RDF front end to the local LDAP database has been developed that represents its data as FOAF profiles.[13] The LDAP database contains information about group membership, and also individual names and e-mail addresses, which can be used to link the personal FOAF profiles to the information in the generated profiles.

For data about publications, openacademia uses the Semantic Web Research Community (SWRC) ontology[14] as a basic schema. However, because most researchers do not have their publication data in RDF, openacademia also accepts BibTeX, a format commonly in use in academia. Authors have to include a BibTeX file with their own publications on a publicly accessible part of their Web site. The BibTeX files are translated to RDF using the BibTeX-2-RDF service,[15] which creates instance data for the SWRC ontology.[16] A simple extension of the SWRC ontology was necessary to preserve the sequence of authors of publications. To this end the properties `swrc-ext:authorList` and `swrc-ext:editorList` are defined, which have `rdf:Seq` as range, comprising an ordered list of authors.

The crawler in openacademia collects the FOAF profiles and publication files. The crawling can be restricted to a specific domain, which can be useful for limiting the data collection to the domain of an institute. All data are subsequently stored in Sesame, an RDF database[17].

---

13. <http://www.cs.vu.nl/swhome/>.
14. <http://ontoware.org/projects/swrc/>.
15. <http://www.cs.vu.nl/~mcaklein/bib2rdf/>.
16. A translator for the EndNote format is being developed.
17. <http://www.openrdf.org/>.

Integration

As the system is designed to reuse information in a distributed, Web-based environment, it has to deal with the increasing semantic heterogeneity of information sources. Heterogeneity affects both the schema and instance levels. The schemas used are stable, lightweight Web ontologies (SWRC and FOAF), so their mapping causes no problem. Openacademia uses a bridging ontology that specifies the relations between important classes in both ontologies, for instance, that `swrc:Author` should be considered a subclass of `foaf:Person`.

Heterogeneity on the instance level arises from using different identifiers in the sources for denoting the same real-world objects. This certainly affects FOAF data collected from the Web (typically each personal profile also contains partial descriptions of the friends of the individual), as well as publication information, (the same author or publication may be referenced in a number of BibTeX sources).

A so-called smusher is used to match `foaf:Person` instances based on name and inverse functional properties. For example, if two persons have the same value for their e-mail addresses (or checksums), we can conclude that the two persons are the same. Publications are matched on a combination of properties. The instance matches that are found are recorded in the RDF store using the `owl:sameAs` property. Since Sesame does not natively support OWL semantics at the moment, the semantics of this single property are expanded using Sesame's custom rule language. These rules express the reflexive, symmetric, and transitive nature of the property as well as the intended meaning, namely, the equality of property values.

Presentation

After all information has been merged, the triple store can be queried to produce publications lists according to a variety of criteria, including personal, group or publication facets. The online interface helps users to build such queries against the publication repository.

In order to appreciate the power of a semantics-based approach, it is illustrative to look at an example query. The query in figure 6.5, formulated in the SeRQL query language[18], returns all publications authored by the members

---

18. a precursor to the SPARQL query language (see chapter 3);
see <http://www.openrdf.org/doc/sesame/users/ch06.html>.

```
SELECT DISTINCT pub
FROM {group} foaf:homepage
{<http://www.cs.vu.nl/ai/>}; foaf:member {person},
{pub} swrc:year {year}; swrc:author {person}
WHERE year="2004"
USING NAMESPACE
   foaf = <http://xmlns.com/foaf/0.1/>,
   swrc = <http://swrc.ontoware.org/ontology#>
```

Figure 6.5 Sample SeRQL query and its graphic representation

of the Artificial Intelligence department in 2004. This department is uniquely identified by its home page.

Note that the successful resolution of this query relies on the schema and instance matching described in the previous section. The query answering requires publication data as well as information on department membership and personal data from either the LDAP database or the self-maintained profile of the researcher. This points to a clear advantage of the Semantic Web approach: a separation of concerns. Researchers can change their personal profiles and update their publication lists without the need to consult or notify anyone. Similarly, the maintainer of the departmental LDAP database can add and remove individuals as before. All this information will be connected and merged automatically.

6.4 Bibster: Data Exchange in a Peer-to-Peer System

6.4.1 The Setting

Section 6.3 discussed a Semantic Web solution to the problem of collecting, storing, and sharing bibliographic information. The openacademia system uses a *semicentralized* solution for this problem. It is *centralized* because it harvests data into a single centralized repository which can then be queried; it's only *semi-centralized* because it harvests the bibliographic data from the files of invidivual researchers.

In this section we describe a fully distributed approach to the same problem in the form of the Bibster system.

6.4.2   The Problem

Any centralized solution relies on the performance of the centralized node in the system: how often does the crawler refresh the collected data-items, how reliable is the central server, will the central server become a performance bottleneck? Also, while many researchers are willing to share their data, they only do so as long as they are able to maintain local control over the information, instead of handing it over to a central server outside their control.

With Bibster, researchers may want to

- query a single specific peer (e.g., their own computer, because it is sometimes hard to find the right entry there), a specific set of peers (e.g., all colleagues at an institute), or the entire network of peers;

- search for bibliographic entries using simple keyword searches but also more advanced, semantic searches (e.g., for publications of a special type, with specific attribute values, or about a certain topic);

- integrate results of a query into a local repository for future use. Such data may in turn be used to answer queries by other peers. They may also be interested in updating items that are already locally stored with additional information about these items obtained from other peers.

6.4.3   The Contribution of Semantic Web Technology

Ontologies are used by Bibster for a number of purposes: importing data, formulating queries, routing queries, and processing answers. First, the system enables users to import their own bibliographic metadata into a local repository. Bibliographic entries made available to Bibster by users are automatically aligned to two ontologies. The first ontology (SWRC[19]) describes different generic aspects of bibliographic metadata (and would be valid across many different research domains); the second ontology (ACM Topic Ontology[20].) describes specific categories of literature for the computer science domain. Second, queries are formulated in terms of the two ontologies. Queries may concern fields like author or publication type (using terms from the SWRC ontology) or specific computer science terms (using the ACM

---

19. <http://ontoware.org/projects/swrc>.
20. <http://www.acm.org/class/1998/>

Topic Ontology). Third, queries are routed through the network depending on the expertise models of the peers describing which concepts from the ACM ontology a peer can answer queries on. A matching function determines how closely the semantic content of a query matches the expertise model of a peer. Routing is then done on the basis of this semantic ranking. Finally, answers are returned for a query. Because of the distributed nature and potentially large size of the peer-to-peer network, this answer set might be very large and contain many duplicate answers. Because of the semistructured nature of bibliographic metadata, such duplicates are often not exactly identical copies. Ontologies help to measure the semantic similarity between the different answers and to remove apparent duplicates as identified by the similarity function.

6.4.4 The Results

The screenshot in figure 6.6 indicates how the use cases are realized in Bibster. The Scope widget allows for defining the targeted peers; the Search and Search Details widgets allow for keyword and semantic search; the Results Table and BibTexView widgets allow for browsing and reusing query results. The query results are visualized in a list grouped by duplicates. They may be integrated into the local repository or exported into formats such as BibTeX and HTML.

6.5 Data Integration at Audi

6.5.1 The Setting

The problem described in section 6.2 is essentially a data integration problem which Elsevier is trying to solve for the benefit of its customers. But data integration is also a huge problem internal to companies. In fact, it is widely seen as the highest cost factor in the information technology budget of large companies. A company the size of Audi (51,000 employees, $22 billion revenue, 700,000 cars produced annually) operates thousands of databases, often duplicating and reduplicating the same information and missing out on opportunities because data sources are not interconnected. Current practice is that corporations rely on costly manual code generation and point-to-point translation scripts for data integration.

Figure 6.6   Bibster peer-to-peer bibliography finder

6.5.2   The Problem

While traditional middleware simplifies the integration process, it does not address the fundamental challenge of integration: the sharing of information based on the intended meaning, the semantics of the data.

6.5.3   The Contribution of Semantic Web Technology

Using ontologies as semantic data models can rationalize disparate data sources into one body of information. By creating ontologies for data and content sources and adding generic domain information, integration of disparate sources in the enterprise can be performed without disturbing existing applications. The ontology is mapped to the data sources (fields, records, files, documents), giving applications direct access to the data through the ontology.

We illustrate the general idea using a camera example.[21] Here is one way in which a particular data source or application may talk about cameras:

```
<SLR rdf:ID="Olympus-OM-10">
    <viewFinder>twin mirror</viewFinder>
    <optics>
       <Lens>
           <focal-length>75-300mm zoom</focal-length>
           <f-stop>4.0-4.5</f-stop>
       </Lens>
    </optics>
    <shutter-speed>1/2000 sec. to 10 sec.</shutter-speed>
</SLR>
```

This can be interpreted (by human readers) to say that Olympus-OM-10 is an SLR (which we know by previous experience to be a type of camera), that it has a twin-mirror viewfinder, and to give values for focal length range, f-stop intervals, and minimal and maximal shutter speed. Note that this interpretation is strictly done by a human reader. There is no way that a computer can know that Olympus-OM-10 is a type of SLR, whereas 75–300 mm is the value of the focal length.

This is just one way of syntactically encoding this information. A second data source may well have chosen an entirely different format:

```
<Camera rdf:ID="Olympus-OM-10">
    <viewFinder>twin mirror</viewFinder>
    <optics>
       <Lens>
           <size>300mm zoom</size>
           <aperture>4.5</aperture>
       </Lens>
    </optics>
    <shutter-speed>1/2000 sec. to 10 sec.</shutter-speed>
</Camera>
```

Human readers can see that these two different formats talk about the same object. After all, we know that SLR is a kind of camera, and that f-stop is a synonym for aperture. Of course, we can provide a simple ad hoc integration of these data sources by simply writing a translator from one to the other. But this would only solve this specific integration problem, and we

---

21. By R. Costello; at <http://www.xfront.com/avoiding-syntactic-rigor-mortis.html>.

would have to do the same again when we encountered the next data format for cameras.

Instead, we might well write a simple camera ontology in OWL:

```
<owl:Class rdf:ID="SLR">
  <rdfs:subClassOf rdf:resource="#Camera"/>
</owl:Class>

<owl:DatatypeProperty rdf:ID="f-stop">
  <rdfs:domain rdf:resource="#Lens"/>
</owl:DatatypeProperty>

<owl:DatatypeProperty> rdf:ID="aperture">
  <owl:equivalentProperty rdf:resource="#f-stop"/>
</owl:DatatypeProperty>>

<owl:DatatypeProperty rdf:ID="focal-length">
  <rdfs:domain rdf:resource="#Lens"/>
</owl:DatatypeProperty>

<owl:DatatypeProperty> rdf:ID="size">
  <owl:equivalentProperty rdf:resource="#focal-length"/>
</owl:DatatypeProperty>>
```

In other words, SLR is a type of camera, f-stop is synonymous with aperture, and focal length is synonymous with lens size.

Now suppose that an application A is using the second encoding (camera, aperture, lens size) and that it is receiving data from an application B using the first encoding (SLR, f-stop, focal length). As application A parses the XML document that it received from application B, it encounters SLR. It doesn't "understand" SLR so it "consults" the camera ontology: "What do you know about SLR?" The ontology returns "SLR is a type of Camera." This knowledge provides the link for application A to "understand" the relation between something it doesn't know (SLR) and something it does know (Camera). When application A continues parsing, it encounters f-stop. Again, application A was not coded to understand f-stop, so it consults the camera ontology: "What do you know about f-stop?" The ontology returns: "f-stop is synonymous with aperture." Once again, this knowledge serves to bridge the terminology gap between something application A doesn't know and something application A does know. And similarly for focal length.

The main point here is that syntactic divergence is no longer a hindrance. In fact, syntactic divergence can be encouraged, so that each application uses the syntactic form that best suits its needs. The ontology provides for a single integration of these different syntactical forms rather n^2 individual mappings between the different formats.

Audi is not the only company investigating Semantic Web technology for solving its data integration problems. The same holds for large companies such as Boeing, Daimler Chrysler, Hewlett Packard, and others (see Suggested Reading). This application scenario is now realistic enough that companies like Unicorn (Israel), Ontoprise (Germany), Network Inference (UK), and others are staking their business interests on this use of Semantic Web technology.

6.6   Skill Finding at Swiss Life

6.6.1   The Setting

Swiss Life is one of Europe's leading life insurers, with 11,000 employees worldwide and some $14 billion of written premiums. Swiss Life has subsidiaries, branches, representative offices, and partners representing its interests in about fifty different countries.

The tacit knowledge, personal competencies, and skills of its employees are the most important resources of any company for solving knowledge-intensive tasks; they are the real substance of the company's success. Establishing an electronically accessible repository of people's capabilities, experiences, and key knowledge areas is one of the major building blocks in setting up enterprise knowledge management. Such a skills repository can be used to enable a search for people with specific skills, expose skill gaps and competency levels, direct training as part of career planning, and document the company's intellectual capital.

6.6.2   The Problem

With such a large and international workforce distributed over many geographical and culturally diverse areas, the construction of a companywide skills repository is a difficult task. How to list the large number of different skills? How to organize them so that they can be retrieved across geographical and cultural boundaries? How to ensure that the repository is updated frequently?

6.6.3   The Contribution of Semantic Web Technology

The experiment at Swiss Life performed in the On-To-Knowledge project (see Suggested Reading) used a handbuilt ontology to cover skills in three organizational units of Swiss Life: information technology, private insurance, and human resources. Across these three sections, the ontology consisted of 700 concepts, with an additional 180 educational concepts and 130 job function concepts that were not subdivided across the three domains.

Here we give a glimpse of part of the ontology, to give a flavor of the kind of expressivity that was used:

```
<owl:Class rdf:ID="Skills">
 <rdfs:subClassOf>
  <owl:Restriction>
   <owl:onProperty rdf:resource="#HasSkillsLevel"/>
   <owl:cardinality rdf:datatype="&xsd;nonNegativeInteger">
    1
   </owl:cardinality>
   </owl:Restriction>
 </rdfs:subClassOf>
</owl:Class>

<owl:ObjectProperty rdf:ID="HasSkills">
 <rdfs:domain rdf:resource="#Employee"/>
 <rdfs:range  rdf:resource="#Skills"/>
</owl:ObjectProperty>

<owl:ObjectProperty rdf:ID="WorksInProject">
 <rdfs:domain rdf:resource="#Employee"/>
 <rdfs:range  rdf:resource="#Project"/>
 <owl:inverseOf rdf:resource="#ProjectMembers"/>
</owl:ObjectProperty>

<owl:ObjectProperty rdf:ID="ManagementLevel">
 <rdfs:domain rdf:resource="#Employee"/>
 <rdfs:range>
  <owl:oneOf rdf:parseType="Collection">
   <owl:Thing rdf:about="#member"/>
   <owl:Thing rdf:about="#HeadOfGroup"/>
   <owl:Thing rdf:about="#HeadOfDept"/>
   <owl:Thing rdf:about="#CEO"/>
  </owl:oneOf>
```

```
  </rdfs:range>
 </owl:ObjectProperty>

 <owl:Class rdf:ID="Publishing">
  <rdfs:subClassOf rdf:resource="#Skills"/>
 </owl:Class>

 <owl:Class rdf:ID="DocumentProcessing">
  <rdfs:subClassOf rdf:resource="#Skills"/>
 </owl:Class>

 <owl:Class rdf:ID="DeskTopPublishing">
  <rdfs:subClassOf rdf:resource="#Publishing"/>
  <rdfs:subClassOf rdf:resource="#DocumentProcessing"/>
 </owl:Class>
```

Individual employees within Swiss Life were asked to create "home pages" based on form filling that was driven by the skills ontology. The corresponding collection of instances could be queried using a form-based interface that generated RQL queries (see chapter 3). Although the system never left the prototype stage, it was in use by initially 100 (later 150) people in selected departments at Swiss Life headquarters.

6.7 Think Tank Portal at EnerSearch

6.7.1 The Setting

EnerSearch is an industrial research consortium focused on information technology in energy. Its aim is to create and disseminate knowledge on how the use of advanced IT will impact the energy utility sector, particularly in view of the liberalization of this sector across Europe.

EnerSearch has a structure that is very different from a traditional research company. Research projects are carried out by a varied and changing group of researchers spread over different countries (Sweden, United States, the Netherlands, Germany, France). Many of them, although funded for their work, are not employees of EnerSearch. Thus, EnerSearch is organized as a virtual organization. The insights derived from the conducted research are intended for interested utility industries and IT suppliers. Here EnerSearch has the structure of a limited company, which is owned by a number of firms in the industry sector that have an express interest in the research being carried out. Shareholding companies include large utility companies in different European countries, including Sweden (Sydkraft), Portugal (EDP), the Netherlands (ENECO), Spain (Iberdrola), and Germany (Eon), as well as some worldwide IT suppliers to this sector (IBM, ABB). Because of this wide geographical spread, EnerSearch also has the character of a virtual organization from a knowledge distribution point of view.

6.7.2   The Problem

Dissemination of knowledge is a key function of EnerSearch. The EnerSearch Web site is an important mechanism for knowledge dissemination. (In fact, one of the shareholding companies actually entered EnerSearch directly as a result of getting to know the Web site). Nevertheless, the information structure of the Web site leaves much to be desired. Its main organization is in terms of "about us" information: what projects have been done, which researchers are involved, papers, reports, and presentations. Consequently, it does not satisfy the needs of information seekers. They are generally not interested in knowing what the projects are or who the authors are, but rather in finding answers to questions that are important in this industry domain, such as: does load management lead to costsavings? If so, how big are they, and what are the required upfront investments? Can powerline communication be technically competitive to ADSL or cable modems?

6.7.3   The Contribution of Semantic Web Technology

The EnerSearch Web site is in fact used by different target groups: researchers in the field, staff and management of utility industries, and so on. It is quite possible to form a clear picture of what kind of topics and questions would be relevant for these target groups. Finally, the knowledge domain in which EnerSearch works is relatively well defined. As a result of these factors, it is possible to define a domain ontology that is sufficiently stable and of good enough quality. In fact, the On-To-Knowledge project ran successful experiments using a lightweight "EnerSearch lunchtime ontology" that took developers no more than a few hours to develop (over lunchtime).

This lightweight ontology consisted only of a taxonomical hierarchy (and therefore only needed RDF Schema expressivity). The following is a snapshot of one of the branches of this ontology in informal notation:

```
      . . .
   IT
     Hardware
```

```
Software
Applications
Communication
   Powerline
   Agent
Electronic Commerce
Agents
   Multi-agent systems
   Intelligent agents
   Market/auction
   Resource allocation
   Algorithms
```

This ontology was used in a number of different ways to drive navigation tools on the EnerSearch Web site. Figure 6.7 shows a semantic map of the EnerSearch Web site for the subtopics of the concept "agent", and figure 6.8 shows the semantic distance between different authors in terms of their disciplinary fields of research and publication.[22]

Figure 6.9 shows how some of the same information is displayed to the user in an entirely different manner with the Spectacle Server semantic browsing software.[23] The user selected the "By Author" option, then chose the author Fredrik Ygge and the concept "cable length". The result lists all the pages with publications on this topic by Fredrik Ygge.

A third way of displaying the information was created by the QuizRDF tool.[24] Rather then choosing between either an entirely ontology-based display (as in the three displayed figures), or a traditional keyword-based search without any semantic grounding, QuizRDF aims to combine both: the user can type in general keywords. This will result in a traditional list of papers containing these keywords. However, it also displays those concepts in the hierarchy that describe these papers, allowing the user to embark on an ontology-driven search starting from the hits that resulted from a keyword-based search.

In this application scenario we have seen how a traditional information source can be disclosed in a number of innovative ways. All these disclosure mechanisms (textual and graphic, searching or browsing) are based on a sin-

---

22. Both figures display results obtained by using semantic clustering visualization software from Aduna; <http://www.aduna-software.com/>.
23. From Aduna, <http://www.aduna.biz/>.
24. Prototyped by British Telecom Research Labs.

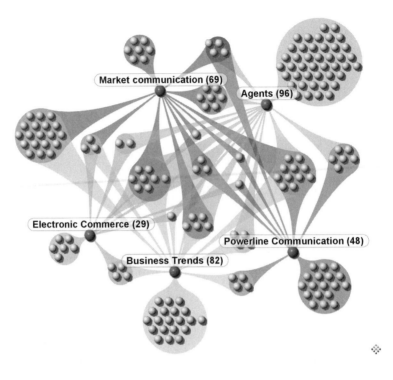

Figure 6.7   Semantic map of part of the EnerSearch Web site

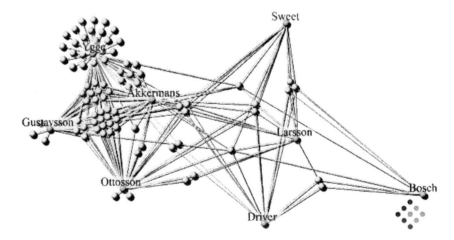

Figure 6.8   Semantic distance between EnerSearch authors

Figure 6.9   Browsing ontologically organized papers in Spectacle

gle underlying lightweight ontology but cater for a broad spectrum of users with different needs and backgrounds.

6.8   e-Learning

6.8.1   The Setting

The World Wide Web is currently changing many areas of human activity, among them learning. Traditionally learning has been characterized by the following properties:

- Educator-driven. The instructor selects the content and the pedagogical means of delivery, and sets the agenda and the pace of learning.

- Linear access. Knowledge is taught in a predetermined order. The learner is not supposed to deviate from this order by selecting pieces of particular interest.

- Time- and locality-dependent. Learning takes place at specific times and specific places.

As a consequence, learning has not been personalized but rather aimed at mass participation. Though efficient and in many instances effective, traditional learning processes have not been suitable for every potential learner. The emergence of the Internet has paved the way for implementing new educational processes.

The changes are already visible in higher education. Increasingly, universities are refocusing their activities to provide more flexibility for learners. Virtual universities and online courses are only a small part of these activities. Flexibility and new educational means are also implemented on traditional campuses, where students' presence is still required but with fewer constraints. Increasingly, students can make choices, determine the content and evaluation procedures, the pace of their learning, and the learning method most suitable for them.

We can also expect e-learning to have an even greater impact on work-related qualifications and lifelong learning activities. One of the critical support mechanisms for increasing an organization's competitiveness is the improvement of the skills of its employees. Organizations require learning processes that are just-in-time, tailored to their specific needs, and ideally integrated into day-to-day work patterns. These requirements are not compatible with traditional learning, but e-learning shows great promise for addressing these concerns.

6.8.2   The Problem

Compared to traditional learning, e-learning is not driven by the instructor. In particular, learners can access material in an order that is not predefined, and can compose individual courses by selecting educational material. For this approach to work, learning material must be equipped with additional information to support effective indexing and retrieval.

The use of metadata is a natural answer and has been followed, in a limited way, by librarians for a long time. In the e-learning community, standards such as IEEE LOM have emerged. They associate with learning materials information, such as educational and pedagogical properties, access rights and conditions of use, and relations to other educational resources. Although these standards are useful, they suffer from a drawback common to all solutions based solely on metadata (XML-like approaches): lack of semantics. As a consequence combining of materials by different authors may be difficult; retrieval may not be optimally supported; and the retrieval and organization of learning resources must be made manually (instead of, say, by a personalized automated agent). These kinds of problems may be avoided if the Semantic Web approach is adopted.

6.8.3 The Contribution of Semantic Web Technology

The key ideas of the Semantic Web, namely, common shared meaning (ontology) and machine-processable metadata, establish a promising approach for satisfying the e-learning requirements. It can support both semantic querying and the conceptual navigation of learning materials:

- Learner-driven. Learning materials, possibly by different authors, can be linked to commonly agreed ontologies. Personalized courses can be designed through semantic querying, and learning materials can be retrieved in the context of actual problems, as decided by the learner.

- Flexible access. Knowledge can be accessed in any order the learner wishes, according to her interests and needs. Of course, appropriate semantic annotation will still set constraints in cases where prerequisites are necessary. But overall nonlinear access will be supported.

- Integration. The Semantic Web can provide a uniform platform for the business processes of organizations, and learning activities can be integrated in these processes. This solution may be particularly valuable for commercial companies.

6.8.4 Ontologies for e-Learning

In an e-learning environment the situation can easily arise that different authors use different terminologies, in which case the combination of learning materials becomes difficult. The retrieval problem is additionally compounded by the fact that typically instructors and learners have very different backgrounds and levels of knowledge. Therefore, some mechanism for establishing a shared understanding is needed. Ontologies are a powerful mechanism for achieving this task. In an e-learning environment it makes sense to distinguish between three types of knowledge, and thus of ontologies: content, pedagogy, and structure.

A *content ontology* describes the basic concepts of the domain in which learning takes place (e.g., history or computer science). It includes also the relations between these concepts, and some basic properties. For example, the study of Classical Athens is part of the history of Ancient Greece, which in turn is part of Ancient History. The ontology should include the relation "is part of" and the fact that it is transitive (e.g., expressed in OWL). In this way, an automated learning support agent can infer that knowledge on Classical Athens can be found under Ancient History. The content ontology can also use relations to capture synonyms, abbreviations, and so on.

Pedagogical issues can be addressed in a *pedagogy ontology*. For example, material can be classified as lecture, tutorial, example, walk-through, exercise, solution, and so on. Finally, a *structure ontology* is used to define the logical structure of the learning materials. Typical knowledge of this kind includes hierarchical and navigational relations like *previous, next, hasPart, isPartOf, requires*, and *isBasedOn*. Relationships between these relations can also be defined; for example, *hasPart* and *isPartOf* are inverse relations. It is natural to develop e-learning systems on the Web; thus a Web ontology language should be used.

We should mention that most of the inferences drawn from learning ontologies cannot be expected to be very deep. Human readers can easily deal with relations such as *hasPart* and *isPartOf* and their interplay. The point is, though, that this kind of reasoning should be exhibited by *automated agents*, and the semantic information is necessary for reasoning to occur in an automated fashion.

6.9   Web Services

6.9.1   The Setting

By Web services we mean Web sites that do not merely provide static information but involve interaction with users and often allow users to effect some action. Usually a distinction is made between simple and complex Web services.

Simple Web services involve a single Web-accessible program, sensor, or device that does not rely upon other Web services nor requires further interaction with the user beyond a simple response. Typical examples are information provision services, such as a flight finder and a service that returns the postal code of a given address.

Complex Web services are composed of simpler services and often require ongoing interaction with the user, whereby the user can make choices or provide information conditionally. For example, user interaction with an

Figure 6.10   Work flow for finding the closest medical supplier

online music store involves searching for CDs and titles by various criteria, reading reviews and listening to samples, adding CDs to a shopping cart, providing credit card details, shipping details, and delivery address.

6.9.2   The Problem

SOAP, WSDL, UDDI, and BPEL4WS are the standard technology combination to build a Web service application. However, they fail to achieve the goals of automation and interoperability because they require humans in the loop. For example, information has to be browsed, and forms need to be filled in. Also, WSDL specifies the functionality of a service only at a syntactic level but does not describe the meaning of the Web service functionality, so other programs cannot make use of this information.

6.9.3   The Contribution of Semantic Web Technology

The Semantic Web community addressed the limitations of current Web service technology by augmenting the service descriptions with a semantic layer in order to achieve automatic discovery, composition, monitoring, and execution. The automation of these tasks is highly desirable.

Example Scenario

The example task is specializing the more generic task of finding the closest medical provider (or provider in any domain). A strategy for performing

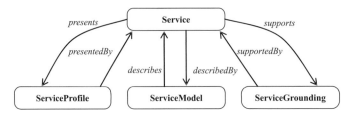

Figure 6.11 OWL-S service ontology

this task is: (1) retrieve the details of all medical providers (of a certain type) and (2) select the closest by computing the distance between the location of the provider and a reference location. This work flow can be schematically represented as in figure 6.10. For the example task it is enough to populate this work flow with the MedicareSupplier service and a Web service that calculates the distance between zip codes.

Semantic Web service technology aims to automate performing such tasks based on the semantic description of Web services. Using these descriptions the right services can be selected and combined in a way that would solve the task at hand.

A common characteristic of all emerging frameworks for semantic Web service descriptions (among them OWL-S, and WSMO[25]) is that they combine two kinds of ontologies to obtain a service description. First, a *generic Web service ontology*, such as OWL-S, specifies generic Web service concepts (e.g., inputs, outputs) and prescribes the backbone of the semantic Web service description. Second, a *domain ontology* specifies knowledge in the domain of the Web service, such as types of service parameters (e.g., *City*) and functionalities (e.g., *FindMedicalSupplier*), that fills in this generic framework. These two kinds of ontologies are discussed in the following sections.

6.9.4 Generic Web Service Ontologies: OWL-S

The OWL-S ontology is conceptually divided into four subontologies for specifying what the service does (Profile[26]), how the service works (Process[27]) and how the service is implemented (Grounding[28]). A fourth ontol-

---

25. <http://www.wsmo.org/>.
26. <http://www.daml.org/services/owl-s/1.0/Profile.owl>.
27. <http://www.daml.org/services/owl-s/1.0/Process.owl>.
28. <http://www.daml.org/services/owl-s/1.0/Grounding.owl>.

ogy (Service[29]) contains the *Service* concept, which links together the *Service-Profile*, *ServiceModel* and *ServiceGrounding* concepts (see Figure 6.11). The last three concepts are all further specialized in the Profile, Process and Grounding ontologies, respectively. In the the following sections, we explain all three parts of the OWL-S ontology by exemplifying their use in describing the MedicareSupplier service.

The Profile Ontology

Profile specifies the functionality offered by the service (e.g., *GetMedicalSupplier*), the semantic type of the inputs and outputs (e.g., *City, MedicareSupplier*), the details of the service provider, and several service parameters, such as quality rating or geographic radius. This description is used for discovering the service. The central concept of this ontology, *Profile*, is a subclass of *ServiceProfile*.

For each *Profile* instance we associate the process it describes (indicated by the *hasProc* relation) and its functional characteristics (inputs, outputs, pre-conditions, effects — referred to as IOPEs) together with their type. In the following example, the *MedicareSupplier* service presents three profiles (i.e., it offers three distinct functionalities). Each profile has a semantic type described by one of the functionality concepts *FindMedicareSupplierByZip*, *FindMedicareSupplierByCity* or *FindMedicareSupplierBySupply*. Each profile describes a process (specified in the process models P1, P2, P3). Finally, all profiles return an output that was described with the *SupplierDetails* concept. The input type varies for each profile: *ZipCode*, *City*, or *SupplyType*. The example is given in an informal, abstract notation because the XML-based code would be too lengthy and would distract from the discussion.

```
Service MedicareSupplier:
 *Profile:FindMedicareSupplierByZip (hasProc P1)
          (I(ZipCode), O(SupplierDetails))
 *Profile:FindMedicareSupplierByCity (hasProc P2)
          (I(City), O(SupplierDetails))
 *Profile:FindMedicareSupplierBySupply (hasProc P3)
          (I(SupplyType), O(SupplierDetails))
 *ProcessModel: ...
 *WSDLGrounding: ...
```

---

29. <http://www.daml.org/services/owl-s/1.0/Service.owl>.

The Process Ontology

Many complex services consist of smaller services executed in a certain order. For example, buying a book at Amazon.com involves using a browsing service (which selects the book) and a paying service. OWL-S allows describing such internal process models. These are useful for several purposes. First, one can check that the business process of the offering service is appropriate (e.g., product selection should always happen before payment). Second, one can monitor the execution stage of a service. Third, these process models can be used to automatically compose Web services.

A *ServiceModel* concept describes the internal working of the service and is further specialized as a *ProcessModel* concept in the Process ontology. A *ProcessModel* has a single *Process*, which can be atomic, simple, or composite (composed from atomic processes through various control constructs). Each process has a set of IOPEs. In our notation, for each service we represent its *ProcessModel* with its *Process*. For each *process* we depict its type, the involved control constructs, the IOPEs and their types. The *MedicareSupplier* service allows a choice from its three *AtomicProcesses* (corresponding to the three profiles), therefore its *ProcessModel* consists of a *CompositeProcess* modeled with the *Choice* control construct.

```
Service MedicareSupplier:
 *Profile:...
 *ProcessModel:
    CompositeProcess: MedicareProcess:Choice

      AtomicProcess:P1 (I(ZipCode),O(SupplierDetails))
      AtomicProcess:P2 (I(City),O(SupplierDetails))
      AtomicProcess:P3 (I(SupplyType),O(SupplierDetails))

 *WSDLGrounding: ...
```

Profile to Process Bridge

A *Profile* contains several links to a *Process*. Figure 6.12 shows these links, where terms in boldface belong to the Profile ontology and the rest to the Process ontology. First, a *Profile* states the *Process* it describes through the unique property *has_process*. Second, the IOPEs of the *Profile* correspond (in some degree) to the IOPEs of the *Process*.

Understanding this correspondence is not so trivial given the fact that the IOPEs play different roles for the *Profile* and for the *Process*. In the Profile on-

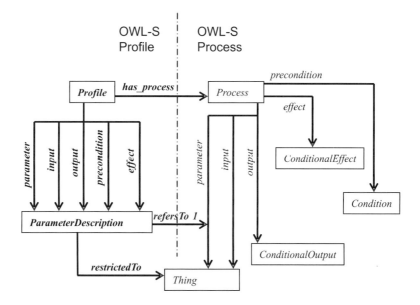

Figure 6.12   Profile to Process bridge

tology they are treated equally as parameters of the *Profile* (they are subproperties of the *profile:parameter* property). In the Process ontology only inputs
and outputs are regarded as subproperties of the *process:parameter* property.
The Preconditions and effects are just simple properties of the *Process*. While
technically the IOPEs are properties both for *Profile* and *Process*, the fact that
they are treated differently at a conceptual level is misleading. The link between the IOPEs in the Profile and Process part of the OWL-S descriptions
is created by the *refersTo* property, which has as domain *ParameterDescription*
and ranges over the *process:parameter*.

The Grounding ontology

Grounding provides the vocabulary to link the conceptual description of the
service specified by Profile and Process to actual implementation details,
such as message exchange formats and network protocols. The grounding
to a WSDL description is performed according to three rules:

1. Each *AtomicProcess* corresponds to one WSDL operation.

2. As a consequence of the first rule, each input of an *AtomicProcess* is
mapped to a corresponding messagepart in the input message of the
WSDL operation. Similarly for outputs: each output of an *AtomicProcess*
is mapped to a corresponding messagepart in the output message of the
WSDL operation.

3. The type of each WSDL message part can be specified in terms of a OWL-S
parameter (i.e., an XML Schema data type or a OWL concept).

The Grounding ontology specializes the *ServiceGrounding* as a *WSDL-
Grounding*, which contains a set of *WsdlAtomicProcessGrounding* elements,
each grounding one of the atomic processes specified in the *ProcessModel*. In
our abstract notation, we depict each atomic process grounding by showing
the link between the atomic process and the corresponding WSDL element.
The *MedicareSupplier* service has three atomic process groundings for each
process of the *ProcessModel*.

```
Service MedicareSupplier:
 *Profile:...
 *ProcessModel:...
 *WSDLGrounding:
    WsdlAtomicProcessGrounding: Gr1 (P1->op:GetSupplierByZipCode)
    WsdlAtomicProcessGrounding: Gr2 (P2->op:GetSupplierByCity)
    WsdlAtomicProcessGrounding: Gr3 (P3->op:GetSupplierBySupplyType)
```

Design Principles of OWL-S

The following design principles underlying OWL-S have been identified in
the literature:

• Semantic versus Syntactic descriptions. OWL-S distinguishes between the
semantic and syntactic aspects of the described entity. The Profile and Process ontologies allow for a semantic description of the Web service, and
the WSDL description encodes its syntactic aspects (such as the names of
the operations and their parameters). The Grounding ontology provides
a mapping between the semantic and the syntactic parts of a description
facilitating flexible associations between them. For example, a certain semantic description can be mapped to several syntactic descriptions if the
same semantic functionality is accessible in different ways. Conversely, a
certain syntactic description can be mapped to different conceptual interpretations that offer different views of the same service.

- Generic versus domain knowledge. OWL-S offers a core set of primitives to specify any type of Web service. These descriptions can be enriched with domain knowledge specified in a separate domain ontology. This modeling choice allows using the core set of primitives across several domains.

- Modularity. Another feature of OWL-S is the partitioning of the description over several concepts. The best demonstration for this is the way the different aspects of a description are partitioned into three concepts. As a result, a *Service* instance will relate to three instances, each of them containing a particular aspect of the service. There are several advantages of this modular modeling. First, since the description is split up over several instances, it is easy to reuse certain parts. For example, one can reuse the *Profile* description of a certain service. Second, service specification becomes flexible because it is possible to specify only the part that is relevant for the service (e.g., if it has no implementation, one does not need the *ServiceModel* and the *ServiceGrounding*). Finally, any OWL-S description is easy to extend by specializing the OWL-S concepts.

6.9.5 Web Service Domain Ontology

Externally defined knowledge plays a major role in each OWL-S description. OWL-S offers a generic framework to describe a service, but to make it truly useful, domain knowledge is required. For example, domain knowledge is used to define the type of functionality the service offers as well as the types of its parameters.

Figure 6.13 depicts the hierarchical structure of the domain ontology used to describe the example Web service. This ontology would usually be expressed in OWL, but we have not provided OWL code here to improve readability. Note that it specifies a DataStructure hierarchy and a Functionality hierarchy. The Functionality hierarchy contains a classification of service capabilities. Two generic classes of service capabilities are shown here, one for finding a medical supplier and the other for calculating distances between two locations. Each of these generic categories has more specialized capabilities either by restricting the type of the output parameters (e.g., find Medicare providers) or the input parameters (e.g., *ZipCode, City, SupplyType*).

The complexity of the reasoning tasks that can be performed with semantic Web service descriptions is conditioned by several factors. First, all Web services in a domain should use concepts from the same domain ontology

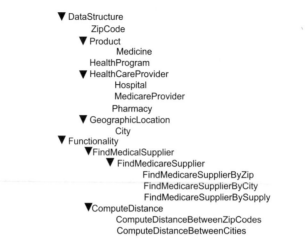

▼ DataStructure
    ZipCode
   ▼ Product
       Medicine
    HealthProgram
   ▼ HealthCareProvider
      Hospital
      MedicareProvider
     Pharmacy
   ▼ GeographicLocation
     City
  ▼ Functionality
    ▼FindMedicalSupplier
      ▼ FindMedicareSupplier
         FindMedicareSupplierByZip
         FindMedicareSupplierByCity
         FindMedicareSupplierBySupply
    ▼ComputeDistance
       ComputeDistanceBetweenZipCodes
       ComputeDistanceBetweenCities

Figure 6.13   Web service domain ontology

(or a small number of coupled ontologies) in their descriptions. Otherwise the issue of ontology mapping has to be solved, which is a difficult problem in itself. This requires that domain ontologies be *broad* enough to provide the concepts needed by any Web service in a certain domain. Second, the richness of the available knowledge is crucial for performing complex reasoning.

Example Scenario

By using the semantic Web service descriptions presented above, the example task can be generalized and automated. The right services for the task can be selected automatically from a collection of services. Semantic metadata allow a flexible selection that can retrieve services that partially match a request but are still potentially interesting. For example, a service that finds details of medical suppliers will be considered a match for a request for services that retrieve details of Medicare suppliers, if the Web service domain ontology specifies that a *MedicareSupplier* is a type of *MedicalSupplier*. This matchmaking is superior to the keyword-based search offered by UDDI. The composition of several services into a more complex service can also be automated. Finally, after being discovered and composed based on their semantic descriptions, the services can be invoked to solve the task at hand.

6.10   Other Scenarios

In this section we mention in somewhat less detail a number of other applications that are being pursued in industry or research.

6.10.1   Multimedia Collection Indexing at Scotland Yard

Police forces such as Scotland Yard and Interpol are concerned with the theft of art and antique objects. It is often hard enough to track down the thieves, but even when this has been done, and when some of the stolen artifacts have been recovered, it turns out to be surprisingly difficult to return the objects to their original owners. Even though international databases of stolen art objects exist, it is difficult to locate specific objects in these databases, because different parties are likely to offer different descriptions. A museum reporting a theft may describe an object as "a Song dynasty Ying Ging lotus vase," whereas a police officer reporting a recovered item may simply enter a "12.5 inch high pale green vase with floral designs." It currently takes human experts to recognize that the vase listed as stolen is indeed the same one reported as recovered.

Part of the solution is to develop controlled vocabularies such as the Art and Architecture Thesaurus (AAT) from the Getty Trust,[30] or the Iconclass thesaurus[31] to extend them into full-blown ontologies, to develop software that can automatically recognize classified objects from descriptions of their physical appearance using ontological background knowledge, and to deal with the ontology-mapping problem that exists when different parties have described the same artifacts using different ontologies.

6.10.2   Online Procurement at Daimler-Chrysler

Like all car-manufacturing companies today, Daimler-Chrysler interacts with hundreds of suppliers in order to obtain all the parts that go into making a single car. In recent years, online procurement has been identified as a major potential cost saver; for instance, the paper-based process of exchanging contracts, orders, invoices, and money transfers can be replaced by an electronic process of data interchange between software applications. Also, static long-term agreements with a fixed set of suppliers can be replaced by

---

30. <http://www.getty.edu/research/conducting_research/vocabularies/aat>.
31. <http://www.iconclass.nl/>.

dynamic short-term agreements in a competitive open marketplace. Whenever a supplier is offering a better deal, Daimler-Chrysler wants to be able to switch rather then being locked into a long-term arrangement with another supplier.

This online procurement is one of the major drivers behind business-to-business (B2B) e-commerce. Current efforts in B2B e-commerce rely heavily on a priori standardization of data formats, that is, off-line industrywide agreements on data formats and their intended semantics. Organizations such as Rosetta Net[32] are dedicated to such standardization efforts. To quote from RosettaNet's Web site:

> RosettaNet [is] a self-funded, non-profit organization. [It] is a consortium of major Information Technology, Electronic Components, Semiconductor Manufacturing, and Telecommunications companies working to create and implement industrywide, open e-business process standards. These standards form a common e-business language, aligning processes between supply chain partners on a global basis.

Since such data formats are specified in XML, no semantics can be read from the file alone, and partners must agree in time-consuming and expensive standards negotiations, followed by hard-coding the intended semantics of the data format into their code.

A more attractive road would use formats such as RDF Schema and OWL, with their explicitly defined formal semantics. This would make product descriptions "carry their semantics on their sleeve," opening the way for much more liberal online B2B procurement processes than currently possible.

6.10.3   Device Interoperability at Nokia

This section is based on a usecase from the OWL Requirements document (see Suggested Reading). Recent years have seen an explosive proliferation of digital devices in our daily environment: PDAs, mobile telephones, digital cameras, laptops, wireless access in public locations, GPS enabled cars. Given this proliferation, interoperability among these devices is becoming highly desirable. The pervasiveness and the wireless nature of these devices require network architectures to support automatic, ad hoc configuration.

A key technology of true ad hoc networks is service discovery, functionality by which services (functions offered by various devices such as cell

---

32. <http://www.rosettanet.org/>.

phones, printers, and sensors) can be described, advertised, and discovered by others. All current service discovery and capability description mechanisms (e.g., Sun's JINI, Microsoft's UPnP) are based on ad hoc representation schemes and rely heavily on standardization (on a priori identification of all those things one would want to communicate or discuss).

More attractive than this a priori standardization is "serendipitous interoperability," interoperability under "unchoreographed" conditions, that is, devices that are not necessarily designed to work together (such as ones built for different purposes, by different manufacturers, at different times) should be able to discover each others' functionality and be able to take advantage of it. Being able to "understand" other devices and reason about their services/functionality is necessary because full-blown ubiquitous computing scenarios involve dozens if not hundreds of devices, and a priori standardization of the usage scenarios is an unmanageable task.

Similar to the scenario of online procurement, ontologies (with their standardized semantics) are required to make such "unchoreographed" understanding of functionalities possible.

Suggested Reading

An excellent and up-to-date collection of Semantic Web usecases has been collected by W3Cs Semantic Web Education and Outreach Interest Group, and can be found at
<http://http://www.w3.org/2001/sw/sweo/public/UseCases/>.

A nontechnical book on the use of ontologies in electronic commerce and knowledge management:

- D. Fensel. *Ontologies: A Silver Bullet for Knowledge Management and Electronic Commerce*. New York: Springer, 2001.

The usecase document for OWL describes a number of usecases that motivated the W3C's Web Ontology Working Group in defining OWL:

- J. Heflin. OWL Web Ontology Language Use Cases and Requirements. W3C Recommendation. February 10, 2004.
<http://www.w3.org/TR/webont-req/>.

The following book describes three different application case-studies that were performed in the On-To-Knowledge project. More information on this project can also be found at <http://www.ontoknowledge.org/>.

- J. Davies, D. Fensel, and F. van Harmelen. *Towards the Semantic Web: Ontology-Driven Knowledge Management.* New York: Wiley, 2003.

A collection of papers on industrial applications of Semantic Web technology can be found in the Industrial Track papers of the International Semantic Web Conferences, starting with the 2003 conference:

- D. Fensel, K. Sycara, J. Mylopoulos, eds. In *Proceedings of the 2nd International Semantic Web Conference,* 2003.

A paper describing the potential benefits of the Semantic Web for e-learning:

- L. Stojanovic, S. Staab, and R. Studer. eLearning Based on the Semantic Web. In *Proceedings of WebNet 2001 — World Conference on the WWW and the Internet.*
  <http://www.aifb.uni-karlsruhe.de/WBS/Publ/2001/
  WebNet_lstsstrst_2001.pdf>.

Two relevant references for Semantic Web portal applications:

- S. Staab et al. Semantic Community Web Portals. In *Proceedings of the 9th International WWW Conference,* 2000.
  <http://www9.org/w9cdrom/134/134.html>.

- N. Stojanovic et al. SEAL — A Framework for Developing SEmantic PortALs. In *Proceedings of the 1st International Conference on Knowledge Capture (K-CAP),* 2001.
  <http://www.aifb.uni-karlsruhe.de/WBS/Publ/2001/sealkcap2.pdf>.

The main page on OWL-S and OWL-enabled Web services is

- <http://www.daml.org/services/owl-s/>

Some relevant publications:

- D. Martin et al. Bringing Semantics to Web Services: The OWL-S Approach. In *Proceedings of the 1st International Workshop on Semantic Web Services and Web Process Composition (SWSWPC 2004),* San Diego, 2004.

- S. McIlraith, T. Son, and H. Zeng. Mobilizing the Semantic Web with DAML-Enabled Web Services. In *Proceedings of the 2nd International Workshop on the Semantic Web (SemWeb 2001).*
  <http://www.daml.org/services/owl-s/pub-archive.html>.

- M. Paolucci et al. Semantic Matching of Web Services Capabilities. In *Proceedings of the 1st International Semantic Web Conference (ISWC)*. New York: Springer, 2002. Lecture Notes in Artificial Intelligence 2342.

The section of this chapter on Web services was based on material from Marta Sabou's Ph.D. dissertation:

- M. Sabou. *Building Web Service Ontologies*. SIKS Dissertation Series No. 2006-04.

Some useful Web sites with collections of tools are:

<http://business.semanticweb.org/>. A very good resource on the use of Semantic Web technolgy in companies, and a list of providers of Semantic Web technology.

<http://www.daml.org/tools/>. An extensive repository of tools.

<http://www.w3.org/2001/sw/WebOnt/impls#Implementations> and <http://www.cs.man.ac.uk/~horrocks/OntoWeb/SIG/node3.html> list the first tools that came out after the OWL specification stabilized.

7 *Ontology Engineering*

7.1   Introduction

So far, we have focused mainly on the techniques that are essential to the Semantic Web: representation languages, query languages, transformation and inference techniques, tools. Clearly, the introduction of such a large volume of new tools and techniques also raises methodological questions: How can tools and techniques best be appliled? Which languages and tools should be used in which circumstances, and in which order? What about issues of quality control and resource management?

Chapter Overview

Many of these questions for the Semantic Web have been studied in other contexts, for example in software engineering, object-oriented design, and knowledge engineering. It is beyond the scope of this book to give a comprehensive treatment of all of these issues. Nevertheless, in this chapter, we briefly discuss some of the methodological issues that arise when building ontologies, in particular, constructing ontologies manually (section 7.2), reusing existing ontologies (section 7.3), and using semiautomatic methods (section 7.4). Section 7.5 discusses ontology mapping, and section 7.6 explains how Semantic Web tools can be integrated into a single architecture.

7.2   Constructing Ontologies Manually

For our discussion of the manual construction of ontologies, we follow mainly Noy and McGuinness, "Ontology Development 101: A Guide to Creating Your First Ontology." Further references are provided in Suggested Reading.

We can distinguish the following main stages in the ontology development process:

1. Determine scope.   5. Define properties.
2. Consider reuse.   6. Define facets.
3. Enumerate terms.   7. Define instances.
4. Define taxonomy.   8. Check for anomalies.

Like any development process, this is in practice not a linear process. These steps will have to be iterated, and backtracking to earlier steps may be necessary at any point in the process. We do not further discuss this complex process management. Instead, we turn to the individual steps.

7.2.1   Determine Scope

Developing an ontology of a domain is not a goal in itself. Developing an ontology is akin to defining a set of data and their structure for other programs to use. In other words, an ontology is a *model* of a particular domain, built for a particular purpose. As a consequence, there is no *correct* ontology of a specific domain. An ontology is by necessity an abstraction of a particular domain, and there are always viable alternatives. What is included in this abstraction should be determined by the use to which the ontology will be put, and by future extensions that are already anticipated. Basic questions to be answered at this stage are, What is the domain that the ontology will cover? For what we are going to use the ontology? For what types of questions should the ontology provide answers? Who will use and maintain the ontology?

7.2.2   Consider Reuse

With the spreading deployment of the Semantic Web, ontologies will become more widely available. Already we rarely have to start from scratch when defining an ontology. There is almost always an ontology available from a third party that provides at least a useful starting point for our own ontology (see section 7.3).

7.2.3 Enumerate Terms

A first step toward the actual definition of the ontology is to write down in an unstructured list all the relevant terms that are expected to appear in the ontology. Typically, nouns form the basis for class names, and verbs (or verb phrases) form the basis for property names (e.g., *is part of*, *has component*).

Traditional knowledge engineering tools such as laddering and grid analysis can be productively used at this stage to obtain both the set of terms and an initial structure for these terms.

7.2.4 Define Taxonomy

After the identification of relevant terms, these terms must be organized in a taxonomic hierarchy. Opinions differ on whether it is more efficient/reliable to do this in a top-down or a bottom-up fashion.

It is, of course, important to ensure that the hierarchy is indeed a taxonomic (subclass) hierarchy. In other words, if A is a subclass of B, then every instance of A must also be an instance of B. Only this will ensure that we respect the built-in semantics of primitives such as `owl:subClassOf` and `rdfs:subClassOf`.

7.2.5 Define Properties

This step is often interleaved with the previous one: it is natural to organize the properties that link the classes while organizing these classes in a hierarchy.

Remember that the semantics of the `subClassOf` relation demands that whenever A is a subclass of B, every property statement that holds for instances of B must also apply to instances of A. Because of this inheritance, it makes sense to attach properties to the highest class in the hierarchy to which they apply.

While attaching properties to classes, it makes sense to immediately provide statements about the domain and range of these properties. There is a methodological tension here between generality and specificity. On the one hand, it is attractive to give properties as general a domain and range as possible, enabling the properties to be used (through inheritance) by subclasses. On the other hand, it is useful to define domain and range as narrowly as possible, enabling us to detect potential inconsistencies and misconceptions in the ontology by spotting domain and range violations.

7.2.6 Define Facets

It is interesting to note that after all these steps, the ontology will only require the expressivity provided by RDF Schema and does not use any of the additional primitives in OWL. This will change in the current step, that of enriching the previously defined properties with facets:

- Cardinality. Specify for as many properties as possible whether they are allowed or required to have a certain number of different values. Often, occurring cases are "at least one value" (i.e., required properties) and "at most one value" (i.e., single-valued properties).

- Required values. Often, classes are defined by virtue of a certain property's having particular values, and such required values can be specified in OWL, using `owl:hasValue`. Sometimes the requirements are less stringent: a property is required to have some values from a given class (and not necessarily a specific value, `owl:someValuesFrom`).

- Relational characteristics. The final family of facets concerns the relational characteristics of properties: symmetry, transitivity, inverse properties, functional values.

After this step in the ontology construction process, it will be possible to check the ontology for internal inconsistencies. (This is not possible before this step, simply because RDF Schema is not rich enough to express inconsistencies.) Examples of often occurring inconsistencies are incompatible domain and range definitions for transitive, symmetric, or inverse properties. Similarly, cardinality properties are frequent sources of inconsistencies. Finally, requirements on property values can conflict with domain and range restrictions, giving yet another source of possible inconsistencies.

7.2.7 Define Instances

Of course, we rarely define ontologies for their own sake. Instead we use ontologies to organize sets of instances, and it is a separate step to fill the ontologies with such intances. Typically, the number of instances is many orders of magnitude larger then the number of classes from the ontology. Ontologies vary in size from a few hundred classes to tens of thousands of classes; the number of instances varies from hundreds to hundreds of thousands, or even larger.

Because of these large numbers, populating an ontology with instances is typically not done manually. Often, instances are retrieved from legacy data sources such as databases. Another often used technique is the automated extraction of instances from a text corpus.

7.2.8   Check for Anomalies

An important advantage of using OWL over RDF Schema is the possibility of detecting inconsistencies in the ontology itself, or in the set of instances that were defined to populate the ontology. Examples of often occurring anomalies are incompatible domain and range definitions for transitive, symmetric, or inverse properties. Similarly, cardinality properties are frequent sources of inconsistencies. Finally, the requirements on property values can conflict with domain and range restrictions, giving yet another source of possible inconsistencies.

7.3   Reusing Existing Ontologies

One should begin with an existing ontology if possible. Existing ontologies come in a wide variety.

7.3.1   Codified Bodies of Expert Knowledge

Some ontologies are carefully crafted by a large team of experts over many years. An example in the medical domain is the cancer ontology from the National Cancer Institute in the United States.[1] Examples in the cultural domain are the Art and Architecture Thesaurus (AAT),[2] containing 125,000 terms, and the Union List of Artist Names (ULAN),[3] with 220,000 entries on artists. Another example is the Iconclass vocabulary of 28,000 terms for describing cultural images.[4] An example from the geographical domain is the Getty Thesaurus of Geographic Names (TGN),[5] containing over 1 million entries.

7.3.2   Integrated Vocabularies

Sometimes attempts have been made to merge a number of independently developed vocabularies into a single large resource. The prime example of

---

1. <http://www.mindswap.org/2003/CancerOntology/>.
2. <http://www.getty.edu/research/tools/vocabulary/aat>.
3. <http://www.getty.edu/research/conducting_research/vocabularies/ulan>.
4. <http://www.iconclass.nl/>.
5. <http://www.getty.edu/research/conducting_research/vocabularies/tgn>.

this is the Unified Medical Language System,[6] which integrates 100 biomedical vocabularies and classifications. The UMLS metathesaurus alone contains 750,000 concepts, with over 10 million links between them. Not surprisingly, the semantics of such a resource that integrates many independently developed vocabularies is rather low, but nevertheless it has turned out to be very useful in many applications, at least as a starting point.

7.3.3   Upper-Level Ontologies

Whereas the preceding ontologies are all highly domain-specific, some attempts have been made to define very generally applicable ontologies (sometimes known as upper-level ontologies). The two prime examples are Cyc,[7] with 60,000 assertions on 6,000 concepts, and the Standard Upperlevel Ontology (SUO).[8]

7.3.4   Topic Hierarchies

Other "ontologies" hardly deserve this name in a strict sense: they are simply sets of terms, loosely organized in a specialization hierarchy. This hierarchy is typically not a strict taxonomy but rather mixes different specialization relations, such as *is-a, part-of, contained-in*. Nevertheless, such resources are often very useful as a starting point. A large example is the Open Directory hierarchy,[9] containing more then 400,000 hierarchically organized categories and available in RDF format.

7.3.5   Linguistic Resources

Some resources were originally built not as abstractions of a particular domain but rather as linguistic resources. Again, these have been shown to be useful as starting places for ontology development. The prime example in this category is WordNet, with over 90,000 word senses.[10]

---

6. <http://umlsinfo.nlm.nih.gov/>.
7. <http://www.opencyc.org/>.
8. <http://suo.ieee.org/>.
9. <http://dmoz.org/>.
10. <http://http://wordnet.princeton.edu/>, available in RDF at <http://www.semanticweb.org/library/>.

7.3.6   Ontology Libraries

Attempts are currently underway to construct online libraries of ontologies. Examples may be found at the Ontology Engineering Group's Web site[11] at the DAML Web site,[12] those provided with the Protégé ontology editor,[13] and at SemWebCentral.[14] Perhaps currenty the best repository of online ontologies is Swoogle,[15] which has cataloged over 10K Semantic Web documents and indexed metadata about their classes, properties, and individuals as well as the relationships among them. Swoogle also defines a ranking property for Semantic Web documents and uses this to help sort search results.

Work on XML Schema development, although strictly speaking not ontologies, may also be a useful starting point for development work.[16]

It is only rarely the case that existing ontologies can be reused without changes. Typically, existing concepts and properties must be refined (using `owl:subClassOf` and `owl:subPropertyOf`). Also, alternative names must be introduced which are better suited to the particular domain (e.g., using `owl:equivalentClass` and `owl:equivalentProperty`). Also, this is an opportunity for fruitfully exploiting the fact that RDF and OWL allow private refinements of classes defined in other ontologies.

The general question of importing ontologies and establishing mappings between different mappings is still wide open, and is considered to be one of the hardest (and most urgent) Semantic Web research issues.

7.4   Semiautomatic Ontology Acquisition

There are two core challenges for putting the vision of the Semantic Web into action.

First, one has to support the re-engineering task of semantic enrichment for building the Web of metadata. The success of the Semantic Web greatly depends on the proliferation of ontologies and relational metadata. This requires that such metadata can be produced at high speed and low cost. To this end, the task of merging and aligning ontologies for establishing semantic interoperability may be supported by machine learning techniques

---

11. <http://www.ontology.or.kr/ontology/onto_lib.asp>.
12. <http://www.daml.org/>.
13. Reachable from <http://protege.stanford.edu/download/ontologies.html>.
14. <http://semwebcentral.org/>.
15. <http://swoogle.umbc.edu/>.
16. See, for example, the DTD/Schema registry at <http://XML.org/>
and Rosetta Net <http://www.rosettanet.org/>.

Second, one has to provide a means for maintaining and adopting the machine-processable data that are the basis for the Semantic Web. Thus, we need mechanisms that support the dynamic nature of the Web.

Although ontology engineering tools have matured over the last decade, manual ontology acquisition remains a time-consuming, expensive, highly skilled, and sometimes cumbersome task that can easily result in a knowledge acquisition bottleneck.

These problems resemble those that knowledge engineers have dealt with over the last two decades as they worked on knowledge acquisition methodologies or workbenches for defining knowledge bases. The integration of knowledge acquisition with machine learning techniques proved beneficial for knowledge acquisition.

The research area of machine learning has a long history, both on knowledge acquisition or extraction and on knowledge revision or maintenance, and it provides a large number of techniques that may be applied to solve these challenges. The following tasks can be supported by machine learning techniques:

- Extraction of ontologies from existing data on the Web

- Extraction of relational data and metadata from existing data on the Web

- Merging and mapping ontologies by analyzing extensions of concepts

- Maintaining ontologies by analyzing instance data

- Improving Semantic Web applications by observing users

Machine learning provides a number of techniques that can be used to support these tasks:

- Clustering

- Incremental ontology updates

- Support for the knowledge engineer

- Improving large natural language ontologies

- Pure (domain) ontology learning

Omelayenko (see Suggested Readings) identifies three types of ontologies that can be supported using machine learning techniques and identifies the current state of the art in these areas

7.4.1 Natural Language Ontologies

Natural language ontologies (NLOs) contain lexical relations between language concepts; they are large in size and do not require frequent updates. Usually they represent the background knowledge of the system and are used to expand user queries. The state of the art in NLO learning looks quite optimistic: not only does a stable general-purpose NLO exist but so do techniques for automatically or semiautomatically constructing and enriching domain-specific NLOs.

7.4.2 Domain Ontologies

Domain ontologies capture knowledge of one particular domain, for instance, pharmacological or printer knowledge. These ontologies provide a detailed description of the domain concepts from a restricted domain. Usually, they are constructed manually, but different learning techniques can assist the (especially the inexperienced) knowledge engineer. Learning of the domain ontologies is far less developed than NLO improvement. The acquisition of the domain ontologies is still guided by a human knowledge engineer, and automated learning techniques play a minor role in knowledge acquisition. They have to find statistically valid dependencies in the domain texts and suggest them to the knowledge engineer.

7.4.3 Ontology Instances

Ontology instances can be generated automatically and frequently updated (e.g., a company profile from the Yellow Pages will be updated frequently) while the ontology remains unchanged. The task of learning of the ontology instances fits nicely into a machine learning framework, and there are several successful applications of machine learning algorithms for this. But these applications are either strictly dependent on the domain ontology or populate the markup without relating to any domain theory. A general-purpose technique for extracting ontology instances from texts given the domain ontology as input has still not been developed.

Besides the different types of ontologies that can be supported, there are also different uses for ontology learning. The first three tasks in the following list (again, taken from Omelayenko) relate to ontology acquisition tasks in knowledge engineering, and the last three to ontology maintenance tasks:

- Ontology creation from scratch by the knowledge engineer. In this task machine learning assists the knowledge engineer by suggesting the most important relations in the field or checking and verifying the constructed knowledge bases.

- Ontology schema extraction from Web documents. In this task machine learning systems take the data and metaknowledge (like a metaontology) as input and generate the ready-to-use ontology as output with the possible help of the knowledge engineer.

- Extraction of ontology instances populates given ontology schemas and extracts the instances of the ontology presented in the Web documents. This task is similar to information extraction and page annotation, and can apply the techniques developed in these areas.

- Ontology integration and navigation deal with reconstructing and navigating in large and possibly machine-learned knowledge bases. For example, the task can be to change the propositional-level knowledge base of the machine learner into a first-order knowledge base.

- An ontology maintenance task is updating some parts of an ontology that are designed to be updated (like formatting tags that have to track the changes made in the page layout).

- Ontology enrichment (or ontology tuning) includes automated modification of minor relations into an existing ontology. This does not change major concepts and structures but makes an ontology more precise.

A wide variety of techniques, algorithms, and tools is available from machine learning. However, an important requirement for ontology representation is that ontologies must be symbolic, human-readable, and understandable. This forces us to deal only with symbolic learning algorithms that make generalizations and to skip other methods like neural networks and genetic algorithms. The following are some potentially applicable algorithms:

- Propositional rule learning algorithms learn association rules or other forms of attribute-value rules.

- Bayesian learning is mostly represented by the Naive Bayes classifier. It is based on the Bayes theorem and generates probabilistic attribute-value rules based on the assumption of conditional independence between the attributes of the training instances.

- First-order logic rules learning induces the rules that contain variables, called first-order Horn clauses.

- Clustering algorithms group the instances together based on the similarity or distance measures between a pair of instances defined in terms of their attribute values.

In conclusion, we can say that although there is much potential for machine learning techniques to be deployed for Semantic Web engineering, this is far from a well-understood area. No off-the-shelf techniques or tools are currently available, although this is likely to change in the near future.

7.5 Ontology Mapping

With reuse rather than development-from-scratch becoming the norm for ontology deployment, ontology integration is an increasingly urgent task. It will rarely be the case that a single ontology fulfills the needs of a particular application; more often than not, multiple ontologies will have to be combined. This raises the problem of ontology integration (also called ontology alignment or ontology mapping). This problem is now widely seen as both a crucial issue for the realization of the Semantic Web and as one of the hardest problems to solve. Consequently, this problem has received wide attention in the research community in recent years.

Current approaches to ontology mapping deploy a whole host of different methods, coming from very different areas. We distinguish linguistic, statistical, structural, and logical methods.

7.5.1 Linguistic Methods

The most basic methods try to exploit the linguistic labels attached to the concepts in source and target ontology in order to discover potential matches. This can be as simple as basic stemming techniques or calculating Hamming distances, or it can use specialized domain knowledge. An example of the latter would be that the difference between *Diabetes Melitus type I* and *Diabetes Melitus type II* is not a negligible difference to be removed by a small Hamming distance.

7.5.2   Statistical Methods

Instead of using the linguistic labels of concepts, other methods use *instance data* to determine correspondences between concepts. If there is a significant statistical correlation between the instances of a source concept and a target concept, there is reason to believe that these concepts are strongly related (by a subsumption relation or perhaps even an equivalence relation). These approaches of course rely on the availability of a sufficiently large corpus of instances that are classified in both the source and the target ontologies.

7.5.3   Structural Methods

Since ontologies have internal structure, it makes sense to exploit the graph structure of the source and target ontologies, and try to determine similarities between these structures, often in coordination with some of the other methods. If a source concept and a target concept have similar linguistic labels, then the dissimilarity of their graph neighborhoods could be used to detect homonym problems where purely linguistic methods would falsely declare a potential mapping.

7.5.4   Logical Methods

The methods that are perhaps most specific to mapping *ontologies* are the logical methods. After all, ontologies are *"formal specifications* of a shared conceptualization," and it makes sense to exploit this formalization of both source and target structures. A serious limitation of this approach is that many practical ontologies are semantically rather lightweight and thus don't carry much logical formalism with them.

Our conclusion from this brief treatment of ontology-mapping techniques must unfortunately be similar to our conclusion about automatic ontology acquisition techniques: although there is much potential, and indeed need, for these techniques to be deployed for Semantic Web engineering, this is far from a well-understood area. No off-the-shelf techniques or tools are currently available, and it is not clear that this is likely to change in the near future.

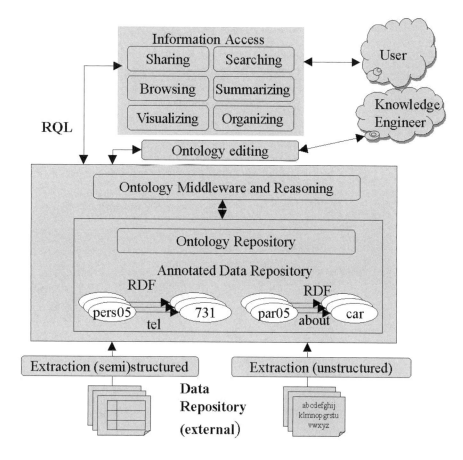

Figure 7.1 Semantic Web knowledge management architecture

7.6 On-To-Knowledge Semantic Web Architecture

Building the Semantic Web not only involves using the new languages described in this book but also a rather different style of engineering and a rather different approach to application integration. To illustrate this, we describe how a number of Semantic Web-related tools can be integrated in a single lightweight architecture using Semantic Web standards to achieve interoperability between independently engineered tools (see figure 7.1).

7.6.1   Knowledge Acquisition

At the bottom of figure 7.1 we find tools that use surface analysis techniques to obtain content from documents. These can be either unstructured natural language documents or structured and semistructured documents (such as HTML tables and spreadsheets).

In the case of unstructured documents, the tools typically use a combination of statistical techniques and shallow natural language technology to extract key concepts from documents.

In the case of more structured documents, the tools use techniques such as wrappers, induction, and pattern recognition to extract the content from the weak structures found in these documents.

7.6.2   Knowledge Storage

The output of the analysis tools is sets of concepts, organized in a shallow concept hierarchy with at best very few cross-taxonomical relationships. RDF and RDF Schema are sufficiently expressive to represent the extracted information.

Besides simply storing the knowledge produced by the extraction tools, the repository must of course provide the ability to retrieve this knowledge, preferably using a structured query language such as SPARQL. Any reasonable RDF Schema repository will also support the RDF model theory, including deduction of class membership based on domain and range definitions, and deriving the transitive closure of the `subClassOf` relationship.

Note that the repository will store both the ontology (class hierarchy, property definitions) and the instances of the ontology (specific individuals that belong to classes, pairs of individuals between which a specific property holds).

7.6.3   Knowledge Maintenance

Besides basic storage and retrieval functionality, a practical Semantic Web repository will have to provide functionality for managing and maintaining the ontology: change management, access and ownership rights, transaction management.

Besides lightweight ontologies that are automatically generated from unstructured and semistructured data, there must be support for human engineering of much more knowledge-intensive ontologies. Sophisticated editing environments must be able to retrieve ontologies from the repository, allow a knowledge engineer to manipulate them, and place them back in the repository.

7.6.4   Knowledge Use

The ontologies and data in the repository are to be used by applications that serve an end user. We have already described a number of such applications.

7.6.5   Technical Interoperability

In the On-To-Knowledge project,[17] the architecture of figure 7.1 was implemented with very lightweight connections between the components. Syntactic interoperability was achieved because all components communicated in RDF. Semantic interoperability was achieved because all semantics was expressed using RDF Schema. Physical interoperability was achieved because all communications between components were established using simple HTTP connections, and all but one of the components (the ontology editor) were implemented as remote services. When operating the On-To-Knowledge system from Amsterdam, the ontology extraction tool, running in Norway, was given a London-based URL of a document to analyze; the resulting RDF and RDF Schema were uploaded to a repository server running in Amersfoort (the Netherlands). These data were uploaded into a locally installed ontology editor, and after editing, downloaded back into the Amersfoort server. The data were then used to drive a Swedish ontology-based Web site generator (see the EnerSearch case study in chapter 6) as well as a U.K.-based search engine, both displaying their results in the browser on the screen in Amsterdam.

In summary, all these tools were running remotely, were independently engineered, and only relied on HTTP and RDF to obtain a high degree of interoperability.

---

17. <http://www.ontoknowledge.org/>.

Suggested Reading

Some key papers that were used as the basis for this chapter:

- N. Noy and D. McGuinness. Ontology Development 101: A Guide to Creating Your First Ontology.
  <http://www.ksl.stanford.edu/people/dlm/papers/ontology101/ontology101-noy-mcguinness.html>.

- M. Uschold and M. Gruninger. Ontologies: Principles, Methods and Applications. *Knowledge Engineering Review*, Volume 11, 2 (1996): 93–155.

- B. Omelayenko. Learning of Ontologies for the Web: The Analysis of Existing Approaches, In *Proceedings of the International Workshop on Web Dynamics, 8th International Conference on Database Theory (ICDT 2001)*. 2001.
  <http://www.cs.vu.nl/~borys/papers/WebDyn01.pdf>.

Two often-cited books:

- A. Maedche. *Ontology Learning for the Semantic Web*. New York: Springer 2002.

- J. Davies, D. Fensel, and F. van Harmelen. *Towards the Semantic Web: Ontology-Driven Knowledge Management*. New York: Wiley, 2003.

Project

This project of medium difficulty can be done by two or three people in about two or three weeks. All required software is freely available. We provide some pointers to software that we have used successfully, but given the very active state of development of the field, the availability of software is likely to change rapidly. Also, if certain software is not mentioned, this does not indicate our disapproval of it.

The assignment consists of three parts.

1. In the first part, you will create an ontology that describes the domain and contains the information needed by your own application. You will use the terms defined in the ontology to describe concrete data. In this step you will be applying the methodology for ontology construction outlined in the first part of this chapter and using OWL as a representation language for your ontology (see chapter 4).

2. In the second part, you will use your ontology to construct different views on your data, and you will query the ontology and the data to extract information needed for each view. In this part, you will be applying RDF storage and querying facilities (see chapter 3).

3. In the third part, you will create different graphic presentations of the extracted data using XSLT technology (see chapter 2).

Part I. Creating an Ontology

As a first step, decide on an application domain, preferably one in which you have sufficient knowledge or for which you have easy access to an expert with that knowledge.

In this description of the project, we use the domain that we use in our own course, namely, radio and television broadcasting, with its programs, broadcasting schedules, channels, genres, and celebrities. Of course, you can replace this with any domain of your own choosing.

Second, you will build an ontology expressed in OWL that describes the domain (for example, your faculty). The ontology does not have to cover the whole domain but should contain at least a few dozen classes. Pay special attention to the quality (breadth, depth) of the ontology, and aim to use as much of OWL's expressiveness as possible. There are a number of possible tools to use at this stage. Arguably the best current editor is Protégé,[18] but we have also had good experiences with OILed,[19] and OntoEdit.[20] If you are ambitious, you may even want to start your ontology development using ontology extraction tools from text (we have no experience with this in our own course) or experiment with tools that allow you to import semistructured data sources, such as Excel sheets or tab-delimited files (see, for example, Excel2RDF and ConvertToRDF).[21] Of course, you may choose to start from some existing ontologies in this area.[22] For the purposes of this exercise, we give our own students a reasonably large amount of semistructured data, generously donated by the Dutch national broadcasting archives.[23] These data are provided in XML format and can be converted to RDFS or OWL by

---

18. <http://protege.stanford.edu/>.
19. <http://oiled.man.ac.uk/>.
20. <http://www.ontoprise.de/>.
21. <http://www.mindswap.org/>.
22. For example, those found in <http://www.daml.org/ontologies/>.
23. <http://www.beeld-en-geluid.nl/>.

writing XSLT style sheets (see section 2.6) that produce XML syntax for either of these languages.

Preferably, also use an inference engine to validate your ontology and to check it for inconsistencies. We have experience using the FaCT reasoning engine that is closely coupled with OILed, but OntoEdit has its own inference engine. If you use Protégé, you may want to exploit some of the available plug-ins for this editor, such as multiple visualizations for your ontology, or reasoning in Prolog or Jess.

Third, export your ontology in RDF Schema. Of course, this will result in information loss from your rich OWL ontology, but this is inevitable given the limited capabilities of the tools used in subsequent steps, and this is also likely to be a realistic scenario in actual Semantic Web applications.

Finally, populate your ontology with concrete instances and their properties. Depending on the choice of editing tool, this can either be done with the same tool (OntoEdit) or in another way (OILed). Given the simple syntactic structure of instances in RDF, you may even decide to write these by hand or to code some simple scripts to extract the instance information from available sources. The XML data set mentioned before can also be used for this purpose (writing XSLT scripts to produce RDF instance data), or you may want to write a scraper for some of the many Web sites that contain information on radio and television schedules, programs, genres, and celebrities. You may want to use the the validation service offered by W3C.[24] This service not only validates your files for syntactic correctness but also provides a visualization of the existing triples. Also, at this stage, you may be able to experiment with some of the tools that allow you to import data from semistructured sources.

At the end of this step, you should be able to produce the following:

- The full OWL ontology

- The reduced version of this ontology as exported in RDF Schema

- Instances of the ontology, described in RDF

- A report describing the scope of the ontology and the main design decisions you took while modeling it.

Part II. Profile Building with RQL Queries

Here you will use query facilities to extract relevant parts of your ontology and data. For this you need some way of storing your ontology in a reposi-

---

24. <http://www.w3.org /RDF/Validator/>.

tory that also supports query facilities. You may use the Sesame RDF storage and query facility,[25] but other options exist, such as the KAON server,[26] or Jena.[27]

The first step is to upload your ontology (in RDF Schema form) and associated instances to the repository. This may involve some installation effort.

Next, use the query language associated with the repository to define different user profiles, and use queries to extract the data relevant for each profile.

Although these programs support different query languages (RQL for Sesame, RDQL for Jena, KAON Query for the KAON server), they all provide sufficient expressiveness to define rich profiles. In the example of modeling your own faculty, you may choose to define viewing guides for people with particular preferences (sports, current affairs) or viewers of particular age groups (e.g., minors), to collect data from multiple television stations (even across nations), to produce presentations for access over broadband or slow modemlines, and so on.

The output of the queries that define a profile will typically be in XML format: RDF/XML or some other form of XML.

Part III. Presenting Profile-Based Information

Use the XML output of the queries from part II to generate a human-readable presentation of the different profiles.

The technology to use is XML style sheets, in particular XSLT (see chapter 2). A variety of editors exist for XSLT, as well as a variety of XSLT processors.[28]

The challenge of this part is to define browsable, highly interlinked presentations of the data that were generated and selected in parts I and II.

Alternative Choice of Domain

Besides using the semistructured dataset describing the broadcasting domain, it is possible to model the domain of a university faculty, with its teachers, courses, and departments. In that case, you can use online sources, such as information from the faculty's phonebook, curriculum descriptions,

---

25. <http://www.openrdf.org/>.
26. <http://kaon.semanticweb.org/>.
27. <http://www.hpl.hp.com/semweb/>.
28. See, for example, <http://www.xslt.com/>.

teaching schedules, and so on to scrape both ontology and instance data. Example profiles for this domain could be profiles for students from different years, profiles for students from abroad, profiles for students and teachers, profiles for access over broadband or slow modemlines, and so on.

Conclusion

After you have finished all parts of this project, you will effectively have implemented large parts of the architecture shown in figure 7.1. You will have used most of the languages described in this book (XML, XSLT, RDF, RDF Schema, OWL), and you will have built a genuine Semantic Web application: modeling a part of the world in an ontology, using querying to define user-specific views on this ontology, and using XML technology to define browsable presentations of such user-specific views.

8 *Conclusion and Outlook*

8.1 Introduction

In the previous chapters we presented the basic ideas, languages and technologies of the Semantic Web initiative and discussed a number of indicative applications. In the following we try to give an analysis and overview of the current state of Semantic Web research.

Chapter Overview

Section 8.2 points to different interpretations of the Semantic Web as the reason underlying many controversies, and section 8.3 examines (and debunks) four false objections often raised against the Semantic Web effort. In section 8.4 we discuss the current status of Semantic Web work, reviewing the current answers to four central research questions and surveying the uptake of Semantic Web technology in different application areas. Finally, in section 8.5, we identify key challenges facing the Semantic Web community.

8.2 Which Semantic Web?

In the current Semantic Web work, we distinguish two main goals. These goals are often unspoken, but the differences between them often account for debates on design choices, on the applicability of various techniques, and on the feasibility of applications.

Interpretation 1: The Semantic Web as the Web of Data

In the first interpretation, the main aim of the Semantic Web is to enable the integration of structured and semistructured data sources over the Web. The main recipe is to expose datasets on the Web in RDF format and to use RDF Schema to express the intended semantics of these datasets, in order to enable the integration and ad hoc reuse of these datasets.

A typical use case for this version of the Semantic Web is the combination of geodata with a set of consumer ratings for restaurants in order to provide an enriched information source.

Interpretation 2: The Semantic Web as an Enrichment of the Current Web

In the second interpretation, the aim of the Semantic Web is to improve the current World Wide Web. Typical use cases here are improved search engines, dynamic personalization of Web sites, and semantic enrichment of existing Web pages.

The sources of the required semantic metadata in this version of the Semantic Web are mostly claimed to be automated sources: concept extraction, named-entity recognition, automatic classification, and so on. More recently the insight is gaining ground that the required semantic markup can also be produced by social mechanisms in communities that provide large-scale human-produced markup.

Of course, there are overlaps between these two versions of the Semantic Web. They both rely on the use of semantic markup, typically in the form of metadata described by ontology-like schemata. But perhaps more noticeable are the significant differences: different goals, different sources of semantics, different usecases, different technologies.

8.3   Four Popular Fallacies

The Semantic Web has been the subject of a stream of strongly and often polemically voiced criticisms. [1] Unfortunately, not all of these are equally well informed. A closer analysis reveals that many of these polemics attribute a number of false assumptions or claims to the Semantic Web program. In this section we aim to identify and debunk these fallacies.

---

1. For instance, <http://www.shirky.com/writings/semantic_syllogism.html> and <http://www.csdl.tamu.edu/~marshall/mc-semantic-web.html>.

Fallacy 1: The Semantic Web tries to enforce meaning from the top.

This fallacy claims that the Semantic Web enforces meaning on users through its standards OWL and RDFS. However, the only meaning that OWL and RDFS enforce is the meaning of the connectives in a language in which users can express their own meanings. Users are free to to choose their own vocabularies, to assign their own meanings to terms in these vocabularies, and to describe whatever domains they choose. OWL and RDFS are entirely neutral in this respect.

The situation is comparable to HTML: HTML does not enforce the lay-out of web-pages "from the top". All HTML enforces is the language that people can use to describe their own lay-out. And HTML has shown that such an agreement on the use of a standardised language (be it HTML for the lay-out of web-pages, or RDFS and OWL for their meaning) is a necessary ingredient for world-wide interoperability.

Fallacy 2: The Semantic Web requires everybody to subscribe to a single predefined meaning for the terms they use.

Of course, the meaning of terms cannot be predefined for global use; in addition, meaning is fluid and contextual. The motto of the Semantic Web is not the enforcement of a single ontology but rather "let a thousand ontologies blossom." That is exactly the reason that the construction of mappings between ontologies is such a core topic in the Semantic Web community. And such mappings are expected to be partial, imperfect and context-dependent.

Fallacy 3: The Semantic Web requires users to understand the complicated details of formalized knowledge representation.

Indeed some of the core technology of the Semantic Web relies on intricate details of formalized knowledge representation. The semantics of RDF Schema and OWL and the layering of the subspecies of OWL are difficult formal matters. The design of good ontologies is a specialized area of Knowledge Engineering. But for most users of (current and future) Semantic Web applications, such details will remain entirely behind the scenes, just as the intricacies of CSS and (X)HTML do. Navigation or personalization engines can be powered by underlying ontologies, expressed in RDF Schema or OWL, without users ever being confronted with the ontologies, let alone their representation languages.

Fallacy 4: The Semantic Web requires the manual markup of all existing Web pages, an impossible task.

It is hard enough for most Web site owners to maintain the human-readable content of their sites. They will certainly not maintain parallel machine-accessible versions of the same information in RDF or OWL. If that were necessary, it would indeed spell bad news for the Semantic Web. Instead, Semantic Web applications rely on large-scale automation for the extraction of such semantic markup from the sources themselves. This will often be very lightweight semantics, but for many applications that is enough.

Note that this fallacy mostly affects interpretation 2 of the Semantic Web (previous section), since massive markup in the "Web of data" is much easier. The data are already available in (semi)structured formats and often already organized by database schemas that can provide the required semantic interpretation.

8.4   Current Status

In this section we briefly survey the current state of work on the Semantic Web in two ways. First, we assess the progress that has been made in answering four key questions on which the success of the Semantic Web relies. Second, we give a quick overview of the main areas in which Semantic Web technology is currently being adopted.

8.4.1   Four Main Questions

Question 1: Where do the metadata come from?

As pointed out in Fallacy No. 4 much of the semantic metadata will come from Natural Language Processing and Machine Learning technology. And indeed these technologies are delivering on this promise. It is now possible with off-the-shelf technology to produce semantic markup for very large corpuses of Web pages (millions of pages) by annotating them with terms from very large ontologies (hundreds of thousands of terms) with sufficient precision and recall to drive semantic navigation interfaces.

More recent (and for many in the Semantic Web community somewhat unexpected) is the capability of social communities to do exactly what Fallacy 4 claims is impossible: providing large amounts of human-generated markup. Millions of images with hundreds of millions of manually provided metadata tags are found on some of the most popular Web 2.0 sites.

Question 2: Where do the ontologies come from?

The term *ontology* as used by the Semantic Web community now covers a wide array of semantic structures, from lightweight hierarchies such as MeSH[2] to heavily axiomatized ontologies such as GALEN.[3]

The lesson of a decade's worth of Knowledge Engineering and half a decade's of Semantic Web research is that indeed the world is full of such "ontologies": companies have product catalogs, organizations have internal glossaries, scientific communities have their public metadata schemata. These have typically been constructed for other purposes, most often predating the Semantic Web, but they are very usable as material for Semantic Web applications.

There are also significant advances in the area of ontology learning, although results there remain mixed. Obtaining the concepts of an ontology is feasible given the appropriate circumstances, but placing them in the appropriate hierarchy with the right mutual relationships remains a topic of active research.

Question 3: What should be done with the many ontologies?

As stated in our rebuttal to Fallacy No. 2, the Semantic Web crucially relies on the possibility of integrating multiple ontologies. This is known as the problem of ontology alignment, ontology mapping, or ontology integration, and it is indeed one of the most active areas of research in the Semantic Web community.

A wide array of techniques is deployed for solving this problem, with ontology-mapping techniques based on natural language technology, machine learning, theorem proving, graph theory, and statistics.

Although there are encouraging results, this problem is by no means solved, and automatically obtained results are not yet good enough in terms of recall and precision to drive many of the intended Semantic Web use cases. Consequently, ontology mapping is seen by many as the Achilles' heel of the Semantic Web.

---

2. <http://www.nlm.nih.gov/mesh/>.
3. <http://www.opengalen.org/>.

Question 4: Where's the "Web" in Semantic Web?

The Semantic Web has sometimes been criticized as being too much about "semantic" (large-scale distributed knowledge bases) and not enough about "Web." This was perhaps true in the early days of Semantic Web development, when there was a focus on applications in rather circumscribed domains like intranets. This initial emphasis is still visible to a large extent. Many of the most successful applications of Semantic Web technology are indeed on company intranets. Of course, the main advantage of such intranet applications is that the ontology-mapping problem can, to a large extent, be avoided.

Recent years have seen a resurgence in the Web aspects of Semantic Web applications. A prime example is the deployment of FOAF technology,[4] and of semantically organized P2P systems.

Of course, the Web is more than just a collection of textual documents: nontextual media such as images and videos are an integral part of the Web. For the application of Semantic Web technology to such nontextual media we currently rely on human-generated semantic markup. However, significant work on deriving annotations through intelligent content analysis in images and videos is under way.

8.4.2   Main Application Areas

An indicative list of applications was presented in chapter 6. It is beyond the scope of this book to give an in-depth, comprehensive overview of all Semantic Web applications. In the following we limit ourselves to a bird's eye survey.

Looking at industrial events, either dedicated events[5] or co-organized with the major international scientific Semantic Web conferences, we observe that a healthy uptake of Semantic Web technologies is beginning to take shape in the following areas:

- Knowledge management, mostly in intranets of large corporations

- Data integration (Boeing, Verizon, and others)

- e-science, in particular the life sciences[6]

---

4. <http://www.foaf-project.org/>.
5. For instance, <http://www.semantic-conference.com/>.
6. See, for example, <http://www2006.org/speakers/stephens/stephens.ppt> for some state-of-the-art industrial work.

- Convergence with Semantic Grid

If we look at the profiles of companies active in this area, we see a transition from small start-up companies such as Aduna, Ontoprise, Network Inference, and Top Quadrant to large vendors such as IBM (Snobase ontology Management System), [7] HP (Jena RDF platform) [8] Adobe (RDF-based XMP metadata framework), and Oracle (support for RDF storage and querying in their prime database product).

However, there is a noticeable lack of uptake in some other areas. In particular, the promise of the Semantic Web for

- personalization,

- large-scale semantic search (on the scale of the World Wide Web),

- mobility and context-awareness

is largely unfulfilled.

A difference that seems to emerge between the successful and unsuccessful application areas is that the successful areas are all aimed at *closed communities* (employees of large corporations, scientists in a particular area), whereas the applications aimed at the general public are still in the laboratory phase at best. The underlying reason for this could well be the difficulty of the ontology mapping.

8.5 Selected Key Research Challenges

Several challenges that were outlined in a 2002 article by van Harmelen have become active areas of research:

- Scale inference and storage technology, now scaling to the order of billions of RDF triples

- Ontology evolution and change

- Ontology mapping.

A number of items on the research agenda, though hardly developed, have had a crucial impact on the feasibility of the Semantic Web vision:

---

7. <http://www.alphaworks.ibm.com/tech/snobase>.
8. <http://jena.sourceforge.net/>.

- Interaction between machine-processable representations and the dynamics of social networks of human users

- Mechanisms to deal with trust, reputation, integrity, and provenance in a semiautomated way

- Inference and query facilities that are sufficiently robust to work in the face of limited resources (computation time, network latency, memory, or storage space) and that can make intelligent trade-off decisions between resource use and output quality.

Suggested Reading

This chapter is based on a paper by van Harmelen:

- F. van Harmelen. Semantic Web Research anno 2006: main streams, popular fallacies, current status, and future challenges. In *Proceedings of the 10th International Workshop on Cooperative Information Agents (CIA-2006)*. LNAI 4149. New York: Springer, 2006.

An earlier paper outlining research directions for the Semantic Web is:

- F. van Harmelen. How the semantic web will change KR: challenges and opportunities for a new research agenda. *Knowledge Engineering Review* 17, 1 (2002): 93–96.

Excellent surveys of the current state of the art in ontology mappings are

- Y. Kalfoglou and M. Schorlemmer. Ontology mapping: the state of the art. *Knowledge Engineering Review* 18, 1 (2003): 1–31.

- E. Rehm and P. Bernstein. A survey of approaches to automatic schema matching. *VLDB Journal* 10, 4 (2001): 334–350.

- P. Shvaiko and J. Euzenat. A survey of schema-based matching approaches. *Journal of Data Semantics* IV (2005): 146–171.

Information on semantic-based P2P systems is found in

- S. Staab and H. Stuckenschmidt. *Semantic Web and Peer-to Peer: Decentralized Management and Exchange of Knowledge and Information*. New York: Springer, 2005.

A Abstract OWL Syntax

The XML syntax for OWL, as we have used it in chapter 4 is rather verbose, and hard to read. OWL also has an abstract syntax[1], which is much easier to read.

This appendix lists the abstract syntax for all the OWL code discussed in chapter 4.

4.4.2: Header

```
Ontology(
  Annotation(rdfs:comment "An example OWL ontology")
  Annotation(rdfs:label "University Ontology")
  Annotation(owl:imports http://www.mydomain.org/persons)
)
```

4.4.3: Class Elements

```
Class(associateProfessor partial academicStaffMember)

Class(professor partial)
DisjointClasses(associateProfessor assistantProfessor)
DisjointClasses(professor associateProfessor)

Class(faculty complete academicStaffMember)
```

---

1. Defined in <http://www.w3.org/TR/owl-semantics/>

4.4.4: Property Elements

```
DatatypeProperty(age range(xsd:nonNegativeInteger))

ObjectProperty(isTaughtBy
 domain(course)
 range(academicStaffMember))
SubPropertyOf(isTaughtBy involves)

ObjectProperty(teaches
 inverseOf(isTaughtBy)
 domain(academicStaffMember)
 range(course))

ObjectProperty(lecturesIn)
EquivalentProperties(lecturesIn teaches)
```

4.4.5: Property Restrictions

```
Class(firstYearCourse partial
 restriction(isTaughtBy allValuesFrom (Professor)))

Class(mathCourse partial
 restriction(isTaughtBy hasValue (949352)))

Class(academicStaffMember partial
 restriction(teaches someValuesFrom (undergraduateCourse)))
card
 Class(course partial
 restriction(isTaughtBy minCardinality(1)))

Class(department partial
 restriction(hasMember minCardinality(10))
 restriction(hasMember maxCardinality(30)))
```

4.4.6: Special Properties

```
ObjectProperty(hasSameGradeAs Transitive Symmetric
 domain(student)
 range(student))
```

4.4.7: Boolean Combinations

```
Class(course partial
 complementOf(staffMember))

Class(peopleAtUni complete
 unionOf(staffMember student))

Class(facultyInCS complete
 intersectionOf(faculty
               restriction(belongsTo
                           hasValue
                           (CSDepartment)))))

Class(adminStaff complete
 intersectionOf(staffMember
               complementOf(unionOf(faculty
                                   techSupportStaff)))))
```

4.4.8: Enumerations

```
EnumeratedClass(weekdays Monday
                        Tuesday
                        Wednesday
                        Thursday
                        Friday
                        Saturday
                        Sunday)
```

4.4.9: Instances

```
Individual(949352
 type(academicStaffMember))

Individual(949352
 type(academicStaffMember)
 value(age "39"^^&xsd;integer))

ObjectProperty(isTaughtBy Functional)

Individual(CIT1111
 type(course)
```

```
    value(isTaughtBy 949352)
    value(isTaughtBy 949318))

Individual(949318
 type(lecturer))
DifferentIndividuals(949318 949352)

DifferentIndividuals(949352 949111 949318)
```

4.6.1: African Wildlife Ontology

```
Ontology(

ObjectProperty(eaten-by inverseOf(eats))
ObjectProperty(eats domain(animal))
ObjectProperty(is-part-of Transitive)

Class(animal partial
 annotation(rdfs:comment "Animals form a class."))

Class(branch partial
 annotation(rdfs:comment "Branches are parts of trees.")
 restriction(is-part-of allValuesFrom (tree)))

Class(carnivore complete
 annotation(rdfs:comment
            "Carnivores are exactly those animals that eat
             animals.")
 intersectionOf(animal
                restriction(eats someValuesFrom (animal))))

Class(giraffe partial
 annotation(rdfs:comment
            "Giraffes are herbivores,
             and they eat only leaves.")
 herbivore
 restriction(eats allValuesFrom (leaf)))

Class(herbivore complete
 annotation(rdfs:comment
             "Herbivores are exactly those animals that
              eat only plants or parts of plants.")
```

```
    intersectionOf(
        animal
        restriction(eats
                    allValuesFrom
                    (unionOf(plant
                             restriction(is-part-of
                                          allValuesFrom
                                          (plant)))))))

Class(leaf partial
  annotation(rdfs:comment "Leaves are parts of branches.")
  restriction(is-part-of allValuesFrom (branch)))

Class(lion partial
  annotation(rdfs:comment
              "Lions are animals that eat only herbivores.")
  carnivore
  restriction(eats allValuesFrom (herbivore)))

Class(plant partial
  annotation(rdfs:comment
              "Plants form a class disjoint from animals."))

Class(tasty-plant partial
  annotation(rdfs:comment
              "Tasty plants are plants that are eaten
               both by herbivores and carnivores.")
  plant
  restriction(eaten-by someValuesFrom (herbivore))
  restriction(eaten-by someValuesFrom (carnivore)))


Class(tree partial
  annotation(rdfs:comment "Trees are a type of plant.")
  plant)

AnnotationProperty(rdfs:comment)
DisjointClasses(plant animal)
)
```

4.6.2: Printer Ontology

```
Ontology(

  Annotation(owl:versionInfo
               "My example version 1.2, 17 October 2002")

  DatatypeProperty(manufactured-by
    domain(product)
    range(xsd:string))

  DatatypeProperty(price
    domain(product)
    range(xsd:nonNegativeInteger))

  DatatypeProperty(printingResolution
    domain(printer)
    range(xsd:string))

  DatatypeProperty(printingSpeed
    domain(printer)
    range(xsd:string))

  DatatypeProperty(printingTechnology
    domain(printer)
    range(xsd:string))

  Class(1100se partial
    annotation(rdfs:comment
                "1100se printers belong to the 1100 series
                 and cost $450.")
    1100series
    restriction(price hasValue ("450"^^&xsd;integer)))

  Class(1100series partial
    annotation(rdfs:comment
                "1100series printers are HP laser jet
                 printers with 8ppm printing speed and 600dpi
                 printing resolution.")
    hpLaserJetPrinter
    restriction(printingSpeed hasValue ("8ppm"^^&xsd;string))
    restriction(printingResolution
```

```
                    hasValue ("600dpi"^^&xsd;string)))

Class(1100xi partial
 annotation(rdfs:comment
            "1100xi printers belong to the 1100 series
             and cost $350.")
 1100series
 restriction(price hasValue ("350"^^&xsd;integer)))

Class(hpLaserJetPrinter partial
 annotation(rdfs:comment
            "HP laser jet printers are HP products
             and laser jet printers.")
 laserJetPrinter
 hpPrinter)

Class(hpPrinter partial
 annotation(rdfs:comment
            "HP printers are  HP products and printers.")
 hpProduct
 printer)

Class(hpProduct complete
 annotation(rdfs:comment
            "HP products are exactly those products
              that are manufactured by Hewlett Packard.")
 intersectionOf(
     product
     restriction(manufactured-by
                  hasValue ("Hewlett Packard"^^&xsd;string))))

Class(laserJetPrinter complete
 annotation(rdfs:comment
            "Laser jet printers are exactly those printers
              that use laser jet printing technology.")
 intersectionOf(
     printer
     restriction(printingTechnology
                  hasValue ("laser jet"^^&xsd;string))))

Class(padid partial
 annotation(rdfs:comment
```

```
                      "Printing and digital imaging devices
                       form a subclass of products.")
       annotation(rdfs:label "Device")
       product)

     Class(personalPrinter partial
       annotation(rdfs:comment "Printers for personal use form
                                a subclass of printers.")
       printer)

     Class(printer partial
       annotation(rdfs:comment "Printers are printing and
                                digital imaging devices.")
       padid)

     Class(product partial
       annotation(rdfs:comment "Products form a class."))
     )
```

Index